CHRISTINE DE PISAN

Autobiography
Of A
Medieval Woman
(1363-1430)

Translated and annotated by
Anil De Silva-Vigier

Documentation compiled by
Daphne Vaudoyer-Doublet

Edited by
Rummana Futehally Denby

MINERVA PRESS
MONTREUX   LONDON   WASHINGTON

CHRISTINE DE PISAN
Copyright © Anil de Silva Vigier 1996

ISBN 1 86106 186 2

First Published 1996 by
MINERVA PRESS
195 Knightsbridge
London SW7 1RE

Printed in Great Britain by
Antony Rowe Ltd, Chippenham, Wiltshire

CHRISTINE DE PISAN

Autobiography
Of A
Medieval Woman
(1363-1430)

Contents

Anil de Silva-Vigier was born in Sri Lanka into a distinguished political family and is one of the few Asian writers to have written on European history.

She studied the History of Art at the Ecole du Louvre and, while working as a diplomat in Paris, co-edited for UNESCO an educational series, "Man through his Art". Many of her works have been published in several languages and she was also editor and co-founder of "Marg", a journal of Art and Architecture from Mumbai (Bombay).

Previous publications include:

The Life of Buddha through Painting and Sculpture

Landscape Painting in the Caves of Tun-Huang, North-West China

Journey to the Caves of Maicheshan in Southern Kansu, China

Research Expedition to the Temples of Pagan in Upper Burma

This Moste Highe Prince, John of Gaunt

Although now retired and living in Cambridge, Anil de Silva-Vigier continues her writing.

Daphne Vaudoyer-Doublet is the daughter of Jean-Louis Vaudoyer, who was director of the Musée Carnavalet, Paris, and noted art critic and friend of Proust. Daphne edited her grandmother's diaries: *The Diary of Genevieve Bréton 1867-1871* (Edition Ramsay, Paris 1985). The USA edition, translated from the French, entitled *In the Solitude of my Soul* was published by Southern Illinois University Press.

Rummana Futehally Denby was born in India into a large and prestigious family. Her mother was a writer. She studied art in Paris and returned to India to paint and to teach art. She came to live in England having married an Englishman and joined the Tate Gallery as a curator in the Information Department. She is now retired and lives in York. With her husband, she is at present engaged in the study of the Medieval period of Indian history, relating to the Delhi Sultanate and the Bahmani Kingdom of the Deccan.

Authors' Note

The extracts included in this edited biography of Christine de Pisan have been selected by us from the totality of her works and though they may appear to be arbitrarily arranged, it was essential to follow a chronological sequence.

We have tried to include in Christine's own words, a representative selection of the great variety of works which she wrote during her lifetime. The descriptions of her early life and struggles are taken mostly from *'La Mutacion de Fortune'*, *'Lavision Christine'* and her ballads.

We must emphasise that there has been no effort to translate Christine's poems as poetry, but it is hoped that with a faithful literary translation rather than the rhythm and rhyme of the poetry, we have been able to convey the meaning with all its nuances. The exception is *'Le Livre du Duc des Vrais Amants'*, where the poems have been translated by Laurence Binyon. The poems, of course, are better appreciated in French and both the French version and the translation should be read together.

The illustrations are miniatures from Christine's original manuscripts of the fourteenth and early fifteenth centuries or from late fifteenth century copies. Christine herself took a great deal of trouble over the illustrations of her books.

List of Illustrations

1. Portrait of Christine in her blue dress sitting in her open study
   – a tree overhead.
   British Library, London.
   (Front cover)

2. Charles V in his study
   Bibliothèque National, Paris.

3. Louis d'Orléans
   French School c.1421 – Private Collection
   Photo: Giraudon

4. Valentine Visconti, Duchess d'Orléans, receiving a book from
   the author Honoré Bonet
   14th Century drawing
   Bibliothèque Nationale, Paris.

5. Portrait of Galeazzo Visconti by Antione Pisanello
   Musée du Louvre, Paris.
   Photo: Giraudon

6. The Duke de Berry by Holbein, the Younger
   Musée de Basle, Switzerland.
   Photo: Bulloz

7. Philippe the Bold, Duke of Burgundy, anonymous portrait
   Musée du Versailles.
   Photo: R.M.N.

8. Jean Gerson, preaching (detail)
   Biliothèque Municipale, Valenciennes.
   Photo: Giraudon

9. Marie de Berry
   Musée du Louvre, Paris.
   Photo: Giraudon

Acknowledgements

My special thanks are due to the late Dr Phillipe Vigier for his enduring affection and constant support to enable me to continue my work. Without his help, my books, and this one in particular would not have been possible.

Adieu Summer,
Autumn lasts so short a time.
Winter comes to me... for this I am sad,
I say, Adieu Youth...

Eustace Deschamps.

Anil de Silva Vigier

We would like to acknowledge the help we have received from so many friends; particularly from Dr Carmen Blacker, Laurent Vigier and Peter Khoroche, who helped us in getting books and documentation, and showed so much interest in our work; and Peter Khoroche's help with difficult translations; also Deborah Chattaway who did various items of translation and Robert Peel for his patience and help in getting the manuscript ready; James Palmes who helped with the verification and proof reading of all the Medieval French poems; Robert Knox of the British Museum who advised and helped in various ways, Cynthia Smale-Adams for her pertinent criticism, June Chammugam in Washington for her good offices to us in the USA.

The support given by Raymond Burton at a critical juncture was extremely helpful.

Rummana Futehally Denby has edited our material and welded it so that it reads as a seamless whole; and our gratitude for her conscientious and meticulous work over many months is immense.

Anil de Silva Vigier
Daphne Vaudoyer-Doublet

Cambridge and Paris

Introduction

> When my soul has departed
> from my body, if people, no
> matter where they be, take
> pleasure in my 'petite choses',
> read and listen to them and
> remember me, if they in
> recompense say a Pater Noster
> for me, I shall attain, God be
> thanked, the end for which I
> have striven....
>
> *Christine de Pisan – 1407*

A woman sitting at her desk in a room encumbered with books is an unusual subject in miniatures of the early fifteenth century. Christine de Pisan, whose work has been neglected for the past four centuries but is now being re-appraised, was a woman of letters, the most celebrated of her age. Wife, mother, poet, philosopher, chronicler, literary and political polemist, feminist and patriot, she was all these, not always happy in every one of these roles but always giving to each one the utmost passion and equal ardour.

Christine de Pisan rose above the brutal age in which she lived. By heroic effort she overcame the oppressive, demeaning, legal limitations and social attitudes which fettered her sex. In an age of glaring contrasts, when degradation, squalor and death were seldom far from the colour and pageantry, Christine stands out among the personalities of this age, and her life represents one brilliant facet of this glittering spectacle.

In medieval romances women were portrayed as the object of great courtesy and veneration, but what was their real situation? If one closely studies them as they appear in the work of the chroniclers, one sees that the noble lady as well as the bourgeoisie was considered inferior and kept in a state of subjugation.

Attitudes had hardly changed since Tertuilian (the theologian) writing in the third century (160-225 A.D.), said in one of his sermons: *"The sentence of God on this sex still lives on in our day... This crime (being a woman) must remain as an eternal fault. O woman, you are the door by which the demon entered into this world; you first discovered the tree; you broke the divine law; it was you who seduced man whom the devil had not the courage to attack frontally, you broke him without effort; man, this image of God; finally it was to efface the punishment which you had brought to him, that is to say death, that the son of God himself had to die..."*

As early as 485 A.D. the Council of Macon had discussed whether *"woman could be called 'homo', as she had not been created in the image of God"*. It was decided that in the Bible the creator had given without distinction the name 'homo' to both man and woman. In India, however, where love was seen as the realisation of an all-embracing cosmic principle, male and female appear as the complementary aspects of the Absolute, clearly shown in the myth of the Indian god, Shiva, and his goddess, Parvati. The god embodies virility, power and valour, his goddess the feminine qualities. Neither can exist or be creative without the other; the goddess is Shiva's secret being, his creative principle, for without her he becomes Shama, tranquillity or cessation. In practical terms, however, woman was oppressed as everywhere else, culminating in the custom of sati, where widows were burnt on the funeral pyre of their husbands.

In the Europe of the Middle Ages we read in the *'Fifteen Joys of Marriage'* that *"The wisest of women in the world has as much sense as I have gold in my eye, or as much as in the swish of a tail"*. In the *'Menagère de Paris'*, a book written for his daughter, by the Chevalier de la Tour Landry, there are two treatises for the edification of women, containing moral principles, useful advice and many edifying examples to establish and preserve the happiness of a father or a husband – in other words, man.

The feudal system, as such, did not encourage a chivalrous attitude towards woman. She was tied to her lands and handed over to some man, who took her as an appendage to the property. As a *chanson de geste* clearly says:

"Un de ces jours mourra un de mes pairs	*One of these days one of my knights will die*
Toute la terre vous en voudrait donner	*All the land you want will be given you*
Et la mouillier si prendre le voulez.	*With the woman to be taken with it."*

But, even though medieval woman was kept in the shadows, sold, kidnapped, beaten and brutalised (the husband had the right to physically chastise his wife or daughter), it was she who did most of the work while the men were at war. Miniatures of this period show women at work in every conceivable task, from weaving, cooking, labouring in the fields, open cast mining, earning their living by painting and sculpturing in the artistic *ateliers*, entertaining her employers and their guests by singing and playing musical instruments in the evenings... Women had few escapes from their drab lives, apart from pilgrimages, which brought them comparative freedom.

There were two views of woman, and many poets held them both: one was that she was a combination of all that was pure and unattainable; and the other that she was the root of all evil. The Church disapproved of literature that manifested passion and tried to insist on the ideal of chastity in a woman, for it was she who apparently took man down the path to hell.

In Medieval literature the main subject of many poems was love. In 'Troilus and Criseyde', Geoffrey Chaucer expressed all the anguish, the passion and the ecstasy of love in Troilus' song:

"If there's no love, O God! what am I feeling?
If there is love, who then and what is he?
If love be good, whence comes this sorrow stealing?
If evil, what a wonder it is to me
When every torment and adversity
That comes of him is savoury, to my thinking!
The more I thirst the more I would be drinking..."

Poets such as Chaucer, Deschamps and Christine de Pisan were inspired by, among others, Dante, Petrarch and Boccaccio. Indeed, the literary salons of the great princes and *seigneurs*, their elaborate libraries, their permanent troupes of minstrels, their musicians, their *joueurs de personnages*, the representations of Mysteries, half pious, half burlesque, gave all the encouragement needed by the Arts.

Medieval literary genres reflect different aspects of this society: the earlier *Chanson de geste*, the Miracles, the *fabliaux*, the *Chanson de toile*, the romantic allegories bring to light a life of pilgrimage, of the Church, of the ideal lady, of the chivalrous knight, of the university and of the growing middle-class population of the towns.

The closely knit links between England and France were forged not only in war but on many levels; there were intermarriages between French and English royalty and interchanges between poets and intellectuals of both countries, for they knew each other either personally, or at least through their work. French was still the language of the English courts and the *raconteurs* and *diseurs* travelled from one country to another and were present at poetic gatherings. Hence Eustace Deschamps, Christine's friend, wrote a ballad to the 'Great Chaucer'...

Christine de Pisan started her career as an author by writing poems about love.

'*Le Roman de la Rose*' was arguably the most influential book of Medieval times. It was written in two parts. The first, by Guillaume de Lorris, written in the first half of the thirteenth century but left unfinished, was lyrical and idealistic; the second part, by Jean de Meung, added in the latter half of the fourteenth century, was cynical and, advocating free love, denigrated women.

By 1350, when our period begins, every cultured and educated man or woman could recognise a quotation from '*Le Roman de la Rose*'. Christine shocked the contemporary intellectual world when she attacked the second part of '*Le Roman de la Rose*', and took up the defence of the *feminine sexe*. She started the great polemic of the Medieval world with this attack.

Christine never ceased to defend the *feminine sexe* and this is seen in her long work '*Le Livre de Mutacion de Fortune*'. Two books that followed, '*La Cité des Dames*' and '*Le Livre des Trois Vertus*', sometimes called '*Le Tresor des Dames*', both composed in 1405, possessed neither the libertine aspect of the '*Livre du Chevalier de la*

Tour Landry' nor the purely material side of Landry's *'Menagère de Paris'*. In these two volumes she assembles all her ideas on women; both are moral treatises destined for women and for once written by a woman. Books destined particularly for the edification of women were generally written by men. **Descriptions of married life were not written by women and anyone making a serious enquiry would have another version to report...** she says, answering a treatise by Matheolus describing married life as unbearable.

Jane Austen echoes this several hundred years later when Anne Eliot says in *'Persuasion'*, *"Yes if you please no reference to examples in books, men have had every advantage of us in telling their own story... The pen has been in their hands. I will not allow books to prove anything..."*

But perhaps the greatest burden a woman had to bear, whatever her position, was the complete lack of freedom to own her own body. In this respect the woman of the merchant class had by far the better life for she was comparatively free, whereas the aristocrat and the peasant were equally serfs in their own spheres. Chaucer's redoubtable Wife of Bath asks us:

"What could it be that women wanted most?
...Women desire the self same sovereignty
On husbands as they have on those that love them,
And would be set in mastery above them,
That is their greatest wish..."

At this important phase in the history of European civilisation the merging of various currents is discernible. This is now seen in a country like India today, where earlier pagan forms of eroticism, based on rites and mysteries going far back in man's history, exist side by side with more formalised concepts of love and courtesy. In medieval Europe the first is seen in licentiousness of behaviour, of pagan freedom at various feasts, festivals and marriages, and in the lascivious or obscene verses written by even the most courteous of poets. It is as survivals that we have to regard the obscenities, equivocal sayings, and gross symbols which we meet in the civilisation of the Middle Ages. In participating in them, medieval man felt no

xxiii

contradiction with the courtly forms of expression; they were on a different level of behaviour.

The chivalrous order was dying but, although dying, it gives us some of the finest examples of this ideal. The knightly concept of duty still exercised an influence on important decisions and the concepts embodied in the chivalrous code have inspired the laws under which we live. The knightly concept of duty prevailed when important decisions were made; honour and the values of virtue have influenced the evolution of the rules of war.

As the poet Chastellain put it:

"Honneur semont toute noble nature	*Honour urges every noble nature*
D'aimer tout ce qui noble est son etre	*To love all that is noble in one's being*
Noblesse aussi y adjoint sa nature	*Nobility also adds uprightness to it."*

Christine's profound horror of war and the deep anguish she felt at the misery of the people during war is apparent in all her writings, and this too is very modern. Time and again she begs the princes and nobles of France to stop the civil war and restore the country to its former glory. She fought so well against war and learnt so much about fighting that she wrote Medieval Europe's definitive book on chivalry, *'Le Livre des Faits d'Armes et de Chevalerie'*. In this book she tried to bring back the true ideals of Chivalry, which by then had become corrupt, debased and decadent. Caxton translated it into English and Henry VII said that every gentleman should read it.

Once a woman, I have become a man. Fortune will'd it so.
I was born a woman, but today I am a man...

With these words Christine summed up her stand against misfortune, when she rose above the oppressive social bondage in which medieval women found themselves. Forced to fend for herself, she had the reactions of a modern woman; she became the first European woman in history to make a living by writing; she devoted her energies both to writing and to the defence of her sex against injustice and prejudice. She took it upon herself to defend morality

xxiv

and ethics and to speak out against war at a time when fighting and plunder were regarded as almost welcome diversions from the other hardships of life.

The daughter of Thomas de Pisan, astrologer to Charles V, she was to become critic, moralist, historian and a leading poet. Her total output was prodigious; her reputation, eventually, enormous. Philippe of Burgundy made her the official biographer of the French court. Her work was known abroad and nowhere was it better received than in England and Italy. Henry IV invited her to England. Visconti, Duke of Milan, offered her a post at his court.

Though her ballads and other poems did not appear more advanced than those of her contemporaries, her forward-looking ideas, her vision, and her passionate will to fight to change the state of affairs as they existed, raised Christine far above the writers of her time.

It was at this period that translations into the national languages became an important part of a poet's work. Within three years of Christine's *'Epistre au Dieu d'Amour'* appearing in 1399, Thomas Hoccleve wrote a paraphrase of it in part of his *'Litera Cupidinis dei Amatoris, direita subdetes suies amatoribus'*. Christine's works were continuously translated during the next century. Anthony Woodville rendered her homage in his *'Proverbes Moraux'*, while Caxton and other early printers published her books. Numerous manuscripts of Christine in England testify to her popularity there.

Her ardent patriotism was perhaps the overwhelming motive of her existence during her later years, particularly after 1407. Her passion became the unity and independence of France. Everything else must be subordinated to this crying need. For this task a virtuous prince must lead the people, for she was convinced that a virtuous life was essential to those in authority. Born into a century when patriotism was still to develop, France and the good of France were uppermost in her mind. During the greater part of these hundred years, 1350-1450, it was France that suffered most on her soil. Before Edward III's *chevauchée* or raid in the Cotentin in 1336, this part of France had known no war for a hundred years. *"It was no marvel that they of the country were afraid for, before that time, they had never seen men of war, nor wist not what war or battle meant"*, says Froissart, the chronicler.

Through her work Christine undoubtedly helped in the formation of the National Moderate Party, which was pledged to stop civil strife and unite to face the invader; it was many years later after her death that this was finally achieved.

On the strength of her poetry alone, Christine was much admired and she had a profound influence on both French and English poets. On her purely poetic achievements, she was considered by her peers *"superior to Alain Chartier, sweeter than Eustace Deshamps, less adroit and less spiritual than Charles d'Orléans, but truer and more natural..."*

Christine's influence on poets and writers of the fifteenth century in France and England particularly, was in some ways considerable. Her *'Epistre au Dieu d'Amour'* was the first book that pleaded for her sex; her example was followed by Martin le France, Provost of Lausanne, when he wrote *'Champion des Dames'* in 1442 where he praised Christine and advocated that women should have a place in government.

"Et que les dames trepassees	*And of those women now dead*
Eurent de clergie tresor	*Who had the treasure of learning*
Plus precieux que ne soit or;	*More precious than gold*
Aussi bien que Dame Christine	*None had more than Dame Christine*
De laquelle a trompe et a cor	*Whose name abroad is endlessly*
Le nom partout va et ne fine.	*Trumpeted and proclaimed."*

Clement Marot, a poet writing after the 1460s said that to *"possess the prize in science (knowledge) and doctrine was well merited by Christine de Pisan during her lifetime, but her golden pen would make her nearly adored if she still lived, by divine will..."* In his *'Vrai disarit advocate des Dames'* (The true case for Women) Marot saw no objection to women ecclesiastics. We cite only two authors of the fifteenth century on the rights of women.

Her views on life in general, and on the role of women in particular, were far in advance of anything else being written by her contemporaries. Frustrated she may have been by the lack of apparent effect her works had on those to whom they were addressed, but her hard-earned reputation was universally recognised and applauded in her own lifetime. She was a person deserving respect – not least because she was never afraid to speak her mind. And she continues to speak.

Indeed, she surpassed all her contemporaries in strength of character and single-mindedness of purpose. Her qualities won her the admiration not only of friends but of enemies: the brothers Pierre and Gontier Col, who had attacked her mercilessly in the debate on *'Le Roman de la Rose'*, admitted that she was a *"scholarly woman of great understanding"*. Long after her death, her praises were still being sung.

She continues to have meaning for us because the causes she fought for still preoccupy us today. Her energy, simplicity and humanity speak to us as though she had never died.

Though she had the same humane traditions as Chaucer, Froissart and Deschamps, more than any of them, the inevitable turn of Fortune's Wheel haunted her, the mutability of which so changed her life and which she describes so aptly.

Vous, princes de la haute tour	*You, princes of the high tower*
Considérez un peu au moins	*Consider at least*
En quelle sureté sont les humains	*In what security does humanity live*
Exposés a de tels dangers!	*Exposed to such dangers!*
Peut-on surement les loger?	*Can humanity really be protected?*
Les hommes doivent-ils s'enorgueillir	*Should men become proud*
Pour un bien qui si tôt peut so taillir?	*When Fortune can turn in short an hour?*

In *'Lavision'* Dame Opinion speaks these prophetic words: *And in times to come they will speak more of your work than when you live. For I say again that you have come at a bad time... But after your death will come a Prince with a courageous vision and boldness who will desire to have lived in your time; he will long to have known you...*

Princes of the High Tower
British Library London

Plan of Paris

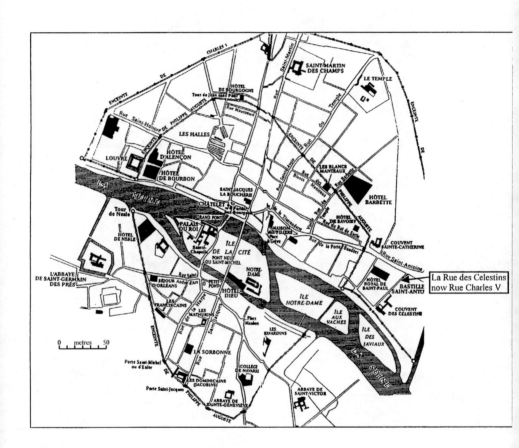

La Rue des Celestins
now Rue Charles V

The Rue des Celestins was where Christine and her parents lived in the
house gifted to them by King Charles V of France.

Genealogical Chart of the Dynasty of Jean le Bon

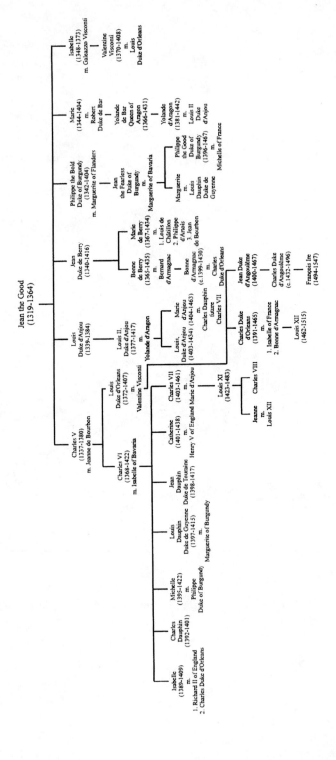

Dedicated to the memory of:

Agnes Nell de Silva (1885 - 1961)
Genèvieve Bréton (1849 - 1918)
Zeenuth Futehally (1903 - 1992)

Chapter One

My Father's Treasures

> Dame Nature herself set a jewelled chaplet on my head. These jewels made me wise... The precious stones were discretion, consideration, retention and a most beautiful stone, memory...

L ord God, open my mouth, enlighten my thoughts, and brighten my understanding, so that what I have to set down from memory is not clouded by ignorance.

Whosoever wishes to give a clear account of himself should start by stating his country of origin, who his parents are or were and if they are rich or poor, whether he is famous on any account, and finally he should give his name. So it is right that I should tell you that I was born near Lombardy, in a city of very great fame whose name is known by many travellers, the city of Venice in the country of Italy, founded in former times by the Trojans. It is a beautiful city.

My father was the son of a nobleman and well-renowned. He was a philosopher too. He was rich in knowledge and a man of great learning, possessed of this amazing wealth. Of this many have spoken that he did not seek to hide his treasure, for the possession of such is worthy of praise. He possessed such virtue, or so people say, that all the thieves in the area never thought of stealing a thing from him. He was never suspicious, nor fearful, nor in trembling, indeed he was in no way weak or timorous, with the result that no one stole his wealth from him, as happens with many other rich men, whom they kill or beat to death. My father, born in the thriving city of Bologna where I was subsequently brought up, had travelled there (Venice) to marry my mother, herself a native of Venice. Theirs had been a long standing acquaintance.

My father was the possessor of the great wealth of knowledge, which was composed of beautiful and precious stones, many noble and virtuous ones, which he drew (and guarded well thereafter) from the fountain which is at the foot of Parnassus, made by the hoof of Pegasus, where the Nine Muses divert themselves, those mentors of so many learned scholars. He repaired to that fountain for so long and worked there so diligently that the wealth, which I have spoken of so highly and which is of much greater value than a province, he gained there, and indeed, so much of it that he amassed a veritable fortune. And of the rich treasures which my father owned, there were amongst them two stones of particularly great value, which I would prize highly. They were not emeralds without imperfection, nor rich rubies. In one of them are contained so many virtues that, since the time of King Arthur, there has been no king or emperor richer than my father.

This stone of knowledge is beautifully resplendent and more glowing than a candle... a beautiful stone... the owner of such understanding could predict future events... often he would give advice to reigning princes on the subject of war and peace, storms, floods, deaths and famines to come... through this stone he knew the course of the planets and their zodiacs... he was always welcome and esteemed among princes because of this stone.

My grandfather, a licensed clerk and doctor, born in the town of Forli and a graduate of the university of Bologna, was a salaried councillor of the city I have mentioned as my birthplace. On the strength of these connections, my father was known to the Venetians, and because of his wide-ranging and authoritative knowledge was given a position like a councillor in the pay of the city of Venice, where for a while he resided on a good salary, in great honour and prosperity.

My mother was solidly built, of a happy disposition, and more valiant than Penthesilea – God really had designed her! Nonetheless, she had more common sense, strength and perception than my father, for all his great learning. She was a queen from the moment of her birth. Her merits and abilities are well enough known. Apparently there is not a lazy moment in her life, and without being a busybody, she occupies herself wherever she is. The proof of her work is all around – every day she does something worthwhile. Whoever would care to list her works past and present would never complete the task. She is old, but she doesn't seem to age: I don't see her relinquishing her life until the Day of Judgement! God gave her sort the task of maintaining and enlarging the workings of his world as soon as he had made it, to sustain all his creatures: she is a sort of Mother Nature to all alike – after all, God calls us brothers and sisters.

Now I have told you of my parents, who can be quite easily described, let me tell you my name, whether you would care to know it or not. It is not a very famous one, but to get it right all you have to do is add the letters I.N.E., and no others, to the name of the most perfect man who ever lived.

My father, whom I have mentioned here, was devoted to the idea of having a male heir to succeed to his fortune 'without throwing it away', as I well remember him saying. He and my mother conceived me in this unanimous expectation. But he did not get his wish, for my mother, more dominant than he, so wanted to have a female child like herself, that I was born a girl, to tell the truth.

My mother, however, did the best she could, for his sake, to make me resemble my father closely in every way except, of course, my sex: our behaviour, bodily mannerisms and faces became so similar that you would have thought, even in the circumstances, that they belonged to one person. So I was given a girl's name, and fed well, and given plenty of affection by my happy mother. She loved me so fondly that she suckled me herself from the moment of my birth, from which nourishment I grew strong, as she gently cared for me throughout my childhood.

I was happy, laughing and singing. As a child I knew how to please and many offered me privileges, presents and services when my mother, gentle and good, fed me. Alas! I used to cry and scream when I lost my wet-nurse who knew how to gently comfort me. Whimpering and crying was my only resource because I felt weak and ignorant, and I did not know how to cope with the situation. For, young as I was, I had spirit and intelligence. Now there is no one who feeds me with her sweet milk and takes care, because I lost my sweet food... Now I languish like an orphan and I must undergo many hurtful and sad moments. I found it difficult at first to learn this new language, different from those of my parents.

My mother, who was Dame Nature herself, set a jewelled chaplet on my head. These jewels made me wise and in all ways more pleasing. It would take pages to describe these precious stones but I must speak of four: discretion; consideration; retention, which helped to retain all I learned and felt, all that my heart conceived; the fourth, a most beautiful stone, was memory, which enabled me to remember all I learnt and read in history and science.

Though I had these gifts, this did not mean that I had them in far greater measure than others, but to add to them I also had the gift of reason and eloquence which compensated for my lack of beauty. These precious gifts increase as the body develops and they get stronger with age.

Quite soon after my birth my father journeyed to Bologna on business and to visit his estates, where immediately he received certain communications from two most excellent kings, who summoned him simultaneously to their presence by virtue of the great fame and authority of his knowledge, promising him large salaries. One of these was the sovereign of Christian kings, the King of France, Charles, the Wise, the fifth of that name. In the manner of the noble emperors of antiquity, this king, wishing to establish in himself the roots of virtue, had serious scholars sought out and summoned to his presence from all countries, philosophers grounded in mathematical and speculative sciences. Since my father's reputation had spread throughout Christendom as an expert in the speculative sciences and as an astrologer of the first order, the King extended his search to Italy and to Bologna, where my father was sent for. The other was the King of Hungary, the one who left behind him such a well deserved reputation that he was called the Good King of Hungary.

My father chose, of course, the more worthy, and besides, he wished to see the schools of Paris, the elevated French court, and possibly the King himself, if only fleetingly. Having obeyed his summons, my father arrived in France, where he was lavishly welcomed and honoured by the wise King Charles. Soon afterwards, having seen the extent of his knowledge, the King made him his esteemed special privy counsellor, an appointment he found so agreeable that at the end of one year he could not bring himself to obtain leave to return home. So the King, to solve all problems, desired him to send for his wife, children, and family, at his own generous expense, to spend the rest of their lives near him in France; and he undertook to provide incomes and pensions to enable them to maintain their standard of living. Nevertheless, my father put off this decision for nearly three years, still hoping that he would return, before he was obliged to take up the King's suggestion.

Thus in 1368 we were conveyed from Italy to France. Riding over strange countries, over high Alps and across wild plains, through deep forests and rushing rivers, past strong forts, rich castles and well kept manors, we travelled towards this second Athens.

The most benevolent and wise King wanted to see us and give us a great and joyful welcome, and this was done soon after our arrival... we wore our best Lombardic costumes, rich with ornaments and finery, as befitted women and children of state. In December the King was in Paris in the Palace of the Louvre, where we were presented to him, the whole household in the company of my good and honourable parents, and he received us with great happiness. We were naturally happy, as any loyal servants would be, to see their good master prosper, for which God be thanked. With the passing of time since my father had entered his service, the King followed his wise advice based on the science of astrology, even in his wars, and on the strength of several victorious campaigns against his enemies, his wealth grew even greater. Those princes and others still living who remember those times can vouch for the truth of these things. The King's generosity was all my father could wish for as his faithful servant, although as is common with all philosophers, he was unable to save anything. At any rate, despite his free spending the good King provided for him in such a way that he wanted for nothing, with everything that was necessary... for the authority, the honour and the great love that the King showed to my father... The King wished it made *"known to all that at the request of our beloved and faithful counsellor and physician Master Thomas de Pisan of Bologna-la-Grasse, and in consideration of the good and agreeable services he has given us and in the hope that he will do so in the times to come, we have given and settled by our royal authority and with especial grace by this present to him and his heirs, in perpetuity and without appeal, a place and a tower belonging to us, with a portion of the wall of the town which adjoins this same place and tower within Paris, behind the Convent of Barbeau; and to know that this same tower is at the corner of the Seine, between the old walls and the new, which pass in front of our Palace of Saint Pol, straight in front of the moat of the Island of Notre Dame."*

At that time I had no cares or worries, nor did I have any need of them: all I had to do was play with other children of my own age, as was usual. But for that which my destiny reserved for me it was better that I did not... because custom was stronger than justice, I acquired no learning and lost my share of this rich treasure... God damn customs! I longed for the treasure I did not have, that of great knowledge... but I had nothing unless I stole it... Although I was a female, if right prevailed, a daughter would gain as much as a son... I had the inclination for it and also a great talent... and I wished to be like my father.

Cristina da Pizzano was born in Venice in 1364. Her father, Tommaso da Pizzano, held a chair of astrology at the University of Bologna, and later became an official in the Republic of Venice, a post which he obtained through the help of an older friend, a scholar called Tommaso di Mondini, who was himself a councillor of the Republic. Tommaso da Pizzano subsequently married his friend's daughter.

By the year of Christine's birth the Hundred Years War, between England and France, begun in 1346, was already eighteen years old. When King Jean le Bon was taken prisoner at the Battle of Poitiers in 1356, his son Charles was made Regent at a very young age. The administration of France, and of Paris in particular, was so corrupt that discontent was rife, reaching a climax when riots broke out, led by Etienne Marcel the provost of the merchants (or bourgeois) of Paris. The rioters forced their way into the Palace of the Louvre in 1358 and murdered the ministers in front of the young Charles. His clothes, it was said, were splashed with their blood. As Regent he took firm command of the situation and went alone to face the burgesses at the Halles. He gradually brought about stability and prosperity to the city.

On the death of Jean le Bon in 1364, Charles became king after eight years as Dauphin. He was a sickly individual. He had suffered from ill health in childhood, which had left him thin and frail, and with a crippled hand. Unusually, he preferred intellectual pursuits rather than those considered more appropriate for a monarch: campaigning, jousting and hawking. John of Gaunt thought him *"more a lawyer than a King,"* and an English historian observed that *"the King was far more interested in conversing with his famous astrologer, Thomas de Pisan, than in the battlefield"*. Christine remembered him with affection. He was that phenomenon, an intellectual king who did not lead his armies into battle – unusual in Medieval times.

In 1368, Tommaso's family joined him in Paris and in that same year, the future King Charles VI was born.

King Charles V gave Thomas de Pisan, as he was to be known in France, a house and all the means to keep up a comfortable life. The house was behind the Convent of Barbeau (now the site of 32, Quai des Celestins) and was given to him *"perpetually and without hindrance"*. Here, the family entertained many dignitaries, as the astrologer was a person of importance at court, astrologers being considered vital for advising on matters of State. Christine writes of having been present when, among others, the **sultan of Babylon sent his escort as a delegation, with many beautiful presents. When I was a child, I remember, they visited my father in his house.**

In 1372 the King presented Thomas the fief of Orsonville in the commune of Villiers-en-Bière, east of Melun and south of the Capital. He also received a regular salary of one hundred francs a month and gifts of books, and Thomas was rich enough to buy a chateau called Mémorant.

The Paris in which Christine was brought up was an exciting city. *"What a wonderful thing is Paris,"* said a contemporary commentator and others went into ecstasy describing its bookshops, its artisans, the goldsmiths and silversmiths, the jewellers, the leather workers who bound the richly illustrated volumes, the miniature painters – many of them women – in their ateliers, the skilful wood carvers; other shops contained the linen drapers, the bakers and confectioners, the green grocers, and a host of others, including bird catchers where the nightingales sang, adding their song to calls and street cries.

An English bibliophile, Richard de Bury, writing at that time said, *"O Holy God of Gods in Sion, what a mighty stream of pleasure made glad our hearts whenever we had leisure to visit Paris, the paradise of the world... There are delightful libraries more aromatic than stores of spice; there are abundant orchards of all manner of books... opening our treasures and unfastening our purse strings we scattered money with joyful heart and bought books without price"*.

Charles V had understandably a dislike of the Louvre after his bloody experience there, and he acquired a new palace – the Hôtel de St. Pol which stretched from what is now Boulevard St. Antoine, the convent of the Celestins and the river. The palaces of the royal dukes, Hôtel d'Artois and the Hôtel de Nesles lay within the city, while the outskirts of Paris had the palaces of St. Germain-en-Laye and the Chateau de Vincennes surrounded by the Forest of Vincennes. The King bought several large houses and linked them up with gardens, orchards, covered galleries, courtyards and cloisters. One of these houses still exists, the Hôtel de Sens, the palace of the archbishops of Sens. Some of the street names, rue des Jardins de St. Pol, the rue de la Cerisaie and the rue des Lions, remain the last traces of the Hôtel de St. Pol with its gardens, the great cherry orchard and the animals that the King collected.

The King seems to have kept the Louvre for administrative purposes and formal occasions, such as the presentation of Thomas's family described by Christine, and for other prominent visitors. Apart from his new palace there were other constructions undertaken by the King including a new city wall.

Guillaume de Metz in his *'Description de la Ville de Paris au XVème Siècle'* gives us an account of the great houses around the Hôtel de St. Pol; the Petite-Muele where the Dauphin resided; and others for each of the royal dukes and the Duke de Touraine, younger brother of the Dauphin. *"You can see"*, he says, *"the Kings of France, of Navarre and of Sicile, many dukes, counts, bishops and other notables living there daily."* He describes the lavish sculpture and paintings used to decorate the palaces and the royal chapels. The Queen's chapel was painted with fruit trees and flowers on a background of v*ert gai*, bright green. In the courtyards, he says, were peacocks and other birds of pleasure. Special rooms were reserved for many paintings and tapestries hung from the walls; another hall was filled with instruments of music, harps, organs, viols, guitars and others. One hall was reserved for games, tables for chess and a variety of contemporary games. He refers to the great cavalcades and processions that frequently passed by on their way to the palace, as many foreign kings and princes visited Paris. The emperors of Greece, Rome and others came for pleasure.

As the King had given Thomas a house close to the Hôtel de St. Pol, Christine no doubt played in these delectable surroundings. There are indications that she must have frequently seen and heard the King as she compares his fragile body with his deep voice. She certainly knew the two royal princes, the Dauphin Charles and his brother Louis, the Duke de Touraine, who was later to become the powerful Duke d'Orléans and who was to be one of her future patrons. The young Marie de Berry, the Countess Montpensier, (the daughter of the Duke de Berry who was one of the King's brothers) remained a life-long friend as we shall see.

It was in this exciting and stimulating atmosphere that Christine grew up, making friends in childhood with young people who had influence in later life. Looking at paintings and sculptures, listening to music and the stories read out in the evenings – all this must have inspired and influenced her when she describes the *Salle des Fresques* in *'La Mutacion de Fortune'*.

Christine came from an intellectual climate in Italy far in advance of that in France. Bologna created the first university in Europe which opened its doors to women. Many famous women scholars were well known, particularly one of the lecturers Alessandra Galiano, a woman who was assistant to a famous fourteenth century scientist.

The Italian merchants, who at that period were very powerful, travelled a great deal and they needed to have their business in the hands of someone they could trust; their wives were the obvious choice. But they had to be educated to be able to deal with affairs, and so women in some parts of Italy were far in advance of the rest of Europe. This circumstance had a great deal to do with Christine's upbringing, though she always resented the fact that she was not educated as a son would have been. Nevertheless, she was provided with an education not usually available to women in France.

Christine's upbringing appears to have been mainly in the care of her father, and her education was based more on Italian principles than French. He brought her up as a Renaissance woman, in contrast to the general medieval woman's upbringing. She had a lively intelligence, and was a happy child with the preference of all children to play rather than study.

In truth, though she complains of her lack of erudition, her education was more complete in this respect than that of most French girls of the time, of whom little was expected beyond a knowledge of housekeeping. This was perhaps due to the sort of attitude to women embodied in the following advice, given to a young man about to marry; *"if you wish to take a wife, dear son, consider your own good: take none for her beauty, nor any that have book learning, for they are often deceitful."* Hand in hand with this attitude went the position of marriageable women in political matches: the land and dowry a girl carried with her all too often left her a mere appendage to the true purpose of the marriage, her usefulness and value limited to her ability to care for her husband's material wants. In contrast to this, Christine's education encompassed reading and writing (French and Latin being current then), chess, backgammon, riding and hawking, as well as music and dancing: altogether, the sort of well-rounded instruction someone brought up in the style of the early Italian Renaissance might have had.

Later on in *'Lavision'*, surrounded by the Nine Muses personifying the liberal arts, she reveals through her conversations on philosophy and astrology that she had indeed absorbed some of her father's knowledge.

Then, when she was fifteen, a husband was chosen for her by her father. He was a young student, born of a noble family from Picardy, and his name was Etienne du Castel.

The King's approval of the match was sought, as required, and obtained, as expected, and Charles V made himself responsible for the wedding festivities.

Chapter Two

The Court of Hymen

Marriage is so sweet a
thing...
I can prove it as my own
life shows...

Now I come to the high point of my fortunes: the time came
when I was approaching the age suitable for marriage. I was still
quite young, although my hand had been asked for by several knights,
rich men and nobles – and let no one say that in stating this I am
boasting. For the cause was the authority granted to my father by the
King's great love and honour for him, and nothing to do with my own
worth. My father esteemed the man who combined the greatest
wisdom with good manners: he noted a young graduate scholar, well-
born of noble parents from Picardy, whose virtues exceeded his
wealth; to this man whom he esteemed as his own son, I was given.
(Etienne du Castel).

Tant avez fait par votre
grant doulceur,
Tres doulz amy, que vous
m'avez conquise
Plus n'y convient complaints,
ni clamour
Je n'y aura par moy défense
mise.
Amours le veult par doulce

You have conquered me,
O very sweet friend
By your great tenderness,
which is so powerful
There is no more need of
sweet words, nor of appeals,
I shall raise no defence.

Love wishes it so through

maistrise,
Et moy aussi le veuil; car, se
m'ait Dieux
Au fort c'estoir foleur, quand
je m'avise
De refuser ami si gracieux.

Et j'ay espoir qu'il a tant de
valour
En vous, que bien sera
m'amour assise
Quant de beauté, de grâce et
tout honour
Il y a tant, que, c'est droit
qu'il souffise
Siest bien droit que sur tous
vous eslise,
Car vous estes bien digne
d'avoir mieux
Je ay eu tort, quant tant
m'avez requise,
De refuser ami si gracieux.

Si vous retien, et vous donne
m'amour
Mon fin coeur doulz, et vous
pri que faintise

Ne trouve en vous, ne nul
autre faulz tour
Car toute m'a entierement
acquise

Vo doulz maingtieng, vo
maniere rassise,
Et vos tres doulz et amoureux

sweet mastery
And, I too, am willing. for,
if God be with me,
It would be indeed madness

To refuse so gracious a
friend.

I hope that you possess much
valour
That my love be well placed

As for beauty, grace and all
honour
There is so much that, let it
suffice to say,
It is right that I should
choose you above all others,
For you are truly worthy of
the best.
It would be wrong of me,
who have been much wooed,
To refuse so gracious a
friend.

I accept your allegiance and
give you my love,
My sweet tender heart, and
pray
That there shall be found in
you no deceit,
Nor any other false traits;

For your tender approach
has completely won me
over,
So too your gentle manner
and your
Beautiful eyes, so soft and

beaux yeux,
Je auroye grant tort, en toute guise
De refuser ami si gracieux.

loving.
I would be very wrong, in every way,
To refuse so gracious a friend.

Mon doulz ami, que j'aim sur tous et prise,

J'oy tant de bien de vous dire, en tous lieux,
Que par Raison devroye estre reprise
De refuser ami si gracieux.

My sweet friend, whom I love above all and value so highly,
I hear you so well spoken of in all places,
That I should be reproved by Reason
If I were to refuse so gracious a friend.

I wore a robe of unblemished white silk, its train fixed at the collar by a fine, rich brooch; at my breast I wore a girdle, along with all the adornments a maiden must have on such an occasion. Richly dressed ladies and girls were there, nobly bejewelled and attractively clothed. There were entertainers and musicians with tubas, tambours, timpani, trumpets, lutes, harps, clarinets, clappers and little bells – more than two of each resounded as we were acclaimed on our way... all ringing out together... as we approached the church, the god Hymen (the god of Marriage) was standing at the entrance... He took me by the hand... and presented me with a fine gold ring, which he put with great affection on my finger... it is his custom that whoever stays in his court must wear a ring. With him he had brought a handsome and attractive young man, who had blond hair, over which he wore a clerk's cap, and around his shoulder, a scarf with the device *Castellum meum Deus* (God is my Fortress). He was dressed in sky blue and silver and was escorted by his friends. He was commanded to look after me and keep me in sickness and in health, without abandoning me for someone else, for however long I was to stay at his court and belong to his following. Then the young man swore by his faith that we would be true lovers and loyal companions... and his presence was most dear to me, for he was physically most attractive. Then Hymen led me into his chamber, where there were great festivities, with so many musicians playing horns that one could not have heard God casting thunderbolts. The priest changed his vestments... and sang mass for us, which we heard in good heart, tasting the blessed bread and wine.

While the church bells rang out joyously we returned to the house in procession. Then from all parts rich and beautiful presents were set aside for me, from great and small. Afterwards we took our seats at tables where there were many famous people.

We were served with delicious dishes and attractive side dishes; potage and roasts and *gelée* of fish; *fromentée* (a pastry made from flour and eggs) and little *pâtes*; pewter dishes full of fruit and jars of drinks made from herbs.

All was joy. High spirited speeches were made and after the feast we struck up many joyful songs. New motets were heard and there were numerous instrumental accompaniments; songs and dances in between each service and divertissements of all sorts. Fresh garlands were brought on this day and the next. It was all beautiful, pleasant and full of great happiness.

I was thankful as I was given to him whom my father chose as his own son. In this case I had no complaints about my fortune, for I had the right... to choose if there was another more to my liking...

Cest douce chose que marriage	Marriage is so sweet a thing
Je le pourrais par moi prouver,	I can prove it, as my own life shows
Pour qui a mari bon et sage	With a good and wise husband
Comme Dieu me l'a fait trouver	Such as God found me.
Loué soit celui qui sauver	Praise be to Him who saved him for me
Me le veuille, car son soutien	Giving me support
Chaque jour je l'ai éprouvé,	In my every hour
Et certes, le doux m'aime bien.	In truth, my sweet doth love me well.
La première nuit du marriage	The first night of our marriage
Dès ce moment j'ai pu juger	From that very moment I could judge

Sa bonté, car aucun outrage	His goodness, for he did attempt
Ne tenta qui put me blesser.	No outrage which could hurt me.
Et avant le temps du lever	Before we rose in the morning
Cent fois me baisa, m'en souviens	A hundred times did he kiss me
Sans vilenie dérober	I remember, hiding no guile
Et certes, le doux m'aime bien.	In truth, my sweet doth love me well.
Il parlait cet exquis langage:'	He spoke thus tenderly:
'Dieu m'a fait vers vous arriver,	'God hath brought me to you dear friend,
Tendre amie, et pour votre usage	And for your service,
Je crois qu'il a voulu m'élever.'	So I believe
Ainsi ne cessa de rêver	Did He bring me up.'
Toute la nuit en tel maintien,	Thus did we dream the whole night through
Sans nullement en dévier	Without turning from our purpose
Et certes, le doux m'aime bien.	In truth, my sweet doth love me well.
O Prince, l'amour peut m'affoler	Oh, Prince, love frightened me
Quand il me dit qu'il est tout mien	When he told me he was all mine
De doulceur me fera crever	His tenderness will kill me,
Et certes, le doux m'aime bien.	In truth, my sweet doth love me well.

Soon afterwards, to help him make his living, our good prince gave him the vacant post of secretary, on a good wage, and retained him as the well-beloved servant of the court, a position which he found most congenial. So this prosperity continued for several years.

Bien doit louer amour de ses	Praise be to love and all its

faits	blessings
Qui m'a donné ami si très parfait	Love that has given me so perfect a friend
Qu'en tous lieux, chacun loue ses faits	In all places they speak of his deeds
Et sa beauté, sa grâce et tout son fait	His beauty, his grace and his presence,
Il n'a de lui ni blame, ni méfait	There is in him neither evil nor blame
Dieu l'a parfait en valeur et en grâce,	God has made him perfect in honour and grace,
L'on ne pourrait mieux vouloir par souhait	One could wish for none better
Certes, c'est lui qui tous les autres passe	Truly, he surpasses all others
Si mon coeur a tout a lui attrait	If my heart is drawn to him
Qui est tout sien, c'est bien raison qu'il l'ait	It is all his, and with reason
C'est tout l'a acquis par ses tres doux traits	For all is won by his sweet gentleness
Et son gentil corps, qu'il n'en sera qu'une fois	And his graceful body
Jamais nul jour de ma vie ne passe	Never does a day pass when in truth I say
Car sans mentir dire plus tout à fait	Truly, he surpasses all others
Certes c'est lui qui tous les autres passe.	Truly, it is he who surpasses all others.

Hymen prepared a well-appointed, large ship and put it into the charge of my captain, who along with myself and my household on board, and with his leave, set out... in a short while we were on the high seas, without at any time having had contrary winds or storms, or, if we did have them, my captain was so skilled that he steered the ship well through all winds.

For ten years I was retained at the great court of Hymen, where all pleasure was mine over and above my desires: I was given good servants and a well-educated household – four squires and three maids who were always well turned-out, and who adorned my company. But above all I was honoured by him to whom I had been given: he laboured so that I would be comfortable and at my ease in this court. He was so loyal in his love and so good to me that, on my soul, I could not praise highly enough the goodness I received at his hands. Wherever we were, he was... wise, courteous and dutiful, high-minded and knowledgeable.

As Thomas had long thought of Etienne du Castel as a son, Christine certainly knew him from an early age. She is much attracted to handsome men and writes constantly of manly beauty in her various books. Etienne, Christine says, was beautiful in body as well as in mind. Though Christine admits she was not beautiful, she had, she says, a body that was **pleasant and wholesome and healthy with a good complexion.**

When, within a year of their marriage, the King fell ill, Christine was full of apprehension. Her faith in the ability and integrity of the royal princes was, however, unshakeable. Although it was with a heavy heart that she watched the progress of the King's increasingly debilitating illness, she still had hopes for the recovery of her adopted country which she was growing to love as her own.

Chapter Three

Orphaned am I

Fortune jealous of our
successes caused their source
to dry up...

harles, the fifth king to bear that name, was not without troubles in his youth... but managed by his great wisdom to turn his adversities to his advantage. As fast as the enemies around him built up their strength he swept them out of his sphere.

The King, for the sake of his health, desired to have fresh air; but in all his comings and goings there was order and measure strictly adhered to. For I saw his daily need and his processions. The accustomed manner of his cavalcade was kept in royal state in his almost daily *chevauchée*. A very strict order was maintained with a great number of barons and knights well mounted and richly dressed. (The King) always dressed in his royal robes rode between his people, in general so far from him, but in this manner and maintaining discipline he could see and get to know any man, foreigner or otherwise for whom he was King.

His knights and men rode before him in correct protocol; among his men-at-arms, dressed as for combat, there were a number and a quantity of different lancers. among whom were captains and notable knights all of them receiving good wages for this office.

The banner of the *Fleur-de-Lys* was carried before him by the Esquire of the Mantle of Ermine of the *Chapelle Royale*. This was according to ancient royal custom.

Before and after the King, and closest to him, rode the barons and princes of his blood, his brothers and others, but no one approached him or spoke to him unless he was spoken to.

After the King came many large beautiful stallions readily harnessed and decorated. When he was in the streets of Paris he was received with great joy by the people, where the order of the procession was strict and the appearance was that of a magnificent and very powerful prince. In this manner the wise King clearly showed in all his actions the noble virtues of order and measure; as royal ceremonies should be conducted with taste and joy.

He seemed to preserve and maintain this as an example to his successors; a solemn order which must be maintained to show the great dignity and high majesty symbolised in the Crown of France towards which all magnificence was due... nobly-born princes from all countries seek his love and desire to be his allies.

Many kings and princes visited Paris. As a child I remember seeing in my father's house the knights of the Sultan of Babylon, whom he had sent as a delegation, with many beautiful gifts, and being amazed at their strange clothes.

Fortune smiled on us in the lifetime of the good and wise King Charles, showering us with bountiful gifts that were received into a full, happy and peaceful family life... But then suddenly the door was opened on our misfortunes and at my tender age I had to go through it.

Our good King is ill, doing penance for our sins. It is a great pity: for there is no prince of his age in the world who is more valiant – From his childhood he was loved by all, and, thanks be to God, this love has not grown cold yet, however great his sufferings in his present illness.

It was a great blow to this kingdom and a shock to the household of Master Thomas, when our wise and good prince fell victim to a rapidly fatal illness. He had lived not even his natural term, being no more than forty-four years of age.

We ought well to mourn above all else the state of the kingdom of France, which was and is the foremost Christian kingdom... I do not think that we have ever had an aristocracy more imbued with chivalry than we do now in this kingdom of France, all ready to serve in defence or attack, if this is necessary... I have seen King Charles VI, crowned with great ceremony at the age of twelve, and he would have become a prince in whom every grace came to perfection, had not Fortune... struck him down with illness. I have seen his noble brother, Duke Louis d'Orléans, the darling of Fortune which will never be his downfall! Up to now, thanks be to God, he has nothing to complain of, and his star is still rising:... there is much goodness in him... The noble dukes of Berry, Burgundy, and Bourbon enjoy much good fortune between them, as far as I can see, for which God be thanked, although they have had plenty of setbacks in the past, but at present they are enjoying peace. If it pleases God, France will be kept from grief by the combination of their good advice and carefully weighed words, plans and deeds...

But Fortune, jealous of our successes, caused their source to dry up... At once my father lost his good salary of one hundred francs a month, which had always been fully paid, along with the books and other gifts he received, which, he had learnt, were worth almost as much; gone too was the hope the good King had given him that he would settle on him and his heirs lands to the value of 500 livres and plenty of other goods. But for lack of reminders and due to the untimely death of the King, this promise came to nothing, although my father was retained by the regents on an inadequate and sporadically paid salary...

In the management of their affairs married people should be responsible for the welfare of their household, which may be made destitute on their death because of their extravagance, and in my father's case he was also over generous towards the poor. With all respect, I do not find this at all praiseworthy, for much misery could have been alleviated had he saved what he had spent; this justifies my opinion that wise economies early in life help a man in his old age while his intellect may yet be sound. My father lost his strength in a long illness which caused him great suffering...

Giving thanks as a good Catholic to his Creator to the end, my father passed away at the hour he had previously predicted. His reputation remained among scholars, such that it was thought that there had not lived a man of such understanding in mathematical sciences or astrological judgements for more than a century before him. Among princes and those of his circle his reputation for wisdom, good deeds, loyalty, honesty and other virtues, together with his irreproachability, caused his death to be mourned and his life to be sorely missed, for no blame was attached to it, unless it be that he was

52

excessively liberal towards the poor, despite his dependent wife and children. If you think that I am partial in my judgement, there are many of his acquaintances living today, princes and others, who are certain that there was never a man so justifiably mourned on his own.

Seven years after her father's death Christine wrote this rondeau in 1396.

Com turtre suis sans père toute seulette	Like a dove orphaned without a father all alone
Et com brebis sans pastor esgarée	Like a lost lamb without a shepherd
Car par la mort fus jadis separée	By death am I separated
De mon doulz père, qu'a toute heure regrette	From my dear father, whom I regret each hour
Il a sept ans que le perdi, lassette	It is seven years that I lost him
Mieulx me vaulsist estre lors enterrée	Better for me were I buried also
Com turtre suis sanz père seulette without	Like a dove am I, orphaned a father
Car depuis lors en deuil et en souffrete	Since then in mourning, and suffering
Et en meschief très grief suis demourée	In misfortune and great grief live I
Ne h'ay espoir, tant com j'are durée	Nor do I cherish hope however long I live
D'avoir soulas quen joye me mette;	To turn my sorrow into consolation and joy;
Com turtre suis sans père toute seulette.	Like a dove orphaned without a father all alone.

In 1380 King Charles V died, aged just forty-four. He had brought back prosperity, *"remedies and restoration"* to the desolate garden which had been France. During his reign, England was pushed back till she held only

Bayonne, Bordeaux and Calais. To do all this he was forced to bring in heavy taxation. On his deathbed he said: *'The poor people of our kingdom are tormented grievously by taxes and subsidies... Take them away as soon as it is possible: Though I was forced to establish them, nothing has saddened me more nor weighed so heavily upon my heart..."* On 4th November 1380, the Dauphin was consecrated King Charles VI at Rheims.

During his lifetime, King Charles the Wise had given Thomas de Pisan the admiration and reverence which was justly his due. Now his premature death was to deprive him and his family of all their hopes and aspirations. Christine was seventeen years old.

Though Christine talks of the respect that was accorded to her father's knowledge and although it is true that he was one of the most famous astrologers of his day, there were differing opinions on his medical knowledge. He evidently impressed Charles V, for whom as astrologer and physician at the court he prepared horoscopes and advice on the astrological aspects of royal marriages.

After the King's death, the opposition of some officials, particularly Philippe de Mézieres, who named him as having given false predictions, came into the open. Even King Charles V's former tutor, Nicolas Oresme, warned the King against Italian advisers. It may be that Thomas was treated badly after the King's death because of this opposition.

Thomas himself, writing to a fellow alchemist Bernard de Trèves, mentions that he may be under the displeasure of the new King and the Duke of Burgundy due to an elixir he had made which turned out wrong, the opposite to which it was intended. Charles V and Thomas had common interests in astrology and this would explain the King's admiration and generosity towards the old astrologer. The Royal Library contained numerous books on astrology and he encouraged its study by paying for two scholarships and for various instruments for the study of the heavens. After the King's death the jealousy that his patronage had aroused was manifest by Thomas de Pisan's loss of salary and other forms of neglect. Though Etienne was obviously a junior official under Charles V, he became more important under Charles VI.

Christine had two children – a daughter born in 1381 (whose name, never mentioned in any of her writings, remains unknown), and four years later, a son, Jean. Her young husband, now head of the household, continued to maintain the state of the family. He was loved and respected by all. The god Hymen seems to have blessed this marriage and ensured that it would be a truly happy one.

Chapter Four

The Valley of Tribulation

> O painful Fortune, from
> what heights to what depths
> have you dropped me?

My husband became the head of the family, young, intelligent, wise and prudent, well-loved by the princes and all those who frequented him. Thanks to his prudent wisdom, the state of the family was maintained. But Fortune ill disposed in my regard brought me down on the turn of her wheel annihilating me completely...

Alas, the moment has come to speak of the grief which vanquished my joy, and which pursues me so that I cannot forget it for one moment. Suddenly a high wind blew up... striking the ship, and snatching up our good captain with such force that he was carried off into the sea some distance away. He was in the flower of his life, in this regard both in his knowledge and his wisdom, he was given important tasks... It was a wise and prudent decision and the Government showed it in a marked manner. He was taken in the prime of life at thirty-four... and I at twenty-five was left with two small children and a great house...

I was not even present at the death of my husband who was surprised by a rapid epidemic. However, he received the grace of God as a good Catholic in the city of Beauvais where he accompanied the King; he had no other beside him but a servant and he was in a strange house...

(After this) I desired nothing but death.... The cries, the tears,... the lamentations and moans which came from myself and my household were such that the very air seemed to tremble. Alas, we had good reason to miss the good leader who had looked after all of us and kept several of us from death. He had been so loyal in his love for me that I should never find another one the same; to see him perish in the sea, it was small wonder that we would never reach a safe port...

Just as Fortune had already crushed me beneath her wheel, she wished in her malevolence to cast me down utterly.

So I was truly filled with grief, missing his sweet company and our former happiness that had not even lasted for ten years. Drowned in this torrent of tribulation I was more desirous of death than of life, and remembering my faith and the deep love that I had pledged him, I decided with reason to never have another. I chose therefore the Valley of Tribulation. For it is said that Fortune, when she has decided to hit anything be it an empire, a kingdom or an individual, goes far afield to find sharp venomous arrows with which to pierce the chosen unfortunate and conduct him to the lowest point and this is what happened to me. I found that trouble came full upon me when I was more dead than alive.

Je suis veuve, seulette et noir vêtue	Widowed am I, alone and dressed in black
Et triste vis, simplement habillée	Simply live I, in sorrow plainly dressed
En grand malheur et bien attristée	Most sadly do I bear
Porte le deuil très amer qui me tue.	The bitter mourning which doth kill me.
Il est bien juste que je sois abattue	How could I not be down-hearted
Pleine de pleurs, peu envieuse de parler	Full of tears and quite loathe to speak
Je suis veuve, seulette et noir vêtue.	Widowed am I, alone and dressed in black
Car j'ai perdu celui par qui continue	For I have lost the one whose presence
Cette doubleur dont je suis maltraitée	Would stop this pain which torments me

Tous mes bons et ma joie sont allés	All my happy days and good fortune lost
En dur état ma fortune est rendue	How hard my fate has turned
Je suis veuve, seulette et noir vêtue.	Widowed am I, alone and dressed in black.

People never stop asking me why I am so sad, why they do not see me singing or laughing any more, why instead I live more simply than a nun... but I have good reasons for singing no more... Fortune has transformed my songs and merry making into a life of grief...

Hoping for better, I must for the time being put a brave face on things, however much they seem to run counter to my will. I must wear black and dress simply... if Fortune grieves me, I must bear it and rule myself according to my circumstances... taking all in good heart, and hoping for better.

En cet état très longtemps fus;	Long did I dwell in this state,
Ou tous plaisirs me refusais	Refusing all pleasures
Sans espoir de jamais avoir	Without hope of ever again knowing joy
Bonheur ni joie, à dire ou à voir.	Nor happiness.
Et notre nef désemparée	And our storm-tossed ship
Par ça, par là était portée.	Drifted here and there.

In what sweet amusements do you imagine I spent the early years of my widowhood, having to listen to the gallantries of foolish suitors, but in spite of what I had been obliged to suffer for so long at the hands of disloyal Fortune she was still not satisfied. I who have so often complained of her as I have good reason to do, for one sticks one's tongue into the pain of a toothache! Right up to the present her ebb and flow has governed me unceasingly.

Ha! fortune très douloureuse	Oh! painful Fortune, from what heights,
Que tu m'as mis de haut en bas!	To what depths have you dropped me!
Ta piqûre tres venimeuse	Through what torments has your sting,

A mis mon coeur en mains ebats

Tu ne pouvais me nuire en ce cas.

Ou tu me fusse plus cruel

Que de m'ôter celui-là

Qui rendait ma vie si joyeuse.

Je fus jadis si heureuse;
Il me semblait qu'il n'était pas

Au monde plus bienheureuse,
Alors je ne te craignais pas
Tu ne pouvais me faire du mal
Mais ta très fausse haine envieuse

M'a ôté celui-là
Qui rendait ma vie si joyeuse.

Horrible, inconstante, ténébreuse,
Tu m'as trop jetée à bas.
Par la méchanceté odieuse
Par qui me viennent maux en tas

Que ne vengeais-tu, hélas,

D'une façon plus miséricordieuse
Que de m'ôter celui-là

Qui rendait ma vie si joyeuse?

So poisonous, dragged my
heart.
You could hurt me only one
way…
You could not have been
more cruel
Than to take from me the
one
Who made my life so joyful

I used to be so happy
It seemed there was no one
in the world
So blessed as I.
Then I did not fear you
You could not hurt me
But your false and jealous
hatred
Has taken from me the one
Who made my life so joyful.

Horrid, fickle, and secretive,
You have struck me too low.
With your spiteful hate
Which has brought me a sea
of troubles;
Could you not have found
revenge
more merciful
Than to take from me the
one
Who made my life so joyful?

In 1389 Etienne du Castel suddenly died while out on a mission with the King. In that same year Isabeau of Bavaria, wife of Charles VI, made her state entry into Paris amid much pageantry. Isabeau was in the future to influence the balance of power at the French Court.

In the year his son was born, Charles V had issued an ordinance that in future, a king of France would rule without the aid of regents when he reached the age of fourteen. Perhaps he had had a premonition of the chaos into which France would be hurled if the Princes of the Blood became too powerful.

Cursed is the land where the prince is still a child, Christine was to write, **the guardians and the teachers of such children must possess a great deal of wisdom and prudence; for it is a momentous task to mould and develop a nature destined to rule...**

On the death of the King in 1380 his son Charles VI was only twelve years old, but when he turned fourteen, his uncles, the Duke of Burgundythe Duke de Berry, the Duke de Bourbon and the Duke d'Anjou (known also as the King of Sicily), ignored their brother's wishes and took the opportunity of furthering their own interests. The Duke of Burgundy was busy securing his territory of Flanders, which had come to him through his wife, and creating a power base in the north east of France. The Duke de Berry oppressed his subjects in the south so that he could continue his collection of manuscripts and *objets d'Art*. The Duke de Bourbon was unambitious and therefore had little influence. But it was the son-in-law of Charles V, the Duke d'Anjou, who insisted on the regency and the possession of the young King, against the express wishes of Charles V. The quarrels were finally settled, the royal Dukes dividing the Kingdom under their spheres of influence. The rapacious Duke d'Anjou for some extraordinary reason demanded, and was given, all the treasure of the late King: the plate, the jewels and the furniture, so that the young King Charles VI lost part of his inheritance.

The reign of the royal dukes during these early years was troubled by many popular uprisings in the cities, including Paris, the south and Flanders. They were put down with the utmost brutality. The bourgeois counsellors who had advised Charles V were dismissed. The cities were heavily taxed. The middle classes were put down and the rule of the nobles prevailed over France.

Christine meanwhile continued to live with the deep emotional torment which had resulted from her loss. Etienne's death had also left her in a financial plight. His **prudent wisdom** had, apparently, not extended to providing for his family after his death, and his affairs were to be found in considerable confusion. Christine's great love for her husband and her impregnable loyalty to him, now made her fearful lest in the battle for her rights, his negligence be revealed for all to see.

Chapter Five

Painful Fortune

> Alone am I, and alone I
> want to be
> Alone am I, for my sweet
> friend has left me
> ...Alone am I, whom
> nothing can now please...
> Alone am I, living without
> my friend...

I could not find the precise state of his (her husband's) finances, for it is the custom with married men not to reveal their affairs completely to their wives, which is the source of much wrong, as I can see from experience. It makes no sense with women who are not flippant but wise, and able to manage things well. So I well know that the full extent of his possessions was not revealed to me.

I was subjected to anguish from all sides, and I was surrounded by pleas and court cases, as if these were the emissaries received by widows. Those who owed me money threatened to stop me from proceeding with any claims against them. God knows it is true that one demanded the proof of my husband's investments, such as any honest man should have, for he claimed fraudulently that his debt was paid, but in his lying claim he became confused and dared no longer speak nor sustain his lie.

I was practically living in the Chamber of Finance in interminable complaints against the pitiless men there, the lackey of his lords and masters, from whom I could obtain no justice. By him I was very seriously wronged, and this would be obvious to anyone examining the case. Many do not know this, and still he does not consider it, grown old in his sins, nor does it give him a guilty conscience. Moreover, this was not my only misfortune. For the savings of my little orphans had been given with my permission by their guardians to a respected and clever merchant in order to augment their inheritance. For one year he gave a reasonable account of this and acquired the interest one might have expected on half of it. But then, tempted by the devil, he made out that he had been robbed, and appropriated it all. This led to an expensive case which I lost.

Another case weighed on me, concerning my inheritance, on which they demanded some old interest and large arrears of which there had been no mention in the document of purchase. The best lawyers advised me that I should boldly defend my cause and rest assured that it was a good one, and that the best thing I could do would be to summon the guarantors of the sale; but they had died in poverty and out of the country. There was no solution, so I came to the point where Fortune wanted me.

But this was only half my trouble for I was fighting with all my power for my fortune. I was very shocked at the state of my finances, having checked and sent through the Chamber of Accounts the schedules of a sum of money still owed to my late husband from his wages. Soon I was prevented from touching the inheritance my husband had procured, and as it was put into the hands of the King it was up to him to pay me the pension from it, but still I received none of it.

I demanded a general order from the King that this should be paid to me. So I was forced to go through a tedious court case involving much work and many replies pro and contra for several days. It is a long and boring task, as those who have been through it will know, more unpleasant than ever these days... One could see in me a woman physically weak and naturally timid: making a virtue of necessity was a costly labour for me, as I did not enjoy the company I had to keep. I had to learn to trot after them at their pleasure through their courts and common rooms, musing on my order from the King. Most days nothing came of it, or sometimes after a long wait I had replies that deceived my hope – after a long wait!

Ah, God, when I remember how many times I spent whole mornings at this Palace (Louvre) in winter dying of cold, watching for those I knew, to solicit their help in my need. I realised how difficult it all was. When one misfortune had befallen me another followed it, in so many different ways that to relate the half of it would be boring.

God knows what great suffering comes from this, and indeed has done to many. I vow that the burden of my cares was little revealed to people through my appearance or my clothes: I wore a grey, furred cloak, and a scarlet undercoat frequently repaired: I had to take care not to catch a chill. In a beautifully draped bed I spent restless nights. My meals were simple, as suited a widow who had to live in spite of everything. I felt abandoned by all.

Seulette suis, et seulette veuil êstre,
Seulette m'a mon doulz ami laissée,
Seulette suis, sans compagnon, ni maîstre,
Seulette suis, dolente et corroucée,
Seulette suis, en langour mesaisée
Seulette suis, plus que nulle egarée,
Seulette suis, sans ami demourée.

Alone am I, and alone I want to be,
Alone am I, for my sweet friend has left me
Alone am I, without companion or master
Alone am I, in suffering and anguish
Alone am I, languishing in want,
Alone am I, more than any other
Alone am I, without my friend.

Seulette suis, a huiz, ou a fenêstre,
Seulette suis, en un anglet musée,

Seulette suis, pour moi de pleurs rapaîstre,
Seulette suis, doulente ou apaisée,
Seulette suis, riens n'est qui tant me siée,
Seulette suis, en ma chambre caserée,

Alone am I, whether at door or window,
Alone am I in a hidden corner,
Alone am I, with only tears for nourishment,
Alone am I, sorrowing or soothed,
Alone am I, whom nothing now can please,
Alone am I, a prisoner in my room

Seulette suis, sans ami demourée.	Alone am I, without a friend.
Seulette suis, partout, et en tout estre,	Alone am I, everywhere and in everything,
Seulette suis, ou ne voise, ou je siée,	Alone am I, wherever I go or wherever I stay,
Seulette suis, plus qu'autre rien terrestre	Alone am I, more than any other uprooted,
Seulette suis, de chacun delaissée,	Alone am I, abandoned by all,
Seulette suis, durement abaissée,	Alone am I, cruelly cast down,
Seulette suis, souvent toute esplorée	Alone am I, so often bathed in tears,
Seulette suis, sans ami demourée.	Alone am I, living without a friend.
Princes, or est ma douleur commenciée,	Princes, my grief has now in truth begun,
Seulette suis, de tout deuil manaciée,	Alone am I, vulnerable in my mourning,
Seulette suis, plus teinte que morée,	Alone am I, more than sombre murrey,
Seulette suis, sans ami demourée.	Alone am I, living without my friend.

While waiting in the palace, several times I heard various judgements which brought tears to my eyes, and many strange replies, but above all what grieved me was the sheer difficulty of the whole case. I had the example of Jesus Christ, who was tortured in the whole of his body to help us to learn patience; Fortune desired that my poor heart was tormented in all ways by various hard thoughts. What greater ill, what greater displeasure can befall an innocent person? What greater cause of impatience can there be than to hear oneself slandered without cause, as Boethius relates in his book on consolation?

Was it not said throughout the town that I was having love-affairs, that I gave myself through self-interest? Such rumours circulate wildly and often wrongly when people who know one another meet often and appear to be lovers... But I swear upon my soul that the man in question did not know me, nor had any man or creature seen me publicly or privately in any place that he frequented; our paths did not cross at all. God be my witness that I speak the truth. Such a thing really could not have taken place, given his character and mine: we were not at all similar, and no one had any reason to think we were: I have frequently been astonished at how such calumnies could arise, carried from mouth to mouth saying 'I have heard it said'... I have behaved as if I was ignorant of their gossip. I gave no proof that what they said had troubled me, fully aware of my innocence, and sometimes I smiled at it, telling myself that God and he and I knew that there was nothing in these rumours.

I have made supplications and requests to French princes still living, asking their help on several occasions with various affairs still unconcluded and losses in the swell of misfortune that often broke over me, not seeking to persuade them by my merits, but by the former love which brought my father to serve them from a foreign country... Their help has been slow in coming and has been given in very limited ways; I have had to wait for my salary and chase up their treasurers, the tediousness of which has outweighed the value and merit of their kindness. What agony this is to a woman with my philosophical bent: I do not lust after money or material possessions, but I am forced against my nature to bear the heavy burden of pursuing these financiers, led on from day to day by their fine words.

Today, for example, I am going to attend the legal sessions of the body responsible for the cases of widows... I have little desire to amass wealth or to increase my estate, except to maintain my inheritance, which I am very keen to preserve; and I recognise that all worldly things are as vapours.

What had moved me against my nature to make my demands in person was that if I sent a message I obtained no audience in their presence. However, when I came myself to remind them of my widowed state and, kneeling before them, asked for their compassion and help, I found no pity in them, to say the least. This humiliation, along with others, lasted a long time: I was constantly in this state for more than six years. Next, I tried to obtain a rather modest sum, which I was paid in part after great efforts on my part and intercessions from several lords; but the rest was withheld.

God knows how my heart was tormented when judgement was passed on me and my treasured possessions seized by bailiffs: the loss I suffered was great but the shame greater. When I was forced to raise a loan somewhere to avoid greater evil, I went to find a friend, my face blushing with shame, God knows. I have still not recovered from these misfortunes today; the memory of them is like an attack of fever.

Once I replied to someone who told me I had nothing to complain about, for in my isolation I had no responsibility. I told him that he had not examined my case closely enough, for I had been defrauded several times, and as he refused to understand I emphasised that I had been personally defrauded no less than six times. On top of all this, the fear was gnawing at my heart that my affairs would become common knowledge, and I worried that people I did not know, as well as my neighbours, might see that the unhappy outcome of all this was the doing of my predecessors, and not my own. Embittered with uncertainties, I would rather have chosen death than let this be my undoing. Ah, what a burden for those who seek to bear it against the desires of Fortune, what a wound to an ever-loving heart! There is no grief so great, and one who has not been through it would not believe it. God knows what great suffering comes from this, and indeed has done to many.

How many disagreeable words, how many mocking looks, how many ironic smiles from people filled with wine and corpulent leisure, I have often had to endure, and for fear of worsening my needy situation, I had to dissimulate without replying, turning away or pretending that I had heard nothing... May God set their vile consciences to rights, for I met some evil men. In the course of this affair I found no charity either from great or lowly people, although I had requested several nobles and important people to put in a good word for me, as moral law obliges them to help widows and orphans.

To crown all my adversities at this time a long illness assailed me, like Job, as a result of this case in which I was at fault however hard I pursued it, and for which my resources were insufficient, my cases were lost, and due to their failure I had to meet the expenses at every point from my own finances. It was extraordinary to see how Fortune could be so set against me: losses came in all conceivable ways, although I took action on good advice and followed it, God knows, to the best of my ability; what happened to me generally in all my actions was the contrary of what might have been reasonably expected.

So the leech of Fortune continued to suck away my inheritance. However, one day I had gone through my entire resources, and I had no more to lose: so my pleas ended, but not my misfortunes. With how many tears, sighs, pleas, lamentations and deep wounds did I suffer when I was all alone in my retreat, or when I saw around me at my hearth my little children and my unfortunate relations, thinking of past times and present misfortunes for which I had no remedy, and which crashed over me in waves. I pitied my family more than myself.

My thoughts do not dwell on excessive adornments or luxurious living... only on the labour of love that I have in looking after my mother in her old age, mindful of the great material benefits I received at her hands, and wishing to be duly worthy of them. I am perplexed and aggrieved when Fortune does not allow my wishes to come to anything. Why should not a woman of such perfect honour and of such an exemplary life, as she is and always has been, enjoy her rightful destiny?

I do not see Fortune ready to help me at any point... When I see others in the bosom of their families, brothers and parents rejoicing together, I am reminded that I am in a strange country, far from my own. Even two of my brothers, wise and honest... have decided that, because they were not provided for here, they would go and live on the inherited lands of my father. I, who am tender hearted and honest with my friends, complain before God when I see my mother without the sons she wants near her, and myself without brothers... O patience! – a virtue of which I had not laid up such great reserves – often great bitterness got the better of you in me. There was a time when I was defending cases and prosecuting others in four courts of Paris, and I swear on my soul that I was beleaguered by dishonest people without justification. How was I to have peace, seeing their plots, to overturn my petitions, I who absolutely abhorred such behaviour as against my peace-loving nature, without giving in to them at very great expense? All this lasted more than fourteen years.

I found nothing to my advantage, and one day, depressed by these matters, I composed this ballad:

Hélas ou donc trouveront   Alas! where will they find

reconfort
Pauvres veuves de leurs bien
despouillées
Puis quen France qui seult estre
porte
De leur salu et ou les exillées

Seuient fuir et les desconseillées,

Mais or ny ont mais amistie.

Les nobles gens n'en ont nulle
pitiée
Aussie nont clers ni greigneur
ni mendre.
Ne les princes ne les daignent
entendre.

Des chevaliers nont elles nesun
port.
Par les prélas ne sont bien
conseillées
Ne les juges ne les gardent de
tort.
Des officiers naient deux
maillées.
De bon respons de poissans
traveillées.
Sont en maint cas na la moitié.

Devers les grans naroyent
exploitie.
Jamais nul jour ailleurs ont a
entendre
Ne les princes ne les daignent
entendre.

Où pourront mais fuir puis que
resort.

comfort
Poor widows, despoiled of
their goods?
Since in France, the wonted
haven
Of their salvation, the place
where exiles
Are wont to flee, and the
unprotected,
No friendliness is offered
them any more.
The nobles show them no
pity
Nor the educated - neither
greatest nor least
And the princes deign not to
lend them an ear.

From the knights they get no
support,
By the prelates they are ill-
advised,
The judges do not defend
them from wrong.
From officials they get not
two farthings' worth
Of proper replies; by the
powerful
They are frequently
tormented, nor will half
Their needs be met from the
side of the great
Never at any time; these
have others to attend to;
And the princes deign not to
lend them an ear.

What refuge have they?
Since in France

Nont en France la ou leur sont
baillées
Esperances vaines conseil de
mort
Voies denfer leur sont appareillés

Selles veulent croire voyes
brouillées.

Et faulx consaulx ou appointee.

Nest de leur fait nul nont si
accointie
Qui les aide sanz a aucun mal
tendre
Ne les princes ne les daignent
entendre.

Bons et vaillans or soyent
esveillées
Voz grans bontez ou vesves soit
taillées
Devoir mains maulx de cuer haitie

Secourez les et croiez mou dettié

Car nul voy que vers elles soit
tendre
Ne les princes ne les daignent
entendre

They have no recourse but
are offered
Only vain hopes, counsel of
death.
Voices of Hell are presented
to them
If they are willing to put
their trust in a babel of
voices
And false counsel, with no
real attention paid
To their plight; they have no
one close to them
Who would help them
without threatening ill.
And the princes deign not to
lend them an ear.

Good and valiant men, let
your great bounty
Now be stirred! oh, widows
are destined
To bear many ills with a
glad heart.
Help them! Believe this my
ditty!
For no one shows himself
tender towards them
And the princes deign not to
lend them an ear.

Christine's life at this period was made even more difficult, for to her pain and resentment were added the consequences of a desperate financial situation. She found herself precipitated into dealing with indifferent officials and fraudulent debtors with whom her husband had had business dealings.

The court, without the strong hand of Charles V, had degenerated into corrupt factions struggling for power.

Charles VI, when he was twenty in 1388, announced through his counsellor the Cardinal of Laon that it was now expedient for the King to rule by himself. The young King, aided by his brother Louis d'Orléans, brought back the principles of government practised by Charles V. Unfortunately, this state of affairs ended.

In 1392 while out riding Charles VI was struck down with the first of his fits of madness. The recurrence of these fits helped the regency under his uncle Philippe of Burgundy to maintain its power. Theoretically power would remain in the King's hands as the regency was established only for the duration of his bouts of insanity. In actual fact real power lay permanently with the regent.

The influence at Court of Charles' able and intelligent brother, Louis d'Orléans, cannot be underestimated. The two brothers had always been very close and Charles showed, as he said, *"profound and deep affection"* for Louis by giving him manors, titles, houses and money. Louis d'Orléans felt it was he rather than his uncle Philippe of Burgundy who had a legitimate claim to the regency.

Meanwhile, scandals were whispered daily in the corridors of the Louvre or in the Hôtel de St. Pol where Charles VI and his pleasure-loving wife Isabeau of Bavaria lived. Isabeau herself was a strange evil character, sensual and egotistical. She genuinely seems to have cared for her husband at first or, at least, for her pleasure with him; but during his periods of madness, the King called on his attendants not to let her near him. This growing aversion to her, not unnaturally, changed her feelings. It is not strange that she turned to his brother Louis, so like the King in many ways. Louis' ambition to rule as regent may also have had something to do with her liaison with him.

Louis was already married, and his wife, Valentine, happened to be the only person at court who had any calming influence on the King. A daughter of Galleas Visconti, first duke of Milan, and of Blanche, sister of Charles V, Valentine was also her husband's cousin. She was one of the most accomplished women of her time, speaking several languages, including German, Latin and Greek, was a good musician and played the harp.

Her biographer, Emile Colas, says: *"She was loved by all for she gave pleasure to all creatures; she had a tender heart for the poor... tall, slim, with a long neck and an elegant figure she had infinite grace and distinction; she stood out at the French court as a real daughter of the dawn of the Italian Renaissance".*

Eustace Deschamps wrote a ballad in praise of Valentine, Duchess d'Orléans:

"A bon droit doit de tous estre louée	*By rights you should be praised by all the world*
Celle qui tant a des biens de nature,	*You, to whom nature has given all that is good*

De sens, d'onnour, de bonne renommée,	The sentiment of honour, of good renown
De doulx maintien, l'exemple et la figure	A sweet appearance, an example of a humble
D'umilité. Celle qui met sa cure	Figure – who takes care to honour
A honorer un chacun en droit li;	Each one as they deserve;
Qui gent corps a, juene, fresche, joly,	You, who possess a beautiful body, pure, fresh
De hault atour, de lignié royal,	With the high allure of a royal line
Celle n'a pas à manière failly:	One who does not lack the manner
A bon droit n'est d'elle un coeur plus loyal.	By right, there is no heart more loyal."

Christine was to mention her several times in her books:

What can I say about Valentine Visconti, Duchess d'Orléans, Daughter of the Duke of Milan, and wife of Duke Louis, son of Charles the Wise – a lady filled with wisdom and prudence. Her loyalty to her lord was strong and constant under adversity. She bore her *seigneur* great love. Her excellent knowledge and good doctrine she taught her children and she governed the duchy with justice and economy. She was virtuous in all ways.

Not surprisingly Isabeau became jealous of Valentine out of pique. The regent Philippe of Burgundy became jealous because of policy: he did not want a rival for the King's trust. Moreover his own wife, Marguerite, a woman now about fifty, was very plain, and Philippe had married her because of her extensive lands in Flanders. She was envious of Valentine, who was young, beautiful and gifted.

Valentine had indeed earned the jealousy and envy of Queen Isabeau and the Duke of Burgundy, as her influence over the King was strong. Her gentle presence soothed the King. She brought him books, probably read to him and played on her harp. In the midst of the corrupt court of Charles VI *"she shone by her elevated sentiments, the grace of her person, the strength of her conversation"*. Unfortunately the court of France was unable at that time to assimilate this enlightened presence. Her husband, Louis d'Orléans, was struggling against Burgundy for the right to direct the government during *la maladie du roi*, so that Valentine's influence over the King was deeply resented. So great was the war against her that the people of Paris, easily misled, threatened her safety. An abominable plot was carried out with great efficiency. The calumnies were quite infamous: that Louis had given his brother, the King, a sword that was bewitched; that Valentine had tried to poison the King's son; that when the King asked daily for her presence beside him, and when she was able to cheer him and distract his mind from dark thoughts she had used sorcery so that he could not do without her. All these rumours and more were circulated among the people who in fact had witnessed several trials for sorcery during those years.

Louis took Valentine out of Paris to Blois, the capital of the Duchy of Orléans, where she remained until her death.

In the long rivalry between the House of Orléans and the House of Burgundy, Valentine Visconti was the first victim.

Ambition and jealousy were leading France into a dangerous abyss. The strong passions aroused were to prove disastrous for France. This was the situation at court during Christine's widowhood.

Chapter Six
Solitude Volontaire

> a life of writing, solitude
> behind closed doors, with all
> my senses awakened to the
> things I found in beautiful
> books... I forgot everything
> and one whole day passed like
> an hour

When all my legal struggles were over, along with my days of youth... I returned to the way of life that most naturally suited me, that is the quiet, solitary life.

I am often all alone, sunk in grief and thought, lamenting past times of happiness now removed from me, always remembering him through whom I lived in glorious happiness... I could not have wished for a wiser, better or more handsome person than he: He loved me justly, as I had been given to him young. If our love and our two hearts had the power to do it, we would have become a single being, closer than brother and sister, sharing joys and sorrows. His company was so agreeable to me that when he was near me there could have been no woman so richly endowed; he put me at rest with his easy, pleasant manner.

He pleased me ah, so deeply, that I could not speak well enough of him if I devoted my entire life to it... It was thus most distressing for me to lose him whom I ought to love above all things. I was senseless with grief – I became like a recluse... I could not take a single step without tears coming to my eyes.

It became clear to me that I should have to start working; I who had lived protected, in luxury and pleasure, had not learnt to work. I had to pilot this ship on open seas, in the midst of a storm, without a master. I contemplated a life of writing, of *Solitude Volontaire*, behind closed doors, with all my senses awakened to the things I found in beautiful books... I forgot everything and one whole day passed like an hour. My good mother had to bang on the door of my chamber and call me for dinner.

One day I had hidden myself away in a small study, where I often enjoyed browsing through various works. I looked in one or two books, but soon became tired of them, because I could find nothing in them that was capable of comforting a sorrow that bore in on my mind. The day of this depression was October 5th 1402... I was still settled in there when night drew on; crouching over the light I sought to pass the time and rid myself of my mourning in meditation on some book.

Suddenly there came into my hands a famous book, a favourite of mine, able to take me out of my loneliness and discomfort, Boethius' good book on consolation. As soon as I began to read, my anger and heavy depression passed away... I liked this book more than I had ever done, and it had never before had such a good effect on me... But it was time to go to bed, as midnight had already passed... I tried to sleep, but somehow various thoughts began to enter my mind, and I was unable to stop them. It occurred to me how this world is no more than a vapour, ephemeral, full of sadness, and without security or goodness, where not even the greatest are assured of good fortune and a comfortable life...

In solitude there came to my mind the meditations of Latin authors and those who write on the noble arts, as well as various phrases and fine rhetoric that I had heard in times past on the lips of my friends, my father, my mother and my husband, despite the fact that I had remembered little of it through my stupidity.

For although I was naturally inclined to such study since my birth, I was kept from it by the usual business of married people, along with the responsibility of bearing several children. Likewise youth, that sweet enemy of good sense, often keeps children from their studies, however clever they may be, and gives them a preference for playing games, unless the fear of punishment keeps them at their work. I had no such fear.

Alas, when I had at my side masters of the sciences, I was not interested in learning, and now the time has come when my mind and emotions deceive me by desiring that, which for want of learning I cannot have, that is to say, the art of philosophy. O sweet tasting honeyed philosophy, my dear science, preceding all other treasures as their most worthy sovereign, how happy are those that taste you to satiety! – or so it seems to me, at any rate, in my imaginings of something I have never fully known. Nevertheless, I can smell its delectable fragrance on the small lower branches of science, unable to climb any higher, and this helps me imagine the happiness of those who savour its supreme delights.

As a child my mind and emotions were dominated by a desire for play, and I could not apply myself to the work of learning... Yet I sustained the desire to be entirely devoted to study, seeing all other occupations and pleasures as vanity, and now I gave so much time to it that no woman born for many years can have excelled me.

Thus at this time, when my age has naturally brought me to some maturity, I have surveyed those past experiences behind me, and the goal of everything before me; just as a man who has come by a dangerous path turns round and looks at it in astonishment, declaring that he will never use it again and will strive to find a better one. So, considering the world to be full of perilous paths, I saw that there is only one that leads to my goal, that is, the way of truth which I now followed in the love of learning to which my nature and destiny inclined me. To this end I shut the door of my senses to the vague enticement of matters unfamiliar to me, clutching to me those beautiful books and volumes.

I told myself that nothing would bring back my former losses, and that I should not pretend to be an expert in the profundities of occult sciences full of terms I could not understand. As Cato said, *"to read a book without understanding is worse than reading half of that book."* So like a child confronted for the first time with his A.B.C., I set myself to reading the ancient histories from the beginning of the world, those of the Hebrews and Assyrians, concerning the origins of the kingdoms, proceeding from one to the next, and eventually reached the Romans, the French, the English and other writers of history.

Then I moved on to scientific logic, according to what I was able to understand in the space of time available for my studies. Next I gave myself over to reading the poets, and the usefulness of my knowledge increased all the time. I was pleased to find my own natural style, delighting in subtle finishes and fine themes decorated with attractive and morally sound inventions, their beautifully styled metres and compositions constructed according to the laws of well polished rhetoric and ornamented with subtle turns of phrase. Through this knowledge nature, contented with me, said: "Daughter, console yourself in achieving the desire that I myself put in you". Continuing in this way, and filling every day with study, my understanding of these writings grew ever deeper, until my mind and heart could not be satisfied without them.

Thus was born in me the desire to produce new works, on the basis of what I had already seen and studied. Nature continued with these words: "Take up your tools and temper on the forge the material I will give you, so strongly that neither iron, nor fire, nor any other substance will be able to destroy it, even though its seams are delicately wrought. When you carried your children in your womb, you felt great pain in giving birth to them. I want you to produce new works through which your memory will be illuminated everywhere, for all time, in the eyes of princes and of the world.

"Your memory will give birth to them joyfully, forgetting the labour they cost you as you hear the voice of your creations, just as a woman who has delivered forgets her pain the moment she hears the cry of her child." So then I began to compose pretty little pieces, more of a light nature at first; like the craftsman who produces much fine work the more he practices it. I studied widely all the time and plunged ever deeper into obscure subjects, evolving my style towards a greater finesse and turning it to more elevated subjects.

From the year 1389 when I commenced, up till 1405, the date from which I write, my work together made fifteen principal volumes, not counting *'les autres petites dictez particuliers'* which made an ensemble of about seventy books of a large format. As it is manifest I did not expect great praise for all this, and there is no merit in boasting. God knows that I speak of this but to put down and recount my good and bad fortune.

In the 14th and 15th centuries, the arts flourished, and the artistic world was closely integrated into the political and social life both of the courts and of the people in general. Poetry, theatre, dancing and music were the main forms of entertainment. Artists were much admired and could exert considerable influence through their work. Poets, in particular, were much sought after at the courts of kings and nobles, and poetic accomplishments were appreciated in any man and were not exclusive to professional poets. Any courtier who was not actually a poet was at least expected to be well read and a good raconteur and conversationalist.

It was in this rich, artistic environment that Christine began her career as a poet. It had become clear to her that she would have to work and urged on by her friends she decided to make a living from what had until then been a pastime – her poetry. In 1392 Eustace Deschamps, Christine's friend and a prominent poet attached to the court of Louis d'Orléans, wrote 'L'Art de Dicter', a treatise on poetic forms: the ballad, the rondeau, the lay, the virelay, the complaint. It is most probable that Deschamps was one of those friends who encouraged Christine to take up a career in writing. Christine perfected her ballads and rondeaux – the other forms did not suit her so well. However, what made her achievement quite remarkable was that unlike Eustace Deschamps or other poets of her day – Guillaume de Machault, and Jean Froissart – who were all attached to a princely court, she was a 'freelance'. She had no official position and was thus obliged to place her work as she could, often sending it unsolicited to potential or actual patrons. She had no security, was poor and had to write constantly to survive. Yet she managed to educate herself, write, bring up her children, and support her mother and brothers and, of course, pursue her endless petitions.

Chapter Seven

Cent Ballades

Once I was a woman but now I am a man and man I shall remain.

et me speak and tell you who I am. Once a woman, I've become a man: Fortune wanted it to be that way, I was born a woman but today I'm male, I wouldn't lie to you. My acts will prove my words to you are true. As true as woman I was made. As true as everything I've said. But it would more than please me to be again a woman as I was when Hymen spoke to me. However, Fortune has kept me from that haven, and I shall never lodge there again. I am now a man and man I shall remain.

Even now Fortune had not wounded me as she could, for I took refuge in the company of the poet's muses... under whom I composed poetic lamentations, mourning my good friend and the good days that were past.

Some friends have begged me to write more poems to send to them. They say that the poems I have given them have brought much pleasure. I do not know if I do make beautiful poems but in any case as they request me so strongly and they seem so certain, I have started to write though I am so ignorant, to accede to their desires. Yet I have neither the sentiment nor the spirit to write poems of consolation and joy because my extensive grief has deflected my happiness in all things. I find myself turning away from all things joyous. The great pain I bear makes me morose and melancholy and I can speak of this endlessly. But I will not write of this when I want to give them pleasure and accede to their desires.

To those that ask me why I am in mourning and why it has lost me all my happiness, I can easily say that the sudden death of him that made my happiness is the cause. But I write these poems because I have been asked for them.

My poems hide my true feelings; my eyes would rather weep, and nobody knows what torment my poor heart is enduring. I conceal my grief since I find pity in no one; the less sympathy one meets the more reason one has to weep. So no complaint passes my lips, no pitiful mourning; instead I laugh when I would rather cry, and without rhyme or rhythm I sing these songs that hide my true feelings. There is little worth in showing one's depression. Those whose hearts remain happy in such a state keep them so only by a sort of madness. So I am not concerned to reveal the direction of my wishes, instead to veil my obscure pain, I write poems that hide my true feelings.

Some poets could misjudge me and think that it is of my love that I speak, and say that I could not know the power and capricious turns of love and speak of it so often without feeling these moods myself; but without contradicting them I appeal to other wise poets to support me.

Those who charge me to write these poems, beautiful, pleasant, long or short, with the most delicate sentiments and those emotions that please almost everyone, it is of love that they wish me to speak, however delicately. To those that think there is some merit in my work I do not excuse myself nor do I accuse myself. For if my love poems are some of my best I have neither the torments of love, nor the joy or the pain. Yet many speak of love whose hearts are not engaged. Most wise poets will support me in this.

Le plus bel qui soit en France
Le meilleur et le plus doux
Hélas! que ne venez-vous?

M'amour, ma loial fiancé
Mon Dieu terrain sur tous
Le plus bel qui soit en France
S'il est en votre puissance
Pour quay n'approchiez de nous?

The most beautiful in France
The best, the most gentle
Alas! Why do you not come?

My love, my loyal fiancé
My earthly God above all
The most beautiful in France
If it is in your power
Why then do you not approach?

Si verre lors sans doubtance	If true and without doubt,
Le plus bel qui soit en France.	The most beautiful in France.

The hundred ballads set down in this book are all charged with my feelings, thus I have kept my promises to those who kindly asked for them... Whether the reader would care to know it or not, I have written my name into the hundredth ballad... I pray those who will read them conscientiously, and those who may recite them anywhere, that they do not take them too seriously and do not criticise them too maliciously... I have written them neither for praise nor reward; but I have picked them out of my thoughts. My limited understanding will allow them little reputation, but to show you that I do not disown them, I have written my name into them. It also helped to pass the time and to see if I could bring any happiness to my sad heart by composing gay love-songs, as if it were the emotions of another.

Je Vous Vends.... (dialogue between lovers)

Je vous vends la paserose	I sell you the hollyhock
Belle, dire ne vous ose	Beauty, I dare not tell
Comment Amour vers vous me tire,	How love draws me to you;
Vous apercevez tout sans dire.	You perceive it without words.
Je vous vends le vert muguet;	I sell you the fresh lily of the valley;
Medisants sont aux aguets,	Gossips are alert,
Ami, pour nous gueter;	Love, to watch us,
Si cherchez autre sentier	So look for another path
Quand vers moi venir devrez	When you come to me
Et l'heure sonner ouirez.	And you hear the hour sound.
Je vous vends le cerf volant;	I sell you the flying kite,
De bien aimer ne soyez lent	To love well do not be slow,
Ami, car vous avez amie	Friend, for you have one
Qui desir autre aimer n'a mie	Who desires nothing but to

Ainse soyez lui vrai et entier
Car celle vous aimes sans tiers.

Je vous vends claire fontaine.
Je vois bien que je perds ma
peine,
Dame de tant vous requerir,

Puisque rien n'y puis acquerir.
Que l'heure ou je vous vis soit
maudite.
Je m'en vais et adieu vous dis.

Je vous vends le songe amoureux,

Qui fait joyeux ou douloureux

Etre celui qui l'a songé.
Ma dame, le songe que j'ai
Fait a nuit, je vous ferai voir
Si je puis votre amour avoir.

Je vous vends la fleur d'ancolie.

Je suis en grand melancholie,
Ami que ne m'ayez changée;

Car vous m'avez trop etrangée,

Dites m'en le voir, sans ruser,

Sans plus me faire en vain muser.

Je vous vends du rosier la
branche.

love you,
Be truly and entirely his,
For he loves only you.

I sell you the clear fountain.
I see well the wasted effort

I have spent, lady, to possess
you,
For I have received nothing.
How I curse the hour when I
saw you.
I will leave and say adieu to
you.

I sell you the amorous
dream,
Whether it be joyful or
painful
To him who dreams.
My lady, the dream I had
This night, I could show you
If I can but have your love.

I sell you the columbine
flower.
I am in great melancholy,
Love, for you have changed
me;
But you treat me like a
stranger
Speak and see me without
ruse
Without making me waste
time in vain

I sell you a sprig from the
rose.

Oncques neige ne fut plus blanche,
Ni rose en mai plus colorée

Qu'est la beauté fine mesurée
De celle en qui entierement

Me suis donné tout ligement.

Je vous vends la feuille de tremble.
De peur tout le coeur me tremble

Que pour moi vous ne soyez blamée
Ma belle dame très aimée;

Et si vers vous je n'ose aller

Pour la doutance du parler
De ceux qui nous ont accusés,
Ainsi me'en tenez pour excuser.

Je vous vends la rose vermeille.
Amour me commande et conseille
Que je fasse de vous ma dame,
Dites moi, belle, par votre âme,

Pourai-je votre amour avoir
Si je fais vers vous mon devoir?

Fleurs vous vends de toutes couleurs.
Je suis guéri de mes douleurs
Quand vous me faites bonne chère,
Ma gracieuse dame chère

Never was snow whiter,

Nor rose in May more colourful
Than the harmonious beauty
Of her to whom I have entirely
Given all me allegiance.

I sell you the leaf of the aspen tree.
In fear my whole heart trembles
Lest you be blamed on account of me
My lovely lady much beloved;
And if towards you I daren't draw nigh
For fear of what may be said
By those who slander us,
Then allow me to be excused.

I sell you the vermilion rose.
Love commands and counsels me
To make of you my lady
Tell me, lovely lady, on your soul,
May I possess your love
If to you I am dutiful?

Flowers I sell you of every hue.
I am cured of sorrow
When you treat me graciously,
My dear gracious lady,

Mais quand vers moi etes yrée	But when to me you show your ire
La mort est de moi desirée.	Then death is what I most desire.

It is true that in royal circles rumours were already spreading of my ordered way of life, in other words, my studies – this had been discovered despite my desire to keep it secret – I made the novel present to certain princes of some of my volumes, however insignificant they may have been, which, being benevolent and humble men, they gracefully received with gladness. It was so unusual for a woman to write... in this way my books were rapidly sold and taken to various regions and countries.

If, as I have said, my books were made known to foreign princes, they were offered to them not by me, but by others as something of a novelty in feminine sensibility since it was composed by a woman. As the proverb says, *"New things please more than they should"*. Nor do I say this in any bragging spirit. The foremost Duke of Milan in Lombardy (Galleas Visconti, father of Valentine, Duchess d'Orléans) who was informed of these developments and possibly over-estimating my worth wished to attract me to his country, he ordered a stipend to be payed to me permanently if I went to Milan. In this regard, several gentlemen of his court were sent by him as ambassadors.

However, Fortune as ever did not allow my ruined estate to be repaired: she immediately took him away by death. So I lost a patron who wished to benefit me. Not that I would have lightly contemplated leaving France, whatever the reason, even in order to return to my native country.

There is a great longing to be bound only to the needs of one's horse, to exile oneself, to spend one's money and spoil one's clothes, to feel the rain and snow, to live a life devoted to danger. He who leaves the sweet land of France at great trouble and expense to see Milan or Pavia will he have great profit from it, or value it? As many important people have subsequently told me, the receipts from my books alone would have made it worthwhile for me to stay in this country. But Fortune wounded me deeply in taking from me a good friend whose loss was a great blow.

My life began to change. Not to say that my bad fortune changed for the better, for Fortune's malevolence persisted, as she was grieved

82

by the usefulness of my solitary meditations, not only towards myself but also my nearest and dearest, to spite me... hating my prosperity as much as ever, she took away my good friends from me, denying them a good life... But all at once I found myself to be of strong heart: it felt as though I had become a man... Seeing the ship in danger, I myself began to put things to rights; with nails and joints I repaired the planks... now I really was a man, capable of steering ships. Fortune had taught me this...

When Christine says she became a man in her mind and in the mind of her contemporaries, the idea of a woman who would, or could, undertake a philosophical, literary or scientific work was unthinkable.

The patronage by women of literature and the arts in France and England seems to have started with Eleanor of Aquitaine and her daughter Marie de Champagne, who were both poets in their own right but, unlike Christine, they wrote entirely for pleasure as a pastime; and if in eleventh century Japan Lady Murasaki wrote her masterpiece *'The Tale of Genjii'*, it was certainly not to gain her livelihood. Eleanor inherited Aquitaine from her father, so she was Duchess of Aquitaine in her own right. She was Queen of France as the wife of Louis VII and Queen of England as wife of Henry II. She brought Aquitaine as part of her dowry and subsequently France and England fought over this territory in the Hundred Years War. A procession of famous women not only encouraged the poets but built and endowed colleges in universities like those of Bordeaux, Angers, Oxford and Cambridge.

Commerce and industry were carried on by women while their husbands sought glory and rewards of pillage on the battlefield. Others, more humble, worked hard on their manors, or as nuns they organised and helped to run hospitals. Women mystics like Julian of Norwich and Catherine of Siena came into prominence, while others efficiently administered great convents.

During the first years of widowhood and work Christine says she chose *Solitude Volontaire*. Christine earned her money by her poetry and executed orders for love poems and prepared herself by study for her more serious works. During these two years, 1389-1390, she had not only had her grief to bear; she had to work and she carried on an almost continuous litigation against her creditors in the law courts.

At the time when Christine took up her poetic career, literary life in Paris flourished and she and Eustace Deschamps were both leading spirits in the brilliant literary salon of Louis d'Orléans. On the fringes of the university a whole auxiliary of artisans grew up; the copyists of the encyclopaedia, the *romans*, the *fabliaux*, the bibles, the psalters and many others.

As all writing was still being done in manuscript at this time there was a whole industry of copyists and illuminators who were employed to produce the work of writers. Christine would probably write the first draft of her manuscript in her own hand, as we see her doing in many miniatures, but for subsequent copies she would employ a copyist; very often poor students from the university earned money to continue their studies, in this way.

Ateliers of men and women would fill in the full page illustrations or the vignettes at the top or middle of the page. Colours were carefully prepared with water and the addition of gum from pine trees, the whole bound together with white of egg; usually it was *said "water for frescoes, eggs for manuscripts, oil for wood..."* Seven coats of colour, one over the other, obtained the desired effect. The ateliers had to be well provided with gold leaf for large surfaces; gold powder to use with a brush for the smaller details. The polishing over it all was done with an agate or a wolf's tooth which gave it a durable brilliance.

Christine would have at her disposal a night lamp with a wick, an inkwell, quills, a ruler, a plumb line, a table, a chair, a blackboard, chalk, a pumice stone and a scraper to prepare the parchment. The desk or *pupitre* would usually be made so that it could be raised or lowered; the prepared parchment would be wound around a roller for convenience and the best quality would be supple and white. We know she took great care over the miniatures that accompanied her books and over the illuminators she employed.

The miniatures give us visible testimony of the importance of the arts in everyday life. We see Chaucer, Froissart, Deschamps and Christine and so many others presenting or reading their books to their patrons. Most of Christine's works are lavishly illustrated with miniature paintings, the pages decorated with flowery borders and illuminated in gold. One of her manuscripts, *'L'Epistre d'Othéa à Hector'*, presented to Louis d'Orléans and dedicated to him, contains over a hundred such miniatures. Her favourite illustrator was a woman called Anastasia **who was born in the town of Paris where the rulers of the world reside. She is so expert in the making of vignettes for the illumination of books and illustrating histories that there does not exist another who works so delicately and beautifully as she does, nor one who is employed so frequently and whose books are so precious and expensive.**

Christine would have her work produced in superbly illuminated form and bound in red leather with buttons and clasps of metal which she would present to any noble who had expressed an interest. Usually the noble then felt under some obligation to make a payment. Christine had learnt that patrons needed just such encouragement. The remuneration for each manuscript would vary according to it's quality. Thus, for example, *'La Mutacion de Fortune'* was presented to Philippe of Burgundy and to the Duke de Berry, among others. Whether these were commissioned or sent unsolicited is not clear, but Christine certainly received money as well as encouragement in return, and in the process, she collected several influential and important admirers. We know she received nearly one hundred écus for a copy of *'Le Livre des Faits et Bonnes Moeurs du Sage Roy Charles V'* and fifty gold francs for *"several books in parchment"* from Jean Sans Peur, the son of her friend and patron, Philippe, Duke of Burgundy.

The first phase of her work mainly embraced lyrical poetry, the ballads, virelays, roundels, the *ditties* and *Jeux à vendre*, all of which were the fashion of the time. In 1397, the Earl of Salisbury made his first visit to France. He was to become a good friend to Christine. By 1399 she was able to bring out the *'Cent Ballades'*, a form very popular among the French poets. Prior to this date, she had already made up several manuscripts to give to the Earl of Salisbury. There is a manuscript copy of her work which was presented to Richard II, before that date.

The first twenty poems reflect her deep melancholy, her sorrow, her **overflowing heart,** her **intense solitude and the wound which never really healed.**

By the year 1402, Christine had achieved confidence and maturity in her writing. Her work was beginning to be known outside France, particularly so in England and Italy. It would have been natural for Christine's friend, Valentine Visconti, Duchess d'Orléans to send Christine's books to her father, Galleas Visconti. Galleas, Duke of Milan, protector of Petrarch, builder of the Cathedral of Milan, had a library which was equal to the best in Europe. He must have thought well of Christine's writing for she tells us he invited her to his court with a permanent position which would have ensured her future.

Chapter Eight

My Son goes to England

Be no deceiver of women.
Honour and never abuse them.

he daughter of the King of France (Princess Isabella) was to be married to King Richard of England: the noble count called Salisbury had come for these negotiations. A gracious chevalier, he appreciated *les conteurs* and was himself a *bon diseur* and a gracious writer. After he had heard one of my recitals he begged me very much to consent that I should permit my son, rather clever and a good singer aged about thirteen years, to accompany him to England to be a companion to one of his own sons of the same age. On my son's leaving for England, I wrote this ballad:

Si j'ay le coeur doulant je
 n'en puis mais,
Car mon ami s'en vait en
Angleterre,
Ne je ne scay quant le
reverray mais,
Le bel et bon qui mon coeur
tient on serre;

Car entre luy et moy ara
grant barre
Mais jamais pour joye ne
bien n'ary

If I have a sorrowing heart
there is nothing I can do,
For my friend leaves for
England,
And I know not when I shall
see him again,
That fair and virtuous soul
whom I hold close to my
heart
For between us there exists a
great sympathy
Joy for me there never will
be

Jusques a tant je le reverray.

Until I see him again.

Et quand je pense a ses gracieus
fais
Doulz et plaisans, trop fort le
coeur me serre.
Et comme pour mourir, certes,
jamais
Ne me courcast, et ou pourroye
guerre
Nul plus plaisant? or veuil je
dieu requerre,
Qui le connoit; mais dolente
serey,

Jusques a tant je le reverray.

When I think of his gracious
ways
Gentle and kind my heart is
fiercely gripped
What if he should die,
indeed, never
Should I sleep, for can war
allow
Any happier outcome? I pray
God,
Who knows him and who
knows my need; but
sorrowing I shall be
Until I see him again.

Or et mon coeur chargie de
pesant fais
Dont plains et plours me feront
dure guerre;
Et en lui seul seront tout mes
regrais
Car je l'aim plus que riens qui
soit sur terre.
Si convendre que le renvoye
guère
On a douleur et meschief
lanquinay,
Jusques a tant je le reverray.

Within my heart's heavy
load
Tears and grief exhaust my
spirit;
In him alone are my hopes

For I love him above all else
on earth.
If it comes about that he
does not return
I shall languish in grief,

Until I see him again.

The same count carried himself so well and promised so much for my son and even more for his future; I saw he would not fail in his promises as he was very powerful and indeed he did keep his promises.

I prepared a collection of my ballads for him for he deserved to have them as a present.

This may be one of the ballads included in Salisbury's collection.

Mon chevalier, mon gracieux servent	My cavalier, my gracious servant
Je sais de vrai que de bon coeur m'aimes	I know with what good heart you love me
Et de long temps, je vais m'apercevant	And for a long time I have seen you
L'amoureux mal dont tant vous vous blamez.	In the sickness of love for which you blame me.
Or ne vous faites plus mal chiere	But have no more doubts
Ne pleures plus, ni jour, ni nuit	Do not cry, night or day
Car je vous veux aimer d'amour entière	For I want to love you entirely
Et vous retiens pour mon loyal ami…	And keep you as my loyal friend
Ma douce amour, ma plaisante chérie	My gentle love, my pleasing dear,
Ma douce amie que tant je puis aimée	My sweet friend whom I love so much
Votre doucer m'a de tous maux guérie	Your sweetness has healed all my hurt
Et vraiment, je peux bien vous clamer	And truly I can well claim you
Fontaine dont tout le bien vient	The fountain of all my happiness
Et qui en paix et en joie me soutient	Who in peace and joy sustain me
Et dont plaisirs me viennent en largesse	From whom pleasures come to me generously
Car vous toute seule me tenez en laisse.	For you alone hold me in leash.

Christine's advice to her son was written about this time.

My son I have no great wealth to give you, so I hope instead you will take heed of some advice I have for you. Love God with all your strength, fear Him and put yourself at His service: to this end follow His Ten Commandments, which I hope you have learnt well. If you wish to have nothing to do with love and its dangers, then remove yourself from the company of that person to whom your heart is most inclined. Do not believe all the slanders that some books hurl at women, for there are many admirable women – experience will prove this to you. Flee from riotous company and women of ill-repute, deceivers, scorners and foul-mouthed people, and all others in any way lacking in virtue. Note well and remember this advice; do not play the fool with any woman if you would love and be loved by her, for your suit will only suffer thereby.

Be no deceiver of women. Honour and never abuse them. If you wish to find true love let it suffice for you to love only one and quarrel with none. Do not become besotted with some pretty idiot – you would be better off dead. If you have a wise and virtuous wife, trust her with your household affairs... but do not put your trust in a foolish wife... Make your wife respect you, but do not beat her, for the virtuous one will resent you for it and the bad one will become worse.

If you would take a woman as your wife, you can learn her habits by regarding her mother. This is a little rule which never fails. According to your means clothe your wife in an honest way and, if she is a lady of the house after yourself, she should not serve. See that she is served by your retainers. If you would live chastely and well, do not read 'The Rose', nor Ovid on the art of loving, the which provide only bad examples. If you would read of battles and the struggle for power, then read Vincent and others, the deeds of the Trojans and the Romans. To acquire devotion and if you seek books thereto, then St. Bernard and other authors will be your teachers in this respect.

Do not secure your damnation by acquiring possessions and land for your children; have them acquaint themselves with some branch of knowledge, or the art of good behaviour... See that your sons learn at school, beat them if you see them misbehaving, hold them subject and in awe to you, but show your great love for them.

In whatever condition you are placed by fortune to whom you are bound, regulate your actions in such a way that your life is well ordered. If you wish to pursue a life of learning by the reading of books, accomplish so much and study so well that among learned men you are not ignorant. Read willingly good literature whenever you can, for good examples are often of great value and help to make people intelligent.

If someone does you a service, reward them, if you can, according to their wishes. Do not be ungrateful for that is a great vice. Reveal your secrets to no one without good reason, nor give any news when it should be withheld, for whosoever discovers it will reveal it.

If you are noble and wish yourself instead a life of arms, you must arm yourself often, or you will be taken for a coward, without honour and lacking in virtue. If you are in a position or office concerned with the dispensation of justice, take care how you judge, for you yourself must one day face the great judge.

If you have disciples do not scold them with too great a rigour nor let them go astray; ponder a while on how weak and vain is human fragility. If you are a man of the church or a priest, in a religious order or a monk in cloisters, take care that beneath your habit, generosity and peace do not escape you.

If you become prosperous through profit and inheritance beware that pride does not overcome you and think that one day you must be judged before God. Do not be arrogant for all is but a perilous wind. Have pity on paupers, whom you see naked and destitute, and help them when you can. Remember that you too will die.

****

Soon afterwards there was a great uprising in England against King Richard, as is generally known, in the wake of which Count Salisbury was very wrongfully executed on account of his great loyalty to his rightful lord. Evil fortune could not allow his goodness towards me. So Fortune disinherited me once again by depriving me of a good friend and a happy expectation...

He was humble and sweet and courteous in all his ways, loyal in all places and prudent. He was brave and fierce as a lion. He wrote beautiful ballads and songs, lays and roundels. Though but a layman his deeds were all so gracious that never, I think, in his country shall be a man in whom God put so much good. May his soul be set in paradise among the saints for ever.

And so my son was deprived of happiness when still only a child and in this time of travail he was out of his country and must have been a little lost. Yet now what should happen but that King Henry, having appropriated the crown for himself, saw the poems and books that I had sent to Count Salisbury desiring to please him. He realised the position and very gladly took my son to himself, looking after him very well. In fact he sent me the command, through two of his heralds, the prominent men Lancaster and Faucon, both Kings of Arms, that I should go over to England, beseeching me and promising great benefit. This offer did not tempt me in the least, considering the state of affairs, so I pretended that I would obey the command, thanking him well, in order to get my son back. To cut a long story short, I exerted myself mightily and spent much money in seeking to persuade him that my son should come over from there to fetch me and accompany me to a country I did not know, in this way I thwarted this deed of fortune on behalf of both of us, because I could not believe that any good could come out of the King's treason.

I was happy to see my beloved son, as one returned from the dead: for three years I had been without him, the only one that death had left me...

But expenses were cruel and heavy for I was not affluent. I had to spend much more now to keep him, which I did not find easy. I was afraid that the fine state in which he had lived over there would give him no desire to return, for children are impressionable and attach themselves to what seems superficially better and more comfortable, and he had been retained by a great and powerful master. However, since the limited powers of understanding possessed by a young man cannot develop in the midst of a great court, my conclusion was that he had been well looked after but not fruitfully employed.

During the periods when the sap mounts, striplings do not understand the diverse movements which agitate them; and so their violent desires make them blind... their judgement contrary to a real understanding often makes them believe that dishonour is something enticing... sensuality dominates the hearts of the young who have not yet gained experience nor the possibility of correct judgement... No one can predict what type of man will eventually develop by what he is as a child... Young people do not want to hear of correction.

To those who have children, what could be a more gracious pleasure, what could they demand that would be more delectable than to see them often and to take great care over their diet and their education; it should be in keeping with their status; girls trained in the right manner; what a blessing if a child becomes used to correct habits and through good example learns to live within this discipline; alas! and if the mother is not wise, what example can she give her daughter?"

The Earl of Salisbury played a very important part in Christine's life. Through her connections at court and her reputation as a poet Christine would have been invited to the many literary gatherings arranged at Court. There were frequently visitors from abroad present at them, and it was probably at one of these, given by Louis d'Orléans, that Christine met the Earl of Salisbury in 1397. When the Earl of Salisbury returned to England, Christine's son, Jean du Castel, accompanied him to be brought up in his household.

It may have been at this time, or not long after, that she wrote the first of her poetic discourses, *'Les enseignements moraux donnés a Jehan de Castel, mon fils'* (moral education for my son). This long poem consists of a collection of advice, gleaned mostly from literature and the classics, and coloured, naturally, by Christine's own ideas, on how a young man should lead his life. Much of the advice must have been intended not only for Jean but for wider consumption. What is fascinating about the work is how little the advice it contains has dated.

In 1398, Richard II was deposed and Henry of Bolingbroke seized the throne of England. On 13th January 1400 the Earl of Salisbury was beheaded at Cirencester, by its citizens. Jean du Castel's future now became uncertain.

It was the manuscript copies of Christine's books which the Earl of Salisbury carried back with him that first established her reputation in England and made her popular there for years to come. Thus it was entirely in keeping that King Henry should take an interest in the Earl of Salisbury's library and sit poring over Christine's manuscripts... One instance of his doing so was when he visited the Abbey of Bardney. After mass and breakfast he asked if he might have a look at their bookroom and here we are told that he spent several hours reading. Henry IV was both a musician and a composer (he never travelled with less than twelve musicians in his suite, even when going on a crusade). His interest in Jean du Castel was therefore natural, for the boy was a good musician and nothing could have delighted the King more. He took Jean into his own court and extended an invitation to Christine to join him there. It was a generous impulse on his part. Jean however, persuaded by his mother, returned to France and once more Christine was obliged to give serious thought to his future.

While trying to place her son with Louis d'Orléans Christine wrote to this prince.

Most noble, elevated, powerful and wise Duke Louis d'Orléans, my lord, with great respect and humility I recommend myself to you... desiring to render you an agreeable service, valiant and influential lord. I come to make a gift to you in love of him whom I hold dearest, to place him under your protection, if you would care, noble duke, to receive him. He is a son of mine, who has desired from an early age to make a valuable contribution to the times in which he lives and who wishes to serve you to the best of his limited ability, if that is acceptable to you. May it please you by this request to take him into your service, valiant prince, worthy of love. I present him as a gift to you – make of him what you will; my respectful heart has every wish to be of service to you, if you would care, noble duke, to receive him. Three years the praiseworthy Count of Salisbury took him away to England into his service, in his great wisdom. Amidst the turmoil of that wicked country with its fickle population, his life came to an end. Since then, in truth, my son has remained in that country. So I have exerted myself greatly to get him back, despite the fact that it was King Henry's pleasure to keep him for himself; and now in good faith I make a gift of him to you; if you would care, noble duke, to receive him... My service is always at your command.

One does not know why Louis d'Orléans did not accept Jean du Castel into his household: the state of his own life was so complicated at that time, it is possible it was not convenient. Eventually it was Philippe Le Hardi, Duke of Burgundy, who took Jean under his protection.

Jean du Castel seems to have stayed in the Burgundian household for some time. Later, perhaps it was after 1410, he appears to have been in the King's service as a jurist; he was also a poet for he wrote a poem on his fidelity to the Dauphin and he practised rhetoric like his mother.

He married a young bourgeoise of Paris, Jeanne le Page, and had three children. He was sent on a diplomatic mission to King Jean II of Castille in the early 1420's and appears to have died there. His widow was refused entry into Paris because of her husband's royalist sympathies. This must have been during the English occupation of Paris. The Earl of Salisbury's son, restored to the King's favour after the execution of his father, became one of England's most outstanding commanders in France during the Battle of Agincourt and after, so that the two erstwhile companions were on opposing sides during this bitter period of the war.

Chapter Nine

Le Dit de Poissy (1400)

Discoursing on the theme
of love... As we rode through
the trees the birds sang and we
went on

y eldest child, my daughter, has dedicated herself to God and
given up her life to His service by the divine inspiration of His pure
will: in the flower of her youth and beauty she is leading a remarkable
life of contemplation and devotion in the religious house of the nuns at
Poissy, and more than fulfils my hopes for her. It often gives me
great comfort to tell of her good life.

I receive from her very affectionate and devoted letters full of
discretion and wisdom, which she sends to console me, and in which
despite her youth and innocence she advises me to hate the things of
the world and to despise material wealth.

Towards the end of the merry month of April in this year of 1400,
the woods were bursting with greenery, and one day, wishing to divert
myself, I decided to go and see this daughter of mine, who in the
opinion of all is beautiful and kind, youthful, clever and gracious.
She is a nun in a rich and noble abbey... situated six leagues from
Paris and most beautiful to see: Poissy is the name of the town where
it lies. I made the preparations for my excursion on a Monday,
sending someone out to find me some of my friends for company.

Nous partimes de Paris, notre
voie

We left Paris, riding

Chevauchâmes et moult joyeuse
estoie.
L'étaient tous ceux qu'avec moi
je menoie
Et toutes celles
Qui nous suivaient, gentilles
demoiselles
Douces, plaisantes, gracieuses,
belles…
Du temps nouveau qui alors
commencait;
Et le soleil clairment reluisait
Sur le champs verts,
Notre chemin était plat et couvert

De fleurettes, chacune à l'oeil
ouvert
Vers le soleil qui brillait
découvert,
Or de l'année
On n'avait jamais vu si pure
matinée
La terre entiére etait enluminée

De rosée par le ciel accordée

Qui resplendit
Faisait l'herbe pour les coeurs
ébaudir
Parmi ces prés, nature avait semé

Marguerites et fleurs qu'il sied
nommer
Fleurs de printemps; partout on
vit germer
Poussait le fleur de 'ne
m'oubliez mie'.
Ainsi la terre était toute fleurie,

Full of joy on our way.

All those whom I had taken
with me
And all those
Who followed us, gentle
ladies
Sweet, pleasant, gracious,
Each one rejoiced
At the springtime now
begun;
And the clear sun inundated
The green fields,
Our path was smooth and
covered
With little flowers, each
with eyes open, looking
Towards the sun shining
brilliantly,
Indeed during that year
One had never seen such a
pure morning
The entire earth was
illuminated
The dew gifted us by the sky
made
Everything resplendent
Spring herbs growing on
these meadows
Enlightened our hearts.
Nature had strewn
Daisies and other flowers
which can be named
Flowers of spring;
everywhere one saw
The forget-me-nots.

And so the earth was
carpeted,

Charles V in his study.
Bibliothèque Nationale, Paris.

Louis d'Orléans.
French School c. 1420 – Private Collection.
Photo: Giraudon. (top)

Valentine Visconti, Duchess
d'Orléans, receiving a book from
the author Honoré Bonet.
14th Century drawing.
Bibliothèque Nationale, Paris.
(bottom left)

Portrait of Galeazzo Visconti by
Antoine Pisanello.
Musée de Louvre, Paris.
Photo: Giraudon. (bottom right)

The Duke de Berry by Holbein,
the Younger.
Musée de Basle, Switzerland.
Photo: Bulloz. (top left)

Marie de Berry.
Musée du Louvre, Paris.
Photo: Giraudon. (top right)

Jean Gerson Preaching (detail).
Bibliothèque Municipale de
Valenciennes.
Photo: Giraudon. (bottom left)

Philippe the Bold, Duke of
Burgundy.
Anonymous portrait.
Musée du Versailles.
Photo: RMN. (bottom right)

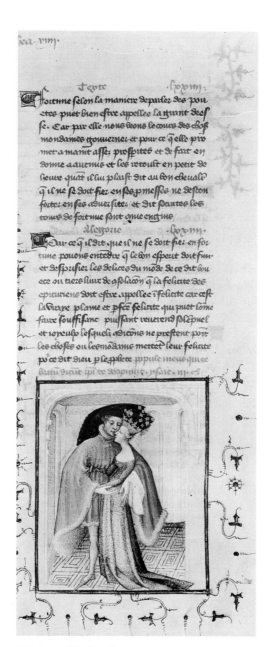

The Lovers ("Epistre d'Othea").
Bibliothèque Nationale, Paris.

The Marriage Bed.
Bibliothèque Nationale, Paris.

King Charles V and his Barons.
Watercolour by François Roger de Gaignières (1642-1715) copy from
a XIV century miniature.
Bibliothèque Nationale, Paris.
Photo: Giraudon.

Texte   Clov viii

En fortune la grant deesse
Ne te fies nen sa promesse
Car en pou de heure elle se change
Le plus hault souuent giette en fange

The Wheel of Fortune ("Epistre d'Othea").
Bibliothèque Nationale, Paris.

Desiring Death more than Life ("Epistre d'Othea").
Bibliothèque Nationale, Paris.

Mais qui pourrait dire la chanterie	But who could describe the singing
Des oisillons qui, avec harmonies	Of the birdlings who with harmony
Notes nouvelles	Modulated new notes,
Modulaient, et des alouetttes belles	And the beautiful larks
En l'air serein qui disaient les nouvelles	In the serene air gave us news
Du printemps, ramageant de voix fluettes...	Of spring with flutelike voices...
Et tellement	And so many
De rossignols hantaient ce lieu bruissant	Nightingales haunted this rustling place.
Qui ca et la allaient en volant,	They flew here and there,
Qu'oncques, je crois, ensemble on n'en vit tant	Never, I believe, could such numbers be seen
Et tant qu'ici	As there were here
Tous gazouillaient: "ocy, ocy, ocy".	All chirped: "ocy, ocy, ocy".

There was not a blemish on the landscape, and it was so beautiful that lovers' love would have grown simply for their being there. Amidst the meadows nature had sown daisies and other spring flowers; everywhere spring grasses and plants were sprouting red, bright green and sea green, yellow and blue... there was the forget-me-not... from which lovers make garlands... We approached the River Seine joyfully. On the bank it was even more beautiful, for the birds in loud chorus were flying by so happily that it gladdened our hearts... and the sweet murmuring of the waters filled the air... We had begun to take our time in order not to arrive before the appointed hour... a mild, pleasant wind arose, lifting our short coats... not wishing to get sunburnt... we rode on... and arrived all holding hands... at the beautiful chateau of St. Germain... continuing into the forest. No one in the world, be he scholar or layman, could believe how pleasing this spot was; I remember there were as many people there as one might see at a procession or a fair... Closely planted were the chestnut trees, tall, wide and beautiful... We never stopped laughing, singing, making merry and inventing love-stories.

Leaving the forest behind us we came straight to Poissy, where we found everything ready for us... when we had relaxed, and set our clothing to rights as best we could... we went together into the abbey... Although it had strongly constructed gates, they had been given permission to open them. Inside there were many nuns... simply dressed and wearing wimples, prepared to do God's bidding. Our friends gave us a great and joyful welcome and she whom I love dearly came towards me, kneeling humbly for me to kiss her sweet face. Then at once we went hand in hand into the church to give thanks to God; having heard mass, we then desired to leave, but the nuns implored us to take some refreshment with them, and led us into a beautiful place, bright and fresh, where we were to eat...

We had not been there long, when the excellent and noble prioress of the abbey, Marie de Bourbon, the aunt of the King, in whom is no vice, being solicitous for our well-being, sent her permission for us to come into her presence to which we gladly responded, as we had not wished to go away without seeing her. In pairs we went up the stairs to the royal chamber, which we found to be richly decorated. Inside her beautiful room we knelt before her, but she humbly beckoned us nearer and spoke to us.

Before long the King's daughter, the noble Princess Marie, arrived, veiled and correctly dressed, for she had been chosen and dedicated to the service of God. Young and tender, she was not alone, but had several ladies in attendance as I well remember. One was the noble daughter of the renowned count of Harcourt, God rest his soul... Immediately the prioress rose and bowed to her, as we did in humility. She received us so graciously that we were put at our ease... We were very glad to see the nuns' way of life; no man attended to them at all or spoke to them, unless he was a relative or accompanied by one; no one could enter the abbey unless by permission... I do not know if they find this inconvenient, but come rain or shine, strangers are not seen to come or go. Some of the nuns are as beautiful as angels... At night they lie on woollen blankets... and their mattresses are covered with beautiful Arras tapestries... but they are hard... In the evening those self-denying nuns lie down on them until morning. Their rooms are adjacent to the dormitory, and they always dine in the refectory, where there are good washing facilities. In the court... there are windows with iron-trellis work, where the nuns with administrative responsibilities may order the provisions necessary for their living.   The abbey holds the appointments for provosts, lords and mayors. It owns towns and castles, and has the income from several well-placed estates; it is wealthy. No one can be admitted to the abbey unless by permission of the King, who must safeguard its authority. It has many other privileges, to relate all of which would take much time.

Before we left, the prioress... gently implored us with great courtesy to take a meal... so we had to accede to her wishes, and were lead by several nuns into an attractive and pleasant room, where billowing white tablecloths and soft carpets were laid out. Without delay wines and meats were brought in large quantities in vessels of gold and silver, and the kindly nuns undertook in their humility to serve us, whether we wished it or not, bringing us delicious dishes but not touching them themselves, which grieved us... Afterwards we returned to the good lady to take our leave and thank her. Then we descended the steps of the palace and went back to the nuns' quarters to take our leave of them... for we did not wish to put a foot wrong... They wanted to show us the beautiful grounds of their buildings... which seemed to us like an earthly paradise. We walked through the cloister, with its pretty little adjacent cells and its great vaults supported by large corbels... underneath us it was paved with thin slabs... A very tall pine-tree had been placed in the middle of the lawn to adorn it... Then we returned to the refectory, and I do not think I have ever seen such a fine and spacious room... To put it briefly, we were taken to such beautiful places that we could not tire of looking... but I must not omit to mention the fact that everywhere there was clear, fresh and sweet running water, for the convenience of all... Within the walls could be seen barrels of wine... ovens... and other necessities... and still the nuns had more to show us... It is clear that this abbey was endowed by a king and other prominent people, for neither gold nor silver was spared in its conception and its building...

Afterwards we went down the fine steps to rejoin the men of our party, and entered the church, which contains many images of the saints... I shall never be able to describe its beauty... It seems to have been built just recently... The stonework is so fine that even gold and silver could not be more finely worked... It is divided into two parts by a screen... those who say mass and read the scriptures are on the near side of it with the townspeople... In the chancel are the good nuns, responding loudly and clearly to those below, and joining their feminine voices in sweet chords... There are so many rich ornaments... and gilt capitals... so many beautiful portraits and images... nothing is there that does not have its place... The nuns... wear robes as white as virgin snow... secured under the breast... and over these, black capes... They have snow white kerchiefs tied over their heads, with a black veil attached to them... When we had fully admired the church... we went once again into their beautiful gardens... which contain more than seventy pairs of fruit-bearing trees... The sound of the birds was deafening... The whole is surrounded by high, well-built walls... we saw many hares and rabbits... and wild goats cropped the grass... By now it was time for the evening meal in the convent... and so a bell pealed out... my daughter who had been walking beside me holding my hand, beseeched me to stay overnight... But we brought our tour and our conversation to a close and gave our most gracious thanks to the warden and those who had been so kind to us. The great gates were opened to let us out and then relocked...

Talking all the while we soon reached Bourbon, which provides accommodation for many visitors. We found a meal ready for us there, and sat down to it straight away, although none of us felt very hungry... After dining we washed and went to take a little rest... Not a half of an hour later we were returned to the great court outside the convent and our arrival announced to the prioress... It is not unusual to make two visits in one day... but we would have liked to have spent all our time there – the men found the sweet nuns in their simple clothes most attractive... We were led to the fountains in the gardens, where we sat down, we spoke little of worldly matters, nor did we touch on love, nor did we dance... we asked them about the rules of their order... it would have been malicious to divert them from their intention to hear nothing but the ordered recital of prayers and the passion story... When it was time to leave, we rose to say goodbye, for we could easily have overstayed our welcome... We were forced to accept gifts from them... little bags of gold and silk... beautifully embroidered... We said to them; "it is time we went... we will never be able to thank you enough, and we will remain your servants..." So saying we came quickly to the gates. My happiness disappeared at the prospect of leaving my dearest one; kissing her I said goodbye.

Immediately we had reached our hostel a beautiful young lady of our company said: "What shall we do? Let us dance and sing..." Her song with its message that we should love one another, was followed by the sweet and pure voice... of a squire... Each one of us sang until night drew near; we did not become at all bored with dancing. The evening meal was ready for us... the tables had been arranged in the gardens... where the dishes were brought to us... The prioress had sent us much lovely food and good wine... including apples and pears of different kinds... we thanked them for their kindness. We arose from the table, said grace... and then walked into the fields, where it was a delight to hear the song of the blackbirds... For one hour we sang there and made merry until night had fallen... Returning to our hostel we went happily to bed. In the morning we heard mass in the abbey, took our leave of the nuns and mounted our fine, large horses... that had eaten well before leaving. On reaching the grass-covered road we made head-garlands from the flowers, and rode on by the forest.

A *dit* or a *dittie* is a descriptive or satiric poem of a happening. In this long poem *'Le Dit de Poissy'*, Christine gives a rare, perhaps unique, description of a personal experience. Chaucer, we know, also went on a pilgrimage to Canterbury, but Christine's *'Le Dit de Poissy'* is the tender poem of a sensitive and passionate woman, giving us a picture of medieval life at one of its most sympathetic moments.

'Le Dit de Poissy' is the account of a group of cultivated medieval men and women on a joyous *chevauchée* and depicts the best of that world where the dark side of medieval life is absent.

The abbey of St. Louis at Poissy was an ancient priory constructed under Philippe le Bel which was in its turn built on an older chateau belonging to the royal family. In 1304, under the Dominicans, it was richly endowed and belonged to the diocese of Chartres. The church was considered one of the most beautiful in France. Around it was the convent run by a royal princess, Marie de Bourbon. It contained inside the first enclosure the sleeping quarters of the nuns, the hospital, the great refectory, the kitchens, the cellars, the cemetery and the gardens; within the second enclosure there were two other chapels, the lodgings of the artisans, the hostelries for the visitors, the park and playing greens, and the farm attached to the convent. Outside this enclosure the fair of St. Denis was held annually.

At the time when Christine's daughter took the veil, the prioress was the widowed Marie de Bourbon, sister to Queen Jeanne and sister-in-law to King Charles V. The nuns at Poissy lived austere lives, slept on hard mattresses and were beaten if they did not rise for matins. Visitors were infrequent and were only allowed to be seen through iron grills. But on the whole this seemed to be a life that suited her daughter, and it was an honour to have been admitted there.

On the way back to Paris Christine and her friends pass through the forest of St. Germain. Here they have a dialogue and a *débat amoureux*: Who is the more unhappy? The lady whose husband or lover is imprisoned by the Turks after the Battle of Nicopolis in 1396, or the chevalier whose lady does not return his love? In effect, one whose love is returned but who suffers the pangs of separation, or one whose love is not returned but who is able to see his love? Christine gives us descriptions of the chevalier and of the lady in question. She describes in such intimate detail male and female beauty that one is certainly inclined to think that she was not quite indifferent to physical beauty. Christine allows herself, in the description of the lover and the lady in question, to be free and sensual, which incidentally shocked her nineteenth century biographer.

Here is the description of the knight given by the lady and the picture of his lady given by the knight.

"Sire, it was a good seven years ago that I gave my love to the most chivalrous and best knight of my choice that is to be found in this world for, by all the good deeds which he performed, he proved himself the best of all. Thus may God save him for me, for I can think of no more perfect man, whether young or old, on this earth at present. For in no place could one hope to find two more perfect eyes, nor a body so tall, straight and broad, and, further, so well made that one could not wish to find one better or in any way change it. His body was well proportioned, also his face, with curly hair dark brown in colour. But his greatest advantage was the beauty of his handsome brow, furrowed in loyalty, for it was deep and especially broad and bore the nobility of fine eyebrows, which were widely arched, brown and narrow. They framed gentle eyes that have so many times allayed my sad sorrow, and still do, for no man has more gentle eyes than he, brown, smiling, piercing and warmly welcoming. Yet, with their large pupils, they have pierced my heart, for his look was so full of sweetness that it has been the cause of the misery I now lament, for when he looked at me full on, I tell you truly, I went quite weak inside, for it seemed to my heart he was saying, 'come', and he took me to him as his possession. His nose was well formed, slim and pointed, without any defect and suited his face in such a perfect way that his whole countenance was thereby doubled in beauty. His lips of red were to be marvelled at and very beautiful, large but not excessively so. He did not have a mouth so big that it reached almost to his ears, but a small one with breath which smelt of the green laurel's leaves or of the rose. His fine teeth were white, small, neat, and complete, his chin rounded; his beard had still to grow for he was young.

Indeed, his countenance, so gently made, in beauty so exemplary, rosy and full, smiling as if to please all, was without any imperfection. His neck too was well made, according perfectly with his head, while his shoulders were of good proportions, wide, straight and muscular and, wherever he went, it was thought that no equal could be found to his arms for dealing blows more forceful, for easily gripping against the walls of castles to seize and take them by force – his arms were long, strong and well made.

His fair hand had no twist but was in every way well turned out, straight, long and harder than bark, firm and large boned, but the beauty of his chest is uppermost in my heart when I am reminded of the great misery which I have so often suffered as a result of tender love. For his fair chest was large and wide, well formed by all standards of beauty, the very paragon of manly grace.

His hips were narrow and buttocks noble, while his big, rounded thighs would allow him to suffer no pain in feats of arms. His legs were long and muscular, straight down to the ankles which were narrow, with no veins prominent, in every way well fashioned. His skin was firm and without any impurity, soft to touch and fair to look at, clear and brown, pleasing and of beauty which could not be rivalled. Thus was he handsome... He who is now alas! a prisoner of the Saracens..."

The knight then spoke of his love:

"This lady had hair like fine gold, blond, curly and daintily covered by a single veil of fine quality. Her forehead was without defect, wide and clear, singularly white and, in truth, it was fashioned like a work of polished ivory, with eyebrows, so ordered by nature, narrow, long, deeply arched and brown, of great beauty. It is impossible to imagine pupils more strikingly large and quite unique, in eyes which were soft and laughing. Pleasing and without pride was her look and sweetly welcoming. A pretty and elegant nose had she, not too large nor too small or long, but straight, well formed, complementing her gracious and kind face.

Her cheeks and jaw were pretty, soft and pleasing, and of a colour which seemed as if mixed with new russets; no other beauty could match them, for such gracious beauty was, and is, without parallel. Her small ears were of rosy hue, and her breath smelt sweet from a mouth that was small and laughing, not large at all, and when she smiled or spoke one could see her tiny teeth, white as pearls from the Orient, well arranged and in good health maintained, sweet and in every respect attractive.

When she smiled there appeared two dimples, of singular sweetness, in her cheeks. But the sweetness of her little chin, rounded and pleasing, gracious and pretty, dimpled and rosy, could not be improved upon, corresponding as well as it did with her fair face, the whole of which was a work of great beauty, gently rounded, and indeed, the sweetest and most beautiful that one could ever see.

Her fair neck was encircled by a gold necklet, which was rich and beautiful and given to her by the King, worn over her elegant chin veil, which was white and exquisitely made and seemed to be sewn with small threads. Nature, who has produced many great works of art and perfection, has never created a work of more beauty.

I think to make no excessive claim here, but her fair bosom was so white and large, it is no exaggeration; in truth, it is something worth seeing, as white as a lily, polished like ivory and with rounded breasts like full-blown pears. And if I dare say it, never in my memory have I seen a sweeter sight. Alas! Happy is he who rests on that bosom!

But more delicate and fresh than the rose, believe me, firm and clear, was her beautiful skin and her fair long arms, slim but not thin, no one could possess a fairer hand than she, long and elegant, white and graceful. Her torso was slim, tall, straight and graceful, her hips small, her buttocks firmly rounded; her stomach felt soft and yielding as I held her. For nature, who has endowed her with all good things, has I believe, forgotten nothing. Thus was she made, thus do I hold her to be – perfect in every way... But alas, she has cruelly turned from me..."

So he told of his woes. The lady immediately replied...

"Enough! What are you trying to tell us? With respect, I certainly suffer more in a single moment than you do in a month... there is no comparison!" To which he answered:... "I am more greatly hurt than you..." Upon which she suggested... "Let us find a judge, wise and fair, who will decide this controversy for us", and he answered: "I agree, let a fair judge be found"...

In this fashion they reached an agreement, and asked me to advise them... afterwards the conversation turned to a discussion of knightly virtues, more than twenty knights from this kingdom and from others were named for their goodness and excellence... We spoke at length of valiant feats of arms and chivalrous deeds...

You, sir, (Jean de Werschin, the Seneschal of Hainault) were named among those good men... When I heard your wisdom spoken of... I vowed to compose a good poem and send it to you... After a little thought, I remembered your gracious reputation, dear Sir... so I told them your name; do not refuse them... They have heard such good reports of you that they would not seek any other judge... They beseech you to give it some thought, Sir, although you are preoccupied with military affairs; in bitter tears they asked me to put the case briefly to you for your decision which of the two lives is in greater suffering...

So our discussion came to an end, as we were approaching Paris, and we rejoined the rest of our company and rode happily to my house in Paris, where amid great rejoicing and festivities we dined. When we had eaten and relaxed, my friends all wished to take their leave, but the two lovers charged me before leaving to write a short account of their love affairs soon. Therefore before long I began work on this present poem, *'Le Dit de Poissy'*. But now it is time to bring it to an end and to include my name in the last line.

Good and kind knight, full of wisdom, since it pleases you to collect my poetry I am sending you this debate between two lovers, upon which you must pass judgement. They have asked me... to find a fair judge for their controversy.

I pray God that he may grant you a long life and that at its end you may be with him in paradise, and that true love holds all faithful lovers... in subjugation and fear.

In order properly to appreciate the simple and moving delight which Christine expressed in the beauty of spring, one should consider the extreme gloom and discomfort of medieval winters; wax or tallow candles were a luxury, heating was virtually non-existent, food was scarce and often bad, and towards the end of winter, only dried meat or fish, and scarcely any vegetables, could be had. Little wonder then, that the whole poem expresses such joy and lightness of spirit.

In French society of the 1400's, love and morality were popular subjects for discussions and debates. Christine now took to writing poems about hypothetical problems of lovers and their actions, and would choose prominent men to whom she would present a manuscript and appoint as judge.

Christine chose to present her manuscript of *'Le Dit de Poissy'* and appoint as judge, Jean de Werschin, the Seneschal of Hainault. It was deemed that in all of France there was no better lover and no braver knight than he. Unfortunately, it is not known how the Seneschal of Hainault responded to this challenge.

These debates were also continued in the courts of love usually held in public places. Just as the crowds watched the tournaments so did they delight in these discussions on the finer points of love and chivalry. To us of the present day, such gatherings, as forms of entertainment for the populace, would seem rather rarefied. Nevertheless, they did have a popular appeal as is evident by a petition presented by the Duke de Bourbon to Charles V in which he asks the King to help the people of Paris to regain their courage and morale after a terrible epidemic of the plague in the city. He suggests that this might be achieved by electing a *Prince d'Amour*, whose court would help to pass the time more graciously and *"would give birth to new joy among the inhabitants"*.

Chapter Ten

Le Debat des Deux Amants

> Let us have a discussion
> about love... let each of us tell
> what he knows of it.

Royal prince... Duke d'Orléans... hear my little poem... do not despise me for my lack of knowledge, or because my subject is trifling and beneath your intellect, which attends to matters of virtue and wisdom. There is no harm at all in hearing of different subjects... joyful matters in rhymes and prose; by hearing of things that are by their nature joyful one can often banish sadness... No human being... could live all the time preoccupied with his cares... the listener derives happiness from hearing pleasant things read... so do not be displeased with me, excellent prince, for bringing to your attention a little poem I have rhymed, to lighten the burdens of your heart. I should like, with God's help, to relate to you a great debate I heard once between two lovers. It will be appreciated by Frenchmen and Germans and all readers of romances; but it needs a judge, and so I humbly ask you to take upon yourself that role.

******

It was in the mild season of May that a group of beautiful young people came together in a very fine house
in Paris... many even-tempered ladies... many gentle maidens, and in truth more than thirty knights and others... intent on making merry. There was more than one group of musicians filling the room with

sound... There was no discord among the people there: they were united and all sadness had been banished... the room had been well decorated... and cleaned... with fresh grass underfoot... Everyone danced, and glances were exchanged that led to hearts being exchanged... Afterwards the musicians, who had been playing beautifully, broke into a well measured song...

I was sitting on a bench without saying a word, observing these attractively gracious lovers, full of the grief that death has caused me, without taking any share in their pleasure, filled with depressing thoughts of the one I shall always hold in my memory, whose soul has gone heavenwards, leaving me all alone to mourn, wherever I may be... I was watching a squire... dancing, singing, making merry as if the world was his own... while near my seat a knight was sitting by a window, his head leaning on his left hand, pensive and depressed... Several times I heard him exclaim 'alas!'... I felt so sorry for him that no man, however close he might have been to me, could have caused me as much grief as this one...

No one seemed to notice his sadness apart from myself... We were the only two not dancing... I could easily see the reason for his position, for more than six times he coloured when the gracious body of a beautiful lady passed near him... Soon he arose from his place and approached me... saying kindly: "What are you thinking of here on your own... without dancing?..." While we were talking in hushed tones the other man I mentioned, came up to us gaily... and said: "Let us have a discussion about love... let each of us tell what he knows of it." The gay young squire I had noticed was in love too, for he looked often towards one of the ladies. Both of them fell to talking of love so earnestly that I suggested we should go outside to talk more peacefully. I proposed that we take another lady with us, a beautiful, pleasant and gracious bourgeoise, and we went into the garden under the beautiful trees.

The knight who had sighed and wept began by saying that he thought love destroyed reason for it can make one forget all that is right, honourable, and customary. Love could reduce a man and even destroy him. The torments of jealousy were terrible. To love too much was to be lost and one should flee from it for the heart which bears this torment and those who love repent of it for it does great damage. He then gave examples from antiquity and history to strengthen his point.

The young bourgeoise said, "Men frequently tell women that they suffer torments from love. But though it may once have been so I cannot but think that today their pains are only light. In stories their sufferings are long and enduring but I believe that money and a pleasant life is what most men think about. No one could bear such suffering and live, but I have heard of no cemetery where those who died of love are buried."

The gay young squire did not agree because for him all pleasure and good things and all joy came from love. He could not be jealous for if one truly loves one trusts the beloved.

Afterwards they said to me: "Compose a poem about our debate."

In the end they decided to choose a judge and I proposed the powerful and noble Duke d'Orléans.

So noble Prince, my redoubtable seigneur, whom God give long life, may this little ditty bring you solace and joy...

This vivid description of an evening's supper and the debate on lovers is only a short passage from the story but it does paint a picture of those times and gives us some idea of the ethical and esoteric questions discussed at these debates.

By 1401 Christine had finished *'Le Debat des Deux Amants'* (The Debate of Two Lovers) and she wanted to go on with her serious philosophical works. Subsequent events and the debate on *'Le Roman de la Rose'* give us an idea that Christine may already have been engaged in this enormous work, so she genuinely did not want to restart her love poems. But as she tells us she could not refuse to relate the true love story of two of her patrons, Jean de Bourbon and her great friend Marie de Berry.

Though at present I have neither the courage nor the inclination to write amorous poems – for I am occupied with other matters – I have undertaken to complete ballads of love at the command of someone held universally in affection, about a lover and his lady... I hope it does not exhaust me, for I would rather attend to other business of more worth for scholarship.

It was impossible, she says, to refuse this young lord *Le plus bel des Fleur de Lys*, who also wrote poetry. Where and how, she asks in a ballad she writes to him, did he learn to write and to know the pleasure that it brings? In 1401 Christine wrote *'Le Livre du Duc des Vrais Amants'* for Marie and Jean.

'Le Livre du Duc des Vrais Amants' (The Book of the Duke of True Lovers) is the story of Jean, Duke de Bourbon, and Marie de Berry as he told it to Christine.

Jean, Duke de Bourbon, one of the members of the royal house, was born in 1380. He had a very active life full of adventure. Jean and Marie de Berry had fallen in love while she was still married to Philippe d'Artois (referred to in the poem as "the jealous one"), and the poem deals with the progress of their love and their secret meetings after Philippe's jealousy had been aroused by malicious tongues. Though they pledged each other undying love, Marie was anxious to preserve her honour, and Jean eventually had to leave to destroy the rumours about them. He left for Spain with the army but he came back to see Marie. When he returned to the war in Spain he was made a prisoner. During the ten years before their marriage he composed ballads and other *dits*; Marie responded in the same fashion.

Chapter Eleven

Le Duc des Vrais Amants (1401)

> And love... took his arrow
> and silently bent his bow.

I have no desire to discourse on love, my mind is filled with matters more pleasing to me. However I am willing to relate a wonderful story at the request of a lord whom it is my duty to obey and who desires me to write on the trouble he endured for these many winters and summers; because his heart was held in love's bondage. He was unwilling that his name should be known. He is content to tell his story and be known as the Duke of True Lovers. I recount, at his pleasure, as he told me, all his joys and sorrows, the adventures through which he passed these long years. He grants me permission to add other matter to that which he tells me. I know he will take my small story and its imperfections with his usual sweet nature and good sense, and with his consent I relate on his behalf the facts as he related them to me:

****

I was really no more than a boy when I already had a great longing to become a lover. I was taught that a lover is above all courteous and so esteemed by men, that I desired to be one. I went to places where I thought I might find a lady whom I could serve but it was a long while and still I could not choose; I had the time but still, upon my soul, I did not know nor could I understand how to achieve this. I frequently sought the company of fair ladies and damsels but still I did not know how or whom to choose. I was, however, happy, pleased with life and gay. But I did not achieve that which I so desired and as the time seemed long, I made a complaint to love:

Vray dieu d'Amours qui des amans es sire,	True god of Love, who art of lovers Lord.
Et toy Venus, l'amoureuse deesse,	And Venus, thou, Love's Lady and goddess,
Veuilles mon coeur briefment mettre en adrece	Since in love only is set my happiness,
D'estre amoreux, Car viens plus ne desire.	Vouchsafe to turn my heart soon thitherward.
A celle fin qu'a vaillance je tyre,	Vouchsafe, that I be with right courage stored,
Vueilles moy tost purveoir de maistrece,	Soon to bring unto me my heart's mistress,
Vray dieu d'Amours qui des amans es sire.	True god of Love, who art of lovers Lord.
Et m'ottroyez grace que puisse eslire	Any may I choose, if thou the grace accord,
Telle qui mon ignorence et j'oennece	One that shall pardon me the simpleness
Sache amender et a honneur me drece,	Of youth and honour on my days impress:
Car le disir que j'en ay me fait dire;	Out of a great desire have I implored,
Vray dieu d'Amours qui des amans es sire.	True god of Love, who art of lovers Lord.

I discoursed on my desire till love heard me and pitied me. I will now tell you in what manner love took possession of me and made my heart its captive for ever after.

One day with one of my kinsmen and four others, we mounted our horses and rode out hunting. I asked the huntsmen to take the ferrets and greyhounds out. We entered a path familiar to me where I knew there were rabbits in plenty; nearby was a strong castle.

A princess of great renown and honour, beautiful and good happened to come to the castle at this time. Her attendants amused themselves singing, walking, exercising. We naturally turned towards them. When they recognised us they came forward and their chief saluted us and many of them went to advise their mistress of our coming. When we were near to the castle a company of ladies came out to meet us and welcomed us graciously.

We greeted them on bended knee and I kissed one of the maidens and a lady who were cousins of the princess. My cousin, who was with me, and I then entered the castle.

A lady had come out of her chamber and stood there with a noble look; she was neither proud nor arrogant, her manner befitted her royal person. As we greeted her she came forward and with her ungloved hand took mine and kissed me saying, "You are welcome. What brings you here?"

Then my cousin answered: "My lady we set out hunting not knowing you were here, but chance brought us to you, and God be praised that we have found so fair a welcome at your hands."

The lady laughed graciously at this and said, "Then let us amuse ourselves".

We walked down into a green meadow and she went with us into a fair place where she took me by her side and bade me sit down beside her.

Large cushions of gold and silk were laid under the shade of a willow and nearby a clear spring flowed through, skilfully cut and planted with green along its banks.

She seated herself beside me, while the others discreetly withdrew and sat beside the stream at a distance. I confess I was then unused to conversing with her, for I was shy and still young but she began to question me.

She enquired of me news of the King and Queen and the Court, from where I had recently come, and the appearance of the ladies. I answered her as best I could and we discoursed on many things.

Now I must confess to the grievous malady which I caught and for which I have so cruelly suffered since, for love's sake. Truly it is a marvellous thing and impossible to comprehend how love came to me for her whom I had seen many times, but never before had she taken possession of my heart.

A man may explore over the seas in strange lands and discover that which he desires is close at hand, but which he had not known to exist till he sees it with new eyes. In truth this is how love came to me, for never before did I perceive the beauty of my lady till love opened my eyes to see her thus. I had seen her often, but until that day I had given her no thought. I had desired love and here it was given me to yield my heart into her keeping. Love had at last released my heart from its anguish and I had before me my precious one, my perfect lady; she troubled me, her gentle words and her bearing so possessed me that I could not speak. I observed her and contemplated her beauty and it seemed to me she held within her more sweetness and grace than I had ever beheld before.

And love, who saw my heart ready and inclined towards love, took his arrow and silently bent his bow. Her tender glance was the arrow which pierced me to the heart. When the loving blow fell I thought myself lost, but it was too late. My heart had yielded to this amorous wound which stung me again and again.

Her laughing eyes stirred my heart and held me in their loving fetters. I could move neither hand nor foot and changed colour at her every glance. If I had longed to be made love's captive, then had I succeeded.

From that hour I ended my early youth. True love now taught me, her captive, to live otherwise. I talked like a child would do in a simple manner for the fire burning in my heart was rekindled afresh time and again as I gazed on her beauty. I was indeed caught as a moth in the light of a candle or the bird in a trap but recklessly I did not heed it.

I had stayed by her side a full third of a summer's day when my cousin said, "Take leave now for, on my soul, you have detained my lady and it is time to sup".

My noble one, the fair, the good, the courteous one, invited us to sup with her but I excused myself. Lingering a short while longer I arose and before departing tasted the wine given to us. I pleaded with my lady that I be permitted to escort her back to the castle but she refused and I took leave of them all.

But before I left my tender heart was pierced again with the arrow of a loving look, for while departing I turned once more to her and her loving eyes looked upon me in such a fashion that never has the memory of it left me to this day and so I left with love's arrow lodged within me.

Outside the castle walls we made haste as night was approaching. My cousin made merry but I could not speak a word and pensively I bowed my head for that glance which had taken possession of my heart burnt like a loving flame and I ceaselessly thought on the gentle beauty and the fair lovely lady to whom my heart was now pledged.

My cousin who got no answer to his speech said to me, "Fair cousin, why do you think on in silence, what is the cause of your thought? Was there no joy in our visit that you do not speak? It is true, God help me, that there could not be a fairer or more perfect lady than the one you now leave. Do I not speak true? Is there one more perfect in all ways, more courteous or kind? She is beautiful to look upon and in nobility and grace, never have I seen equal, except the lady who is in the possession of my own heart, none other can compare with her but the princess we have just spoken of, upon my soul."

When I heard him praise her so, I could no longer refrain and sighing deeply I said, "Cousin, I say that could but God desire to love and possess a friend on earth he could have none other than her, who is beyond compare, for this I will take up combat and throw you my gage. I do swear that all others pale beside her like sparks beside a star."

My cousin understood me and he saw that my heart belonged to her.

Night had fallen as we rode into our house where my father was looking out for me. I saw him at a window overlooking the court. I dreaded his anger. He asked me straight where I had been. I knelt in greeting as he said, "Do you return home when night has come? But it is well, you have now returned."

I said no word in reply and as he left me I departed to my chamber. I sat there with my companions and ate my supper but, though they tried to amuse me with many stories, my thoughts were with her and I saw her face and marvelled with wonder at my captive heart. I slept badly, perhaps an hour or so though my bed was comfortable. I longed for her with the sweet longing which love brings and I feared above all that she would not look upon me as I desired her to; if that be so never would I find comfort. Where would

114

I go to obtain the solace so desired and which would give me so much
joy? I said to myself:

Amours, vertes, assez ne te
purroye
Remercier dece que de ta grace

D'estre amoureux tu ma's mis
en la voye
Et de dame qui toutes autres
passe
Tu ma's pourveu, car de beaulte
et grace

Et de valeur est souvraine, a
voir dire,
Si ne puis dire assez et ne
cessasse.
Graces te rends qui la ma's
fait eslire.

Or ay je ce que je tant desiroye,

C'estoit avoir dame en qui
j'emploiasse
En lui servir mon temps et qui
en joye
Mon coeur tenist, par qui en
toute place

Gay et joilis je fusse et que
l'amasse;
De tout mon coeur, si ay ce que
desire
Choisie l'ay, tu m'en donnas
l'espace,
Graces te rends qui la ma's fait
eslire.

Verily, Love, I have no
language, none
Of thanksgiving sufficient
for thy grace
That moved me unto love,
and such a one
Gave me for mistress as doth
all abase
Beside her, queen of beauty
and of grace

And precious worth: O,
when on her I muse,
Truly my speech with my
thought keeps no pace.
Thanks be to thee, who
mad'st me her to choose.

Now all that I desired so
dear is won,
Having a lady to serve all
my days,
Who holds my heart in joy
to think upon
Her beauty, and in every
hour and place makes my
heart high and glad so to
embrace
Her soul with mine, joy that
I may not lose,
With all my heart, that is
what I desire
Mine was the choice, but
thine shall be the praise,
Thanks be to thee, who
mad'st me her to choose.

Si te suppli, Amours, a qui m'ottroye,	O now, Love, into whose dominion
Que tu me donnes grace que je face	I yield my heart, vouchsafe my service space
Tant par servir qu'encor ma dame voye,	That to my lady I suffice alone,
Que tout sien suy, ey que sa belle face	Being all hers, and that her beauteous face
Et son regard qui tout mon mal efface	And her regard that doth all pain erase,
Três doulcement par pitié vers moy tire,	Bend pitying on me and not refuse
Plus ne demand d'elle ou tout bien s'amasse	Her tender eyes; I ask no other grace,
Grace te rends qui la m'as fait eslire.	Thanks be to thee, who mad'st me her to choose.
Ha! Dieu d'Amours, ainçois que je trespasser	Ah, god of Love, ere that I run my race,
Ottroiez moy que je puisse souffire	Vouchsafe I may alone content her, whose
Pour seul ami a celle qui m'enlasce,	I am always, in good and evil case,
Grace te rends qui la m'as fait eslire.	Thanks be to thee, who mad'st me her to choose.

As I thought about this I wanted to shine in her eyes; be gay, dress well, be generous so that all would praise me to her. I wanted to behave perfectly and change my childish ways, and my thoughtlessness, to appreciate all things noble. I had not come to the point where most lovers find that their longing burns them so that they grow pale or red and slink away. That was still to come. I changed my manners and tried in every way to be courteous and pleasing. And so that I could come to know the ways of love I learnt to dance and sing and to joust, for was it not true that honour comes from the pursuit of love, of arms and of valour?

I determined to choose a device and a motto which would contain my lady's name but which could not be read by others. I begged my parents for more money to spend as I pleased, for I wanted such clothes and a few horses for jousting. And many things did I undertake to try and please her.

I prepared a festival and to this I bade many noble ladies, but I asked the consent of my lady's lord to whom this was due and he consented gladly, inviting me to his castle. I could now see my lady but I never spoke to her of my love. I held my peace, but she could read it in my face; for though love made me silent I was pale and red by turns, my heart pierced by her who was the cause of my love. I endured this sweet pain for it all came from love. My lady did not see this or did little to show me she understood my feelings, but as I saw her often I was happy and found solace in the sight of her and I said to myself but addressing her:

Tres haulte fleur, ma dame
souveraine
De tout honneur et valeur
la deese,
De grant beaulté, sens et bonte
fontaine;
Et celle qui m'est chemin et
adrece.
De pervenir a vaillance, et qui
drece
Tres tous mes fais, dame a qui
je suis lige
Tres humble serf, comme a
douce maistresse,
A vous servir tant com vivray
m'oblige.

Faire le doy, belle de doulceur
pleine,
Car vous passés toutes, et vo
haultece

My lady, and my sovereign,
flower most rare,
In whom honour and worth
are glorified,
Fountain of all things wise,
gracious, and fair;
Who art my way toward
virtue, and the guide.
That over all my goings dost
preside;
Lady, to whom humbly is
vowed my fate,
Serving in that sweet service
at my side,
All of my days to thee I
dedicate.

How else, since none could
with thyself compare?
Thou Beauty filled with
sweetness, O provide

Si me sera exemple et ja me
meine
Au port d'onneur et conduit a
leesce,
Et, pour le doulz plaisir qu'ay,
je ne cease
D'estre joyeux, ma dame, et
pour ce dy je
De coeur et corps, non obstant
ma simplece;
A vous servir tant com vivray
m'oblige.

Vous le verréz et si serez
certaine,
Un temps venra, haulte noble
duchece,
Cement mon cuer de vous
servir se peine,
Et j'aray lors souffisance a
largece
Quant percevrez qu'a tousjours
sanz paresce
Obeiray; dame, l'arbre et la tyge

De tout honneur et de valeur
l'adrece,
A vous servir tant com vivray
m'oblige.

Haulte, puissant, tres louee
princece
A vous amer de tres bonne
heure apris je,
Car j'en vaulz mieulz; pour ce
en tres grand humblece
A vous servir tant com vivray
m'oblige.

Example kindling me to do
and dare
And bring my ship in
honour's port to ride!
So sweet my joy, Lady, it
cannot hide;
Therefore, in my simplicity
elate
Out of my heart and body
have I cried
All of my days to thee I
dedicate.

Most noble Duchess, surely
the hours prepare
That time, when thou shalt
well be certified
How my heart serves thee
with its every prayer,
Then shall my life be
brimmed and satisfied,
When thou its full devotion
having tried
Know'st it all truth; O
honour's path and gate!
Fame's flowering tree! O
valours starry guide!
All of my days to thee I
dedicate.

Princess, who dost in power
and praise abide,
Early I learnt to love thee;
and love, being great,
Lifts up my heart above all
thought of pride.
All of my days to thee I
dedicate.

And now I must turn back to my first subject. With all haste, a great and wonderful fête was prepared, from which many people derived much enjoyment. The jousts were proclaimed, at which those who jousted well might win jewels of great value and a prize, and to this tournament there would arrive twenty knights who would joust with all comers.

And on the day appointed, the assembly was held in a fair meadow where, well placed at the far end of a lake, was a castle with six great towers. And in this meadow were set up many large and spacious tents, scaffolds and pavilions, and all was made ready for the fête and for the jousts. And without adding more to this, I will tell you that when the appointed day came, my sweet lady arrived towards evening, and she was met on the road by a group of noble people and by minstrels too with drums, of which there were more than three pairs, and the trumpets were blown so loudly that the hills and valleys resounded.

I never thought I could have more joy than when I saw my goddess coming. I met her with my retinue and as I approached her litter, I greeted her.

We talked and laughed and with my sweet lady we came near the castle as I rode by her litter. I felt I had already been rewarded by the joy I felt at that moment for it seemed to me she looked at me tenderly. As we came to the castle the ladies there kneeled in greeting her. She descended to the courtyard and I took her to her chamber. Wine and comfits were brought for her refreshment and she invited me to join her. I withdrew after this and left her to rest while I went to dress for the evening. I wanted the dancing to be in the German mode and I had made all preparations to make the evening perfect.

The twenty-five knights wore liveries of green velvet and embroidered with gold chosen from among the hundred that I had made with my own device. Through the day following the jousting, the knights and gentle folk had at whatever cost dressed in satin embroidered in silver.

When all were assembled, the ladies and damsels of the country around, I with my retinue appeared to my lady and boldly said, "My lady it is time to sup". I grew pale as I took her by the hand and drew her into the hall. The knights led the ladies and the sound of trumpets echoed throughout the castle. The banquet was begun and made a wonderful sight.

On a large raised dais I seated my lady and I placed my mother by her side and four countesses to entertain her and each one was seated according to her rank. The gentlewomen and ladies in waiting sat apart from the squires and they were served well with meat and wine.

After supper, as was customary; we took comfits and drank while the minstrels sounded the dance, and soon a gay and joyous dance began. I went to my lady and begged her to dance. She hesitated a while and then consented. I took her by the hand and led her and danced and when it was done took her back to her seat. I was so full of love that to be near her was sheer delight. I desired nothing better and thought myself in paradise. Her face so pleased me and in that sight I rejoiced for it was so sweet, so gentle and looked upon me so tenderly that I thought all I had done seemed to please her. I observed her closely and I knew, I could have cried out in my joy, for I had the happiness of her love for which I longed. We danced again as I asked her and danced a part of the night together and when it ended I led my lady, who was as fair as amber, to her rest and there took leave of her. She looked upon me and her eyes inflamed my desire.

And as we retired to our beds covered with rich brocade, I could not cease to think of her and these words came from my heart:

Tant esjoist mon coeur vostre venue	When you are come, joy is so complete,
Que de parfaitte joye il en sautels,	The heart leaps in my breast, beholding you,
Flour de beaulte, rose fresche, nouvelle,	O flower of beauty, O rose fresh and new,
A qui serf suis par doulce retenue.	Whose slave I am, whose servitude is sweet.
Dame plaisant, et de chascun tenue,	Lady of gracious ways, whom all men greet,
La trés meilleur de toutes et plus belle,	Most beautiful of women and most true,
Tant esjoist mon coeur vostre venue.	When you are come, joy is so complete.
Par vous sera la feste maintenue	For you the happy festival shall meet

En grant boudour; autre je n'y
appelle
Pour m'esjouir, car vous seule
estes celle
Par qui vie et joye m'est
soustenue,
Tant esjoist mon coeur vostre
venue.

In glee; with none else have
I need to do
For my delight, from you
alone I drew
The life and joy that make
my heart to beat,
When you are come, joy is
so complete.

I longed impatiently for morning, I was full of longing to see my mistress. The castle was awake and knights and squires, though it was an early hour, jousted with the foils; I was ready and though mass was said I did not see her, but I found her later, for after hearing mass she had hurried to dress for the jousts. As she came out she greeted me saying, "Fair cousin, take care, for those who would win their lady will take part in the joust".

I smiled and with courage said, "I would ask you my lady to grant me a request. If you grant it I shall be happy. Give me, if it please you, a sleeve off one of your robes and a garland of periwinkle to wear on my helmet. Nothing would give me greater joy, not even the gift of a kingdom."

My lady was pensive and said at last, "Fair cousin, would it not be better for you to ask some other lady for her favour and for whom you can perform bravely? There are present ladies of noble birth and you should receive your tokens from your mistress and friend; not from me, though I would not refuse you indeed I would do more but I do not want anyone to know of it." She drew a dagger and cut a sleeve with ermine from one of her robes of a cloth of gold. I gave her my thanks for this and the garland she presented me, and I told her I would joust for love of her, but I warned her that I was still inexperienced and had much to learn.

She was silent and I could not know if my words gave her pleasure or not.

Dinner was prepared early on that summers day. We all dined hastily in our chambers, then went into the meadow where the jousts were to be held, and dismounted in front of the beautiful pavilions which had been set up all around. The armour was already there, the lances were got ready and the chargers were examined. There were high saddles with stirrups, covered with white, red, and green devices, and shields of various colours and painted lances. And already a great assembly had formed, there being a lot of noise and uproar amongst the common people sitting in many rows. I made ready and armed myself in my pavilion but as I did not begin the joust I waited inside. There were twenty of us, dressed alike, all knights and prepared to joust with all comers. My cousin, about whom I have already spoken, and who was courageous enough, was the first to take the field. He was experienced in this and looked so splendid that he looked truly like a cousin of the King. His helmet was laced correctly and there were gaily painted banners, while the pipes were heard to begin.

I had had many pavilions erected for the strangers who were guests so that they were lodged there and also the knights who joined us at the jousting, while others remained on horseback while watching the tournament. My cousin found that his challenges had been accepted by a knight who touched his shield with the point of his blade. My cousin acknowledged the encounter so that it meant if he was overthrown his blood must be drawn.

The heralds were heard calling out the names of the knights, some known in England and other countries. Five of ours rode out from their tents and did well.

Then the general tourney began in the meadow and, in double file and with our numbers reinforced, our company sallied forth and jousted as bravely as was expected of them. Two minstrels blew the trumpets joyously, the heralds made proclamations, and the knights, on noble chargers, jousted energetically according to their different ranks. My lady and many other ladies, every one of great beauty, were seated apart, in order of rank on sumptuously decorated scaffolds. There were twenty noble born ladies with blond tresses, adorned with chaplets, the sovereign and mistress of whom was she who was uppermost in my thoughts. They were all dressed in white silk, embroidered with a special device in gold and they seemed like goddesses from heaven or fairies created as perfectly as one could wish.

Brave and valorous jousting was done that day and it must have indeed pleased those who watched it. Lances were broken, one overthrew another and the sound of each shock resounded; one was struck on his shield, another through the opening of the visor, others thrown to the ground, the clash of blows resounded and the trumpets sounded so loud that even heaven's thunder would not have been heard.

At last, with my lance at rest, I rode forth from my pavilion swifter than a merlin, well seated in the stirrup and armed all in white on a charger whose caparison was also white. Neither red, nor green, nor any other colour whatsoever was there displayed, except for fine gold. And all the company came out with me and dealt many a good blow. They too were in white as were the lances also, which our side carried. And the sleeve which my lady had given to me, I placed in a suitable position, attaching it firmly to my helm so that it could not be torn off. And having placed the green chaplet on my helm too, I set off with a good company, for I was overcome with a great desire to see my very sweet goddess.

As I reached the jousting ground I turned my eyes to her and her tender glance gave me courage to face even mischance. I closed my helm after I passed her and took my position. A noble count brought me my lance and said to me that I could not shame the worthy crest I bore.

With lowered lance I spurred my horse against another who came towards me. We did not spare each other but it is not seemly that I should tell all my exploits. My lady, however, gave me praise for it and presented me the prize for those of the castle and I took it from her with joy. I did my duty that day in every way I could according to my age. Whatever I achieved was for love and so I do not deserve much praise, for it was love and not myself who performed it. There were others of better renown than myself more worthy but the ladies rewarded me for they saw how eager I was to please.

The prize given to strangers was that day given to a German, a most skilful jouster, one among a thousand.

The tournament continued without ceasing all day as new jousters joined it and the castle men gave good account of themselves. However it is not my intention to detail each blow, but everyone fought fairly and well.

Night came and all returned to the castle where the cooks had hastily prepared the supper. I sent for those who were lodged outside; in the name of the ladies and my own I asked that they should sup with us. Thus, I ordered a round table to be proclaimed on all sides, so that whoever might so desire, might come and keep the fête with us. Everyone came, both those of high and those of low station; none was left out. There were barons from many lands, and there is no need to ask whether the assembly was large, for they were received there, with ever-increasing pleasure. There were so many people that the castle was full. I received them all with a joyful face, and gave honour to each.

The supper was good and plenteous, and when we rose from the table, the minstrels sounded their horns, and those that were of noble rank dressed for the dance. There was no one there who was not dressed in richly embroidered robes, powdered all over with beaten gold and silver, and the ladies were dressed in a similar livery, likewise apparelled to dance gaily. Then began this merry fête. Many a gracious lady and fair maiden courteously invited the strangers to dance and led them onto the floor. The dancing began throughout the hall and everyone strove to dance gaily. But I, whom love had filled with a burning passion, thought only of my lady, and paid no attention to this. I tried to dance a little so that my thoughts might not be perceived or known. Then I retired with the older knights until my lady sent for me. I returned to the hall where all was merry.

When I came to her my lady said, "Fair cousin, why do you not dance?" and I answered: "Do you dance, my lady, and set me an example." but she said I must dance and start first. So I danced with a fair lady one round or two and then I took my lady's hand and we went out gaily in the dance.

The dance lasted most of the night and at last, it ended. Each one retired to rest and lay down in fine white sheets. But I who had a lady and mistress and who felt in my heart the torment of desire to be loved by her who was always in my thoughts, spoke thus to myself:

Rians vairs yeulx dont je porte l'emprainte Dedens mon coeur, par plaisant souvenir, Tant m'esjoist l'espart a souvenir	Laughing grey eyes, whose light in me I bear Deep in my heart's remembrance and delight, Remembrance is such infinite delight
De vous, tres douls qui me tenes en crainte Et d'amoreux mal fust vie exteintte,	Of your brightness, O soft eyes that I fear. Of love-sickness my life had perished here,

Mais vous faites ma vigour
soustenir
Rians vairs yeux dont je porte
l'emprainte.

But you raise up my strength
in death's despite,
Laughing grey eyes, whose
light in me I bear.

Car il m'est vis que par vous
l'atteinte
Venray de ce ou desir avenir,

Certain, by you my heart, I
see full clear.
Shall of desire attain at last
the height,

C'est qu'a son serf ma dame
retenir
Me vueille, et que sera par vous
contrainte
Rians vairs yeux dont je porte
l'emprainte.

Even that my lady, through
your sovereign might,
May me continue in her
service dear
Laughing grey eyes, whose
light in me I bear.

The next day dawned, what can I say about it? Should I talk of other things except my own? This whole day there was jousting. Twenty knights dressed in green held combat and the ladies watched and bestowed the prizes.

Twenty young ladies dressed also in green with golden chaplets on their flowing hair were fair to look upon. That day many high-saddled horses were thrown down, shields were hit and lances broken, many praises were given but I will not go further into this for I want to keep to the reason for which I began this story in the first place and all I thought and felt and did in this affair of love.

Our fête lasted three whole days, all had been made welcome and were at ease. The revel then ended but my lady stayed the length of a whole month. I begged of her lord to grant this and he consented. I wish that I could have given him a recompense for this.

You can well imagine what joy I derived from this pleasing stay! Not an hour passed when I was not thinking of how perfectly I could devise some means of best entertaining her. One day I ordered baths to be made ready and the stoves to be heated. The tubes were placed in a suitable spot in white pavilions. And I happened to be passing when my lady was in the bath. She received me with no great pleasure but I felt perfect joy when I gazed upon her fair flesh, as white as a lily. This delighted me greatly, as you who hear it told can well imagine. On another day we went hunting, and on another we went down to the river to fish. In this way we passed the whole month, partaking of many such happy pursuits.

In this happiness however, love held me in bondage stronger than ever, indeed so violent a hold had she that to be loved in return became my strongest desire. My anguish of mind was scarce endurable. I could never weary of her face and no happiness could I have when I could not gaze on her. It seemed that I could never tire of her presence. This mood gave me great pain and I knew I was not experienced enough to hide my anguish or my love. Never, however, could I speak to any man or woman of what so troubled me but my face in spite of all my reticence, revealed my feelings. My moods changed I was now merry, now thoughtful. I often wept bitterly as if I were forsaken of all the world and I thought to die in my sorrow and despair and with no hope of gaining my lady's love. My courage deserted me, I changed colour growing pale and red by turn, trembled, sweated and became calm. I could not drink or eat with appetite nor could I sleep much and so I grew worse and worse. No one knew my secret for I would speak to no one not even to her who was the cause of my love. She often asked me, enquiring, begging me to confide in her and not hide my trouble from her. She assured me I could speak to her without fear and told me she would do all in her power to comfort and ease me.

But I dare not tell her, for all the gold in the world, nor confide my secret and bare my heart to her. So I wept and sorrowed.

I became so filled with love that I can only say how painful my knowledge of it was and that my peace and quiet had been taken from me. Sorrow was my pitiless guest for I rejected all comfort. I remained like this not daring to beg for mercy from her, for I feared she would refuse me. Bewailing my state I made my complaint:

Amours, jamais ne cuidasse	Love, I had not ever thought,
Qu'a ton servant procurer	Thou would'st bid thy servant share
Deusses tel doleur qui passe	Grief to which all else is naught,
Toutes, car ne puis durer,	Grief whereunder I despair;
Si ne puis sur sains jurer	Thus unfaltering I declare
Qu'a la mort m'en vois le cours	That in death I pass away

Si de toy n'ay brief secours.   If thy saving grace delay.

Car ardent desir me lassee Tant que ne puis endurer	In a burning passion caught I grow faint, and may not bear
La peine qu'il me porchace	All the torment it hath wrought;
C'est par toy; vueillez curer	Thine be the fault, be thine the care!
Mon mal et de moy curer,	Loose me from this evil snare!
Car aillours ne scay recours Si de toy n'ay brief secours.	Other help is none to pray, If thy saving grace delay.
Et certes mieulz mort amasse, Je te jure sans parjurer, Que souffrir long temps la masse	Rather had I death besought, So without deceit I swear, Since my heart is all distraught
D'ardeur que fais enmurer	With thy flame enkindled there,
En mon coeur, et murmurer	Murmuring is not mine to dare;
N'ose; si vain en decours Si de toy n'ay brief secours.	I must perish as I may, If thy saving grace delay.
De joys veulz espurer,	Love, with gladness meet my prayer,
Amours, mon coeur et purer,	Cleanse my soul and make it fair,
Si qu'a a doleur je recours Si de toy n'ay brief secours.	Since in sorrow I must stay If thy saving grace delay.

My mistress left at the end of the month for she could no longer remain and she for whom I lived in anguish departed. Then was I truly in despair for I lost the sight of my perfect one without whom I could not live. I had got so used to looking upon her at all times, now was my happiness ended.

When would I see her again? Not for months perhaps. This grieved me to the quick. I felt such pain at her departure I lost control, and yearned for her so that I grew pale. This caused comment from many and I think caused her trouble. This in turn added to my grief and when I heard that it was rumoured abroad that I loved my lady I thought I would die in despair. Because of this gossip there was talk and discussion among her people and it was perhaps because of this that she left. I tried to hide my anger and my sorrow and sighing I said:

Orest du tort ma joye aneantie

Et mon soulas tourné en armertume
Trés doulce flour, puis que la departie
Je voy de vous, et la doulce coustume,
Las! que j'avoye
De tous les jours vous veoir, qui en joye
Me soustenoit, sera tourné en yre.
Helas! comment vous pourray je a Dieu dire!

Ma doulce amour, ma dame et ma partie
Celle de qui ardent desir m'alume,
Et que feray quant, n'en tout n'en partie
Ne recevray d'amours fors que l'escume?
C'est que ou que soye
N'aray confort ne chose qui m'esjoye
De vo beaulte qui loing de moy se tire.
Helas! comment vous pourray je a Dieu dire!

Now in good sooth my joy is vanished clean,
And all my gladness changed to grievous ire;
What profits it, dear flower! since I have seen
Thy going hence, that I could never tire
When thou wast here
To greet thee every day in every year?
Delight that was is grown disaster fell
Alas! How can I bid thee now farewell!

My love, my choice, my lady and my queen,
For whom my heart is kindled in desire,
What shall I do when love from what hath been
Take the gold and leaveth me the mire?
Not far nor near
Is comfort found, nor any pleasant cheer,
Gone is thy beauty, that did all excel;
Alas! How can I bid thee now farewell!

Ha mesdisans, ceste euvre avez bastie
Et pour ma mort forgée a dure enclume,
Fortune s'est a mon mal consentie,
Qui chiere n'a ne ma char ne ma plume,
Or n'y scay voye
Fors que morir, Dieu prie qu'il m'y convoye;
Car sans vous n'est riens qui me peust souf fire,
Helas! comment vous pourray je a Dieu dire!

Thine is the deed O evil tongue and keen!
Forged for my fate upon an anvil dire;
Fortune, that loveth not my hand, I ween,
Nor yet my pen, did in the task conspire.
No help is clear save death,
When God shall grant him to appear;
Else thou alone couldst win me out of hell.
Alas! How can I bid thee now farewell!

Ah simple et coye,
Au moins voiez comment plour et larmoye
Pour vo depart qui me met a martire,
Helas! comment vous pourray je a Dieu dire!

Ah simple and dear!
At least behold me and my mourning drear,
Thy loss is torment more than I can tell,
Alas! How can I bid thee now farewell!

I truly believe she would have lingered longer, but with these rumours she was forced to leave for it was her duty to obey her lord and guard his good name. The day came when she took her leave and left the castle. I attended her and rode beside her litter and she could well understand without words that I loved her. She looked long at me with a tender look for she wanted to comfort my painful and sorrowful heart. She would no doubt have spoken to me but that on the left side of her litter rode one of her suite. He was always so close to us that no conversation was possible. I hated him well and realised how much of this I would have to bear in the future. We rode for a whole day and a half. It did not seem long to me but ended only too soon and I was not tired though I suffered so much. At her castle her lord pretended to welcome me and falsely pressed me to stay. But I knew that he was eaten up with jealousy which had begun when I had welcomed a guest at the fête to whom I had even given a gift, never thinking that he would maliciously spy on her. He was in charge of my lady, my fair one, for whom I truly believe I was dying of grief and whom I worshipped. I hid my grief for it was necessary to dissimulate my feelings for fear of malicious gossip. I departed saying to myself:

A Dieu, ma redoubteé dame,	Farewell, my lady dear and dread,
A Dieu, sur toutes souveraine,	Farewell, of all sovereign and queen,
A Dieu, perfaitte et sanz nul blasme,	Farewell, perfect and sacred head,
A Dieu, trés noble et d'onneur honour pleine,	Farewell, who dost all mean,
A Dieu, vraye loyal certaine,	Farewell, true heart, loyal and clean,
A Dieu, en flour de tout le monde,	Farewell, best flower the world doth bear,
A Dieu sans a Dieu, blanche et blonde!	Farewell, yet not farewell, o white and fair!
A Dieu, sage et qui hait diffame,	Farewell, o wise, that no ill said,
A Dieu, fleuve qui grant joye ameine,	Farewell, river that made life green,
A Dieu, le port de noble fame,	Farewell, in whom fame harboured,
A Dieu, doulz voix de seraine,	Farewell, sweet voice so serene,
A Dieu, doulz loyer de ma peine,	Farewell, solace of all my pain,
A Dieu, celle en qui grace habonde,	Farewell, whose grace is wide as air,
A Dieu sans a Dieu, blanche et blonde!	Farewell, yet not farewell, o white and fair!
A Dieu, tres doulz ceil qui m'entame,	Farewell, soft look that through me sped,

A Dieu, trop plus belle qu'Helaine,	Farewell, more fair than Helen queen,
A Dieu, bonne de corps et d'ame,	Farewell, body and sweet soul wed,
A Dieu, tres gracleux demesne	Farewell, thou most gracious domaine,
A Dieu, joyeuse trés moutaine,	Farewell, pole-star, joyous and keen,
A Dieu, de toute valeur l'onde,	Farewell, fountain of valour rare,
A Dieu sans a Dieu, blanche et blonde!	Farewell, yet not farewell, o white and fair!
A Dieu, princesse tres haultaine,	Farewell, Princess of noblest mien,
A Dieu, accueil que crainte meine,	Farewell, thou aweing smile serene,
A Dieu, de tous les vices monde,	Farewell, without fault, sin's despair,
A Dieu, sans a Dieu, blanche et blonde!	Farewell, yet not farewell, o white and fair!

I hurried to my castle, full of sorrow for, no longer would she be near me, she who was so dear to my heart my lady, my fair one.

I had always known when I chose to be a lover that from this wound of love's choosing I would never be free; my sickness grew apace. I grew pale and thin and sighed so often for I found no comfort, no solace. I knew not how I could meet her or see my sweet one. I was on my sick bed when I composed this ballad.

Puis que veoir vo beaulté souveraine,	Since, O my love, I may behold no more,
No puis, m'amour, ma dame et soule joye,	Thy sovereign beauty that was all my cheer,
Mon coeur livre est a mortelle peine,	My heart is given up to sorrows sore,
Car se les biens de tout le monde avoie	For though the wealth of all the world were here,
Sans vous veoir souffisance	There is no ease but in

n'aroye,
Et j'en suis loing! dont me
convenient complaindre
En regraitant le bien qu'avoir
souloie;
Si ne m'en scay a autre que vous
plaindre.

Car vraye amour, de ce soyez
certaine,
Le souvenir comment je vous
veoye
Ne laist partir de moy qui me
rameine
Vostre beaulté au devant, simple
et coye,
Par quoy desir si durement
guerroye
Mon povre coeur que je le sens
esteindre
Ne plue de mal en mourant je
n'aroye,
Si ne m'en scay a autre que vous
plaindre.

Helas! au moins, belle, pour qui
j'ay peine,
Se pour vous muir, de quoy je
suis en voye,
Priez pour moy, et m'ame sera
saine,
Et se vo doulz oeil un pou en
larmoye,
M'ame en sera plus ayse, se la
moye
Doleur vous fait par de pitie
containdre
Un pou gemir, car pour vous
plour me noye

beholding thee
Who art afar! Whence I of
tears am fain
Mourning the happy days
that used to be,
Yet unto none but thee may I
complain.

Doubt not of this, true love
whom I adore,
Thine image in my soul is
ever clear,
I think but on the
blessedness of yore
And on thy beauty, simple
sweet and clear,
So fiercely smiteth love, I
may not flee
Nor may my soul the dread
assault sustain,
Death could not bring a
sorrier weird to dree,
Yet unto none but thee may I
complain.

Alas! one only mercy I
implore
When I am dead (as I to
death am near),
Pray for me, and they
praying shall restore,
My wounded spirit; shed one
tender tear
Great were my comfort if
my pious plea
Might touch thy heart, if
sorrow might constrain
Thy lips to sigh, such need
of sighs have we

Si ne m'en scay a autre que vous plaindre.	Yet unto none but thee may I complain.

Ha! doulce flour a qui tout je m'ottroye, Je sens mon coeur par trop amer estraindre Et Fortune ne veult que vous revoye; Si ne m'en scay a autre que vous plaindre.	Sweet flower, to whom I do abandon me, My heart is broken down with bitter pain For one whom Fortune would not have me see, Yet unto none but thee may I complain.

I was in torment, and knew not how I would have recovered, but God helped me. And my cousin, of whom I have spoken, came back and soon understood what ailed me. He found me sick and he came often. I was truly happy to see him for he was dear to me. He wept to see me as I was and as I embraced him he said, "Cousin, what face is this? My God, what is the cause of it? You must tell me all without restraint as you would do to your confessor; this trouble sickens you and your peace of mind is fled. I understand for I too had this same illness, but it is rather passion that consumes you as straw is consumed in a fire. I would not betray your secret and I would indeed help you and shelter you as I would do myself. Your trouble causes you the greater pain for you are unable to confide in another. Tell me all my dear cousin, do not indeed hide it from me. If you do not I shall perhaps go to Germany on a long voyage. I cannot rest while you are in this condition."

He urged me so pressingly to make known my secret thoughts and he held me so dear that he touched my heart and I wept almost enough to kill me, for in spite of his gentle words, I felt I could not speak of my grief. Seeing me weeping and sobbing he too out of his concern wept bitterly offering himself and his possessions if this could in anyway lessen my grief.

His council to take heart and weep no more calmed me. "Sweet cousin, I know that even as I love you so do you love me. I shall therefore not keep secrets from you, as you must not from me, and tell my joys and griefs. I can speak of this to no other and so you shall know the secrets of my heart. Dear Cousin you must remember our visit to a lady not long ago and for which I have paid with my youth, for love brought me this trouble, it is so terrible that I feel I am dying. I blame no one, not her for there is no other in the world who is her equal in worth, in discretion, in beauty. You know well how I arranged our fête, which was to show my love of her. After it ended I begged her lord to allow my lady to remain the summer at our castle, for pleasure and to hunt; the forest was green then and it is even now. He gave consent to this but you left soon after. However it was a joy to me for I saw my lady with no restraint. But alas! Misfortune which brings hurt to all lovers did not spare me either. There was one full of malice, who saw my state, (for I could not but show my love upon my face) and saw that I was under her spell; may he be damned in the fire of hell. I cannot guess how he knew for I tried to dissemble, hid my feelings, talked and sought other ladies and spoke to no one of my secret, not even to her whose vassal I have now become. This malicious treacherous one spread such rumours that her lord ordered her departure from our castle. I would force repentance on him who started such gossip but that I dare not bring scandal upon my lady. I have lived for three months in this stress and I would rather die than live with no sight of her. I know she has made gracious enquiry of me, letting me know that affairs will change and I will in future see her again, so I should be hopeful. I know my lady realises that my love is sincere but I cannot stay this longing which possesses me. I long for her and I even saw her from a distance in disguise so that none should know me, when she passed by. I do not know how anyone can help me, for the jealous one has spies and would soon know if I visited her. Even though I know I must endure this grief or die I cannot but tell you that I rejoice over my love and I will give you this ballad:

Ha! Amours, bien m'as tray	Thou, O Love, the traitor art!
Qui au premier pour moy prendre	Tender once as any may,
Me fus doulz, puis envay	Then the wielder of the dart
M'as si qu'il me fault mort pendre,	That is pointed out to slay,
Par toy, l'en te doit reprendre	Thee with reason, by my fay,
De porter double visage;	Double-visaged we declare;
Mis l'un a couleur de cendre	One is as the ashes grey,

Et l'autre a d'un ange ymage.   But one is an angel fair.

Dont je me truis esbay   Loth am I to find my part
D'en tel obscurté descendre   In the night without a ray,
Par desir qui esmay   Yet desire hath stung my heart

M'a, mais desespoir fait fendre   And I sigh in sorrow's sway,
Mon coeur, et espoir entendre   Gentle hope will never stay
A moy ne veult; l'un fait rage   In the mansions of despair
Et a mort obscure tendre,   One to death would point the way

Et l'autre a d'un ange ymage.   But one is an angel fair.

Mais bon espoir enhay   Hope might in my spirit start,

M'a, et desir et toy rendre   Death thy servant bide her nay

Me voulez mort, dont hay!   While beneath thy scourge I smart!

Mi dolent, diz de coeur tendre,   Doleful still must be my lay
Car tu pris pour mieulx m'esprendre   Since to set my steps astray
Accueil et dongier sauvage;   Thou at once art wheat and tare;

L'un est diable gendere   One is like a devil, yea,
Et l'autre a d'un ange ymage.   But one is an angel fair.

Amours, tu m'as fait entendre   Love, thou teachest me to say

Qu'apres joye ducil attendre   Double tribute is to pay
Peut cil qui te fait hommage;   For thy servants everywhere,

Deux manoirs as; l'un d'esclandre   One is grievous, well-a-day!
Et l'autre a d'un ange ymage.   But one is an angel fair.

"I realise that I must either endure this or die of it," I said, "but whatever my suffering, you will understand that I rejoice in love when you listen to my song.

"Dame plaisant, sur toutes belle
et bonne,
Ayez mercy de moy qui tout
m'ottrie
A vous servir, ame et corps
abandonne
A vo vouloir, et humblement
deprie
Que tost courir,
Faciez pitie pour mon mal
secourir,
Ou pour vous muir, vueillez
l'apercevoir
Si me daignez pour ami recevoir.

Helas! plaisant flour a qui je me
donne,
Ne m'occiez pas, mercy je vous
crye,
Priant, pour Dieu! que le mal
qui s'estonne
En moy vueilliez garir, je vous
en prie,
Car recourir
Ne scay ailleurs, ne me laissiez
perir,
Et regardez que j'aim senz
decevoir,
Si me daignez pour ami recevoir.

Ne voiz vous comment en plours
m'ordonne
Et que si vo secours trop me
detrie
Je suis perdu, dont, sans que
plus sermonne,
Vueilliez m'amer, car Amours

Sweet lady, fair and gentle
without peer,
Have mercy on me, who all
thy words obey,
Body and soul do I abandon
here
Unto thy will, and humbly
thus I pray,
Come quickly nigh,
Have pity, and cure my
sickness when I cry;
Oh, I beseech thee,
graciously attend
And so consent to take me
for thy friend.

To thee I give myself, O
flower most dear,
For mercy I beseech, and
wilt thou slay?
I charge thee by that Lord
whom we revere
To lift this wrong that
crushes me away,
No help have I
From any other; leave me
not to die!
See, faithfully I serve thee to
the end,
And so consent to take me
for thy friend.

Seest thou not how I shed
full many a tear,
And if thy help for longer
shall delay
I am but lost, what need to
speak more clear.
Ah, love me, Love so holds

136

me maistrie,	me in his sway!
Dont acourir	Then hither hie,
Faites mercis, car je suis au morir	Be merciful, for near to death I lie,
Et vous savz que je dy de ce voir,	'Tis truth, thou knowest, I have no hope to mend,
Si me daignez pour ami recevoir.	And so consent to take me for thy friend.
Dame, mercis, et quant fais mon devoir,	Lady, I thank thee, and all my duty send,
Si me daignez pour ami recevoir.	And so consent to take me for thy friend."

My cousin was enchanted, but when he saw my distress which however was much eased after I had confessed my thoughts, he chided me angrily: "Alas! I see clearly you have little courage or discernment. Why do you cry out against your state with so little reason? Your lady sends you a message, promises you comfort, and yet you foolishly decry her message. It is certain she thinks of your love and intends to give you joy. How could you then allow despair to enter into your soul? How many lovers are there, who with no hope of a return continue with no comfort, no single glance and no possible approach to her whom he loves for fear of scandal? Have patience, believe me when I say to you that you have to speak to her and she will help you. It is certain that your silence on this subject may harm you in her eyes. She will never speak to you of it. I cannot understand how you could be so foolish as not to speak of your love to her when you could so easily have done so, but you gave yourself up to dreams instead!"

"Alas, cousin!" I said, "I was afraid. I dared not speak to her when I had the chance for I feared her answer and I could not for my life speak to her. I do repent my silence now, but I never had courage enough, and in her presence I was so troubled that though I always meant to speak I remained tongue tied. Each loving glance filled me with ecstasy. So I thought she would realise my distress without words!" But my cousin said it was foolish for a lover to keep from his lady the love he bore her. "If you dare not speak why did you not write? I am amazed that receiving her messenger you sent her no

word of the real state of your mind. She certainly had you in her
thoughts to send to know of your news and may be surprised that she
had no answer back from you! Speak no more of sadness, be cheerful
and I will devise a means for your meeting. Indeed may I to a
monastery go if I cannot do this without anyone knowing it. Now no
more grief, no more sighs, I swear to you that within a week you shall
see her if God guides me in this enterprise, surely I shall find a way to
help you!"

My cousin's words so truly brought me hope and comfort that even
as the sun banishes the dark so indeed my cruel anguish was
diminished. He kept his promise so promptly that within the hour he
left to see her. He spoke to her discreetly, but told her the true state
of affairs, how he had found me on my sick bed nigh to death. Indeed
he told her that he could bring me no solace and begged her not to
leave me without hope for she may then be the cause of my death for
the great love I bore her. He pleaded with her to relieve my sad state
and my longing to see her which never wavered.

She grew pale and grave and he saw this news troubled her sorely,
but she would not let me know it and after a while she said, "You tell
me that my cousin and yours is in this distress. It is a surprising thing
for I can hardly credit it. I swear by the apostle Paul I never thought
of this; that he should be in sore distress. Perhaps it is only his youth
and lack of experience that throws him into this state and maybe it will
pass away. Try and counsel him and turn his mind from this. He can
never come near me if the spy (God's curse upon him) were to get
knowledge of it . For great trouble will arise.

"If he were here I would not dare talk to you, I dare not in fact
speak to any man. For he has so filled my lord with angry jealous
thoughts, since he knew that my cousin loved me, he is at my heels
and is set to watch me. I know this is because of the suspicion
aroused by your cousin. He keeps so close a watch that he often goes
to the gate to see who would enter here and follows closely all that is
said to me. I sometimes fear I will get him well beaten by my own
people so that he would not care to return. But my conscience
prevents me. This spying is so odious to me that I think that an end
would come only when your cousin refrains from visiting me here and
so indeed I sent him word. Only by degrees will this come to an end
and my lord cease to be jealous. Then alone can he come to me; if he

cares for my honour, let him keep away. Love, which is only of the mind, will fade away."

No other word would she say, no other word for my solace. My cousin however answered her saying, "My lady, surely you will not leave him to waste away in body and soul. You are too full of compassion to allow this. You say that I can divert him from this love. Yes so I can if I tear his soul from his body. I have tried to turn him to other thoughts, but I tell you straight, my lady, that he will surely die if no word of comfort comes from you. What will you gain by his untimely death for love of you? Give me your response, lady, for I swear that neither the jealous one nor his spies with all their cunning, will see through my plan. I know you pity him. Then grant him a meeting. I shall disguise him so that none will know him, but you must tell me how he should come so that he can see you. Do not say nay; time moves slowly for him."

She answered saying, "I am in no way his enemy and his torment grieves me sorely, for in truth you know that I do love him well. He rightly guards my honour and I will do all in my power to assent to his request. But at present he must be wise, and conduct himself prudently. You yourself may often come, but have little talk with me before this spy. I shall send you a loyal messenger; send me news through him, for him alone can I trust. But now I cannot be sure if we are not watched and we have talked long enough. Tell your friend to be joyful and happy for you have succeeded in your quest. If no violence prevents it, his request will not fail. Commend me to him and let him be comforted for before eight days have passed he shall see me. Trouble yourself no more, and let us cease this discussion; we have indeed been fortunate to have spoken together at leisure. Do not leave however, wait and meet my lord, who will have great pleasure I know in your visit. Now let us pass the time with a game of chess."

They started at a chess table, and when they had done, the lord of the castle entered greeting him warmly. He told my cousin he was very welcome and invited him to lodge at his castle whenever he was in these parts. He would be displeased he said if he did not come again as it would please him above all things. The next day after a meal he left the castle and hurried back to me, knowing of my longing for news of his mission. He related all to me and said that this affair would go right well if, as he had promised my lady, he would arrange all details of it himself.

My heart was filled with joy after this long period of anguish. He advised that I should write a letter to my lady telling her of my love, its heavy burden upon me and beg her to listen to the complaint of herself, beseeching her love asking nothing but her love. He said that I should put all down in a sealed letter which he should take to her himself so that it would in some measure relieve my grief. And I, believing in him, wrote to my lady and enclosed a ballad with my letter which I sealed. To all those who love, I give here a copy of the letter and the accompanying ballad:

> To her who surpasses all, and whom my
> heart fears and yet worships.

Lady, the flower of all noble ones, renowned and respected princess, the desire of my heart, my exalted one, my beloved and much desired. Lady, have pity and listen to the sorrowful complaint of your servant, who under this constraint is like one who is near to death and therefore takes perilous steps so that he may either die or live; sweet lady, by your consent, you can bring me comfort and life, a hasty death or quick remedy for my pain. Beautiful one, I well know that through your sensibility you must have seen how love for you has pierced my heart. I became the captive of love and am still its captive. My courage fled before the fear this great love brought me, this love which fills my heart, sweet lady; I know that you, who are all grace, knowing all the pain and torment that I have suffered and still suffer in longing for your sweet love, though I have not yet performed enough valorous deeds worthy of you or even one less worthy, in the compassion of your gentle heart would not have let me suffer so. Ah! my lady if because of my youth and inexperience I have not yet the rumour of valorous deeds, and if then you think me unworthy of your great worth it will be my death! But my noble lady you must know that you can so enrich me that courage and strength will be given me to undertake and achieve according to my power, all honourable pursuits that a loving heart may dare undertake and perform for the honour of his lady. Oh my sweet lady, my worthy goddess, you can so easily gladden the heart of one who loves and adores

140

you as his most precious joy. Will you by your sweet comfort save him from death and render him his life? And if you demand to know what and how he has been brought to this point I shall say that it is your sweet, pleasant, beautiful, laughing and loving eyes. Ah my lady it is by them that I received this mortal wound and it is only your sweet compassion that can heal and soothe this hurt. My dear and honoured lady let me know your will in this, shall you want me to love or die? I would not weary you longer but I promise you I am not well able to write or speak of all I feel. If I fail to win you I shall die, if by grace I win, then you will see the strength of my loving in my devoted service to you. I send you this ballad which I hope you will receive kindly I pray. My beautiful, wonderful one whom I cannot praise as I should, I pray God that he bestows on you as many joys as the tears I have shed for love of you.

    Written with an ardent and longing heart.

    Your very humble and obedient serf.

Here is the accompanying ballad:

Ayes pitié de moy, ma dame chiere;
Chiere vous ay plus que dame du monde,
Monde d'orgueil, ne me faites let vo chiere
Chiere achater par reffus, blanche et blonde
L'onde de plour m'ostez si que revoye
Voye d'avoir soulas qui me ravoye.

Et si jey fail, pour ce qu'a moy n'affiere,
Fiere moy mort, et en dolour parfonde
Fonde mon coeur et plus vivre

In this sad world have pity my lady dear,
Dear to me more than any other there;
Their pride you know not; not gracious cheer
Cheer me at so great cost, oh white and fair!
Fare I thus ill, yet canst thou bid me see
Seasons of solace that may comfort me.

If for unfitness I be slighted here,
Hé am I dead, and arrows of despair
Spare not to pierce my heart,

ne quiere,
Quiere doleur ou tout
meschief responder
Responde a tous: Amours
point ne m'envoye
Voye d'avoir soulas qui me
ravoye.

Belle plaisant et de tous biens
rentiere,
Entiere en foy, sans pareille
ou seconde,
Com de vo serf faites, sans
m'estre fiere,
Fierement non, qu'en doleur
je n'affonde,
Fonde qui fert mon coeur,
faites que voye,
Voye d'avoir soulas qui me
ravoye.

Dame, vueillez que vo secours
m'avoye,
Voye d'avoir soulas qui me
ravoye.

and life grows drear
Drear as my brooding on the
doom I bear,
Bear witness, Love
withholds in obduracy
Seasons of solace that may
comfort me.

O loveliest one and sweetest,
without peer,
Peerless in honour, of all
bounties heir,
Ere I thy servant pine in
sorry fear
Fear not a kind and gentle
guise to wear
Where shall I find, 'mid this
deep dolorous sea
Seasons of solace that may
comfort me.

Dear Lady, grant in gracious
courtesy
Seasons of solace that may
comfort me.

My cousin bore my letter to my lady. He watched prudently for
the moment he could speak to her alone. He told her of my letter and
she received it gladly. Reading the letter and the ballads several times
she smiled and graciously said: "I will reply to your cousin. More I
cannot say to you now; while I write to him play a game of chess with
my cousin here". She then retired to her chamber with her trusted
confidential secretary, and in the following letter expressed her
thoughts:

My Lady's Reply:

To my Gracious Friend,

Fair, courteous knight, I received your sweet, loving letter and ballads where you assure me that unless you receive comfort and solace your life is in danger. Therefore I write you this reply. If you are sure that I am the cause of your grievous pain I am indeed sorry for you with all my heart, for I would not be the cause of sorrow to anyone and to you more than another for I have known you so long. My dear friend, when you demand that I give you solace for your pain I do know the true meaning of your request, but you must know my intention.

Be sure that if you requested or I found that you expected any action that is dishonourable I would then be a stranger to you and never would you attain your desire, you can be certain that for nothing in the world would I besmirch my honour. I would rather die. But if a love given in honour and without evil intent will please you, then through love will I hold you for ever. When I know for certain that your love will be satisfied with what I may grant you, I will think of you as my only beloved friend and hold to you, if I see you keep to your loving purpose and good intent. And if indeed as you say in your letter I will help the cause of your valour, I will ask of God no greater grace. Write to me and make plain your will, but have a care that no desire will make you ever act against your vows and to the word you will give, for you will then be banished from me. And now I bid you chase all melancholy and sadness, be joyful, merry and content, but I warn you above all to be discreet, and as much as it is in my power I forbid you to act as in the custom of youth; that is, unable to keep secret their affairs and to commonly boast of their conquests. Speak to no one, not even your usual friends and companions, but only to whom it is necessary and which is necessary for your intimate confidante to know. If you do this and keep to it love will not fail you. My dear fair friend, I pray that God gives you all you wish. I feel this is not more than I can hope for you with propriety.

Written with joyful thoughts, your friend.

The letter ended, my lady rose and came to my cousin. She gave him the letter and charged him to say to me that I must no longer linger in melancholy, that she would try to heal my sickness and before too long would fix an hour and a place where I could speak to her. She sent me this message with her letter, that she put her honour into my hands and told me I must indeed banish all care.

My cousin thanked her and left to return to me where he told me how gracious and good he thought my lady to be. I had waited his return with great longing and like a flame. I held out my hands and joyfully said, "God, I thank thee for your mercy to me". My cousin gave me the letter and I, filled with happiness, took it and read it, kissing it a hundred times, I think, and reading it not once but more than twenty times, for I could never tire of reading it. I was almost drunk with joy, when I understood all its meaning. As my lady had commanded I ceased my melancholy, no longer afraid of her reply, hope sprang and restored me fully. I longed to answer her and with joy and without constraint I wrote to her as I now describe:

To the Most Beautiful Flower
My Very Honoured Mistress
Very beautiful and good, more indeed than my loving heart can express, beloved, honoured and desired love, for your radiant eyes have made me a willing slave. I am yours to command and in whose sweet service I would spend all my life as best I can. I thank you for your very tender and pleasing letter which has brought vigour, force and comfort to my poor melancholy heart when I was almost at the end of despair. My greatly desired and honoured lady, in reply to one of the points touched on in your letter, where you are uncertain of the true meaning of my request and where you say you would rather die than act with dishonour, I would have you know, my sweet dear mistress, and assure you that my desire is truly the same as yours. I desire nothing more than your good will, or never could I hold you the mistress of my heart or myself as your subject. As for your warning that I should guard my secret closely and not boast of this affair, my sweet lady, I solemnly promise you that as your liegeman, all my life I shall keep to this. I swear upon my honour. If I fail I shall be admonished,

144

banished by you from all joy and accept dishonour. As for secrecy except from the one who is my confidante and from whom I may not hide it, rest assured I shall follow your good counsel and you shall not find me break my word, gentle lady.

As I assure you on these matters regarding your honour I beg that the promise in your letter be granted me, that is that you will, by your grace, take me as your only beloved friend; if in any way you find me at fault, I am willing to be banished and dishonoured if I am untrue to these vows. God will not suffer me to live if I am untrue. And as for my advancement in valour, sweet lady, it is only through you, and none other that I can achieve this, for you can either make or break me. Sweet lady, comfort me, give me happiness, accord me your love and give my hungry eyes a sight of your beloved face. Send me this joyous news, that which I long for so much. Sweet one, pleasing above all others, I beg and pray for your help more times than I can say. May God grant you a good life and the good will to love me well. Written joyously and in hope of good fortune.

Your humble slave

At the end of this letter I added a short ballad, listen to it for it is not in the normal manner.

Plaisant et belle.	Kind and fair saint.
Ou se repose,	My heart's repose.
Mon coeur, et celle	Whose sweet constraint
En qui enclose	Doth all enclose
Est toute et close	That the world knows
Bonte et grace	Of graciousness,
Prenez m'en grace.	Vouchsafe me grace!
Freche nouvelle	Fresh without taint
Plus que la rose	As the new rose
A la querelle	This my heart's plaint
Que j'ay desclose	That overflows,
Pitie forclose	Ere my breath goes,
Ne soit, ains passe;	Pity and bless
Prenez m'en grace.	Vouchsafe me grace!

Ha! turterelle	Ah, sweet dove pent,
Doucle et reclose	Shy dove, for whose
Vous seule appelle	Dear grace I faint
A qui m'expose,	So my heart glows
Et, se dire ose	It dares disclose
Que vous amasse,	Love, Love, nought less,
Prenez m'en grace.	Vouchsafe me grace!
Sanz que s'oppose	Save thy heart close
Vo coeur a hose	To longing's throes,
Que desirasse,	O Loveliness,
Prenez m'en grace.	Vouchsafe me grace!

My cousin departed with the letter to the one I loved. I begged him to pray my lady that I might speak to her before long, for I could scarce wait longer or my poor life would end.

He sped to her castle and was made welcome but prudently waited till he could speak to her alone, prayed of her for God's sake to lose no time in granting my wish for I was languishing for love and surely would I take irrevocable hurt from this painful state. He gave her the letter which she read leisurely and said to him that she truly believed me for surely I spoke from the depths of my heart when I begged for her love. It was difficult for one so young to dissemble. The jealous one would leave the castle in three days' time on a long journey, and this danger ended, we could see and speak at leisure. At the proper time, I should come secretly disguised as my cousin's valet. She would then find concealment for me so that none of her people, except her secretary, would know of it. She would send him to me and he would explain how I should come. But she asked my cousin to counsel me to bear myself wisely toward her so that I should provoke no reproach or displeasure.

My cousin told her she might be assured that all would be well for I would rather die than displease her. When he returned to me and told me all this good and wonderful news I was filled with joy and it seemed that I lived in a happy dream.

But the days appeared unending to me. She, to whom my heart was given, did not forget her promise and sent this messenger to me and I gave him welcome. He brought the agreeable news which I so desired. That night I was to go towards her to whom my heart tended; I was to speak to no one except my cousin and the secretary and set out with them and no other.

We set out very soon after telling our households that business took us away which would keep us busy till our return on the next day.

We rode swiftly with joy and arrived at the hour agreed upon at a dwelling which my dear lady sometimes used. We descended without light and I took off my robe and put on another. My cousin, kind and wise went forward boldly and I guarded the horses, hiding my face the while.

He excused himself for the late hour of his arrival but said he had pressing business which he must speak of to the lord as urgently as may be. They answered that the lord was away and not due back for months. He said it was a great pity for much harm would come to him. Then it was my sweet lady looked out of a trellised window and said, "What matter brings you my cousin? Go quick and let down the bridge for I must learn the reason of this visit. It is surely some urgent news for me?"

Two damsels led my cousin towards my lady and she asked anxiously, "Is someone dead? What brings you here so late? You have been absent for a week. Tell me what the matter is?" My cousin answered saying it was a grave matter for the lord and master, but as he could not meet him it was good that he departed. But she said that he must tell her what it was. "My valet," he said, "who guards my horse has in his keeping a letter that he must bring me in all haste." Then my lady addressing her secretary commanded him to bring me. The secretary hastened to lead the horses to the stable and brought me up. My cousin came to the chamber door and said, "Give me the letter quickly" and turning to the secretary said, "Let him go". While saying this, he took a long letter from me, and turned towards my lady, for a light in the chamber may have revealed my identity. The secretary still without a light took me into a chamber of a lady, wise, secret and irreproachable and who knew everything. When the letter had been read for my lady in the presence of her household, my cousin decided to leave and pretended regrets. But she forbade him to leave saying she would complain to her lord and so she retained him a while, and at last she said the time had come to sleep, and she let her household go. My cousin's chambers being ready in a distant wing, he was escorted by her esquires to his rest, for at this late hour they had no need to wait on her.

She went to bed, disrobed by her women and she lay down, but soon rose and demanded that a fire was made in the room where I was. I hid till the fire was ready. My lady wrapped in a long robe came in with only the lady mentioned before, in whom she had chosen to confide in this matter, dismissing her serving woman telling her she did not want her to wait so she should not be over-tired. Her companion fetched me and took me to my lady. I hardly knew what to do I was so bewildered but managed to greet her saying, "Sweet lady, God keep you both body and soul".

"Friend, welcome," she replied and made me sit beside her. No sooner had I looked on her I was as a man lost in ecstasy. She divined my state and kissed me welcome and I humbly thanked her for this many times. My lady, sole possessor of my fearful and doubting heart started to say, "Have I granted your wish, fair sir, bringing you secretly to me, is this the gesture of a friend? Do not deceive me, tell me all your desires, now, while you can speak to me of all your thoughts, I pray you be frank". I trembled with joy and sighing said, "Ah sweet lady, by my faith, I know not how to tell you. All I can say is, that I am yours body and soul. I know not how to say more". She came closer to me, laughing she put her arm around me and said, "Then shall I speak for us both? for you can remember nothing to tell me. And yet I think love sent me many of his favours. I believe I cannot speak a word that you might say to me, and I cannot go beyond what it is wise for me to say." The lady who had accompanied her smiled and said, "I do believe that love makes fools of the wisest, though I perceive you are in accord in this matter".

My lady then said to me, "Friend, since love has caged our hearts together we do not need to ask if we love one another. Love has chained us both and claims us his servant. I am not sorry for this. But dear friend though I trust you I want to confide all my thought, with no concealment, hiding nothing, I do not know all your intentions, but believe me whatever love you see in me, whatever sweetness or joy, whatever words I may use, however I may kiss and embrace you, never in my life will I have the desire to do aught that would dishonour me, or could bring me reproach in any way. Sweet friend, I tell you this so that you may never say I surrendered to you, for never can I do that which will smirch my honour. I swear to you this is true. If ever I find you have other thoughts beyond this I shall never see you again. But of all other pleasure which a loving friend can give I will not refuse you. If it were not wrong and indeed foolish I should abandon my heart entirely to you. I promise you loyalty and loving friendship and to cling to you above all others. Will this be sufficient for you? Tell me truly now while we can talk for I must understand all your mind in this matter."

When she, whom I revered, ceased speaking I answered, "Ah! My lady, my heart breaks to hear you say all this. It will suffice, the love, the gentleness and the grace which you offer me. Never think that I will not entirely obey your commands and as I wrote to you in my letter I swear on oath that I shall be dishonoured for ever if in word or deed or thought, in public or in secret, I shall ever do that which will displease you. All that your heart desires will content me, and cannot grieve me, for are you not the beloved of my heart? If ever I think differently may I perish and be brought to shame. God in heaven! You love me and call me 'friend', I possess my heart's desire, am I not fulfilled? In your service I shall do such valorous deeds that your love for me will grow. Therefore, command me now, for I am your liegeman, and my heart, soul and body are all pledged to you, fair one. Command me now as you will, or send me whither you please, and I will go and obey in all things, without opposing your wishes. You can thus do with me what you will, more than I can say, and may God watch over you and reward you abundantly for having promised wholly to love me. I ought not to speak ill of love for it has been the means of my attaining such great joy. Thus, O kind and fair one, I thank you humbly, for I shall henceforth wear the lover's crown and shall cast aside every evil habit of mine, and take virtue into my service. This I seek above all else for I would strive to be valiant. Thus you will make me a prudent man. So, sweet lady, I could not be happier, however much I might discourse upon it." Then my lady, who possesses every virtue, embraced me tenderly and kissed me more than a hundred times. I remained thus happy all night and, believe me, you lovers who hear this, I was most contented. That night we spoke the sweet words of love's delight and my goddess told me how I might see her often in secret. I had all I desired. She cautioned me to change the time of our meeting should there ever be danger to her honour, however disagreeable this may be. If I was not prudent she would be in peril. I should choose carefully the hour and time to arrive and always leave when she asked me. The night was so short the dawn arrived and we embraced a thousand times. Sweet, loving words were said, "Adieu, my dear love," she said, as she left for her bed and locked the door. Alone, I put on the cloak of a page when the secretary came to see me out, and though unaccustomed to this office I resumed my role as a valet but as she said I had received a sweet reward; I took charge of the horses by the gate and often I took this role in the future. You see that sometimes it is necessary for the master to become his valet if this will bring him to his heart's desire.

My cousin had woken early and stole out softly, that he should not wake the household. He had bid adieu to my lady before retiring for the night. I walked the horses up and down as a valet should while I waited for him and he called, "Come here boy, how angry it makes me when you saddle my horse!" He said this for the benefit of some knights and men-at-arms who wanted to escort him back, but he said that he had come alone with his valet for good reason and bemoaned the fact that he did not see the lord, for he greatly desired to speak to him. He refused an escort and we set out towards our dwelling. I changed my clothes on the way and we talked and laughed together. My heart was so light, comforted by my sweet meeting. We were welcomed back by my people who were happy to see us safe, and in great joy we sang this new virelay:

Belle ou est toute ma joye,

Pour vostre amour se resjoye
Mon coeur, dont a chiere lie

Je chante: Dame jolye
Pour qui tout vif j'enragoye;

Mais vous m'avez envoye
Doulx secours qui conforte:
M'a dont je suis convoye,
A joye et bien cnorté.

Si est drois que faire doye
Gaye chiere, car perdoye

Sweet, in whom my joy
must be,
Now my heart is full of glee
For thy love: and loosed
from care
All my song is, "Lady fair,
Living I consume for thee."

But thy gentle love hath sent
The fair comfort that I need:
I therewith am well content
Gladness doth my spirit lead.

Rightly am I glad, pardie!
For of old my jollity

150

Soulas par melancolie,

Mais tout mon mal amolie,
Vo secours que j'attendoie
Belle ou est toute ma joye.

Puis que m'avez ottroyé

Vo doulx coeur, je suis porté

Hors d'anuy et ravoye
A joye et reconforte.

Ha! ma dame, Avous m'envoye
Doulx secours quant par tel voye

Suis ressours, chiere palie

Plus n'aray quant il m'alie
A espoir que vous revoie,

Belle ou est toute ma joye.

Drowned in woes I had to
bear:
Of thy help when I was ware
Gone was all my misery,
Sweet, in whom my joy
must be.

Since the day that thou hast
lent
Thy dear heart, my life is
freed
From the sorrows I lament:
Peace and gladness are my
mead.

Lady, Love despatcheth me
Succour sweet, who thus am
free
From my sickness: pale
despair
Rules no longer when I share
Hope that I thy face may
see,
Sweet, in whom my joy
must be.

I have told you of the different stages of my love; first the surprise
and wonder which subdued me; then the pain and longing and how my
dear cousin and my lady's mercy relieved me of this; now I was
happy and in my joy I wrote this ballad:

Il n'est de moy plus heureux en
ce monde,
Car joye n'est autre per a la
moye
Quant celle qui n'a pareille ou
seconde
M'a a mercy pris, et se je
l'amoye

In all the world is none so
happy here
Nor is there any joy to
match with mine
Since she that hath no rival
and no peer
Doth mercifully to my suit
incline

Jusqu'au morir; certes bien m'est la moye
Peine et doleur granment guerdonnée
Or m'a gari celle que reclamoye,

Puis qu'elle m'a sa doulce amour donnée.

Ha! belle, en qui toute valeur habonde
Vous ne voulez plus que pour vous l'armoye
Aincois vous plaist qu'a tous amans responde;
"Je suis cellui qui des biens affamoie."
Qu'Amours depart, dont dolent me clamoye
Mais la belle de bonte couronnée

M'a respite: Amours a tort blassmoye
Puis qu'elle m'a sa doulce amour donnée

Or est en jeux et ris retourné l'onde
Du tres grief plour qu'en desespoir semoye
Dont gay, jolis et de pensée monde,
Plus qu'oncques mais seray, Amours en voye,
M'en a mis et ma dame qui m'envoye
Tant de plaisirs que joye abandonnée
M'est de tous lez, et a tous bien

Her slave I am till death, for all my pain
In very truth hath met with guerdon meet;
She was my help on whom I called amain,
For she hath granted me her love so sweet.

Fair queen, in whom all nobleness is clear
Thou woulds't not have me for thy presence pain:
Nay, bid me cry in every lovers ear,
"Thirsty was I for Love's immortal wine!"
Not all my weeping might the gift obtain
Yet she, enthroned on beauty's mercy-seat
Hath pardoned all: too soon did I complain,
For she hath granted me her love so sweet.

Now to delight return the torrent drear
That of my mourning was the sorry sign;
Now that I am joyous and of merry cheer,
More than aforetime in her grace divine,
Love bade me follow in his chosen train
Where gladness walks beside my lady's feet,
Nor any loss is mingled with

m'avoie
Puis qu'elle m'a sa doulce
amour donnée.

my gain,
For she hath granted me her
love so sweet.

Princess d'Amours, plaindre ne
me devoye
Pour peine avoir quant joye
redonnée
M'a celle qui mon coeur de tout
avoye
Puis qu'elle m'a sa doulce
amour donnée.

Princess of Love, my sorrow
I disdain,
Since out of mourning
cometh joy complete
By grace of him who is
love's suzerain,
For she hath granted me her
love so sweet.

I behaved carefully and wisely and desired a thousand beautiful things, and took care to learn all that which would become me, and I tried to avoid those that would not, and burned to achieve fame, so that my lady would know herself the beloved of a valiant knight. I spent generously making it appear that I cared not for money.

Briefly I will say that only one thought held me, and that was to follow the path of a true lover. Thank God, I often enjoyed those favours which love and ladies bestow on those who are true to them.

I know well how to be true, though I had to be extremely prudent when I went to her every week so that no one, except those trusted ones knew of it. At the first of such meetings I took her this ballad and brought one back from her.

Comandez moy, ma dame
redoubtée,
Vo bon plaisir, prest suis a le
parfaire,
Com de vo serf; dont amée et
doubtée
Estes, pouez de moy vo vouloir
faire
A bon droit est ce,
Je ye suis tenus, car par vous
j'ay leesce
Plus qu'oncques n'ot, certes, nul
amoreux

Command of me, my lady
and my queen
All thy good pleasure, as I
were thy slave,
Which I shall do with glad
and humble mien
That whatsoever thou
willest, thou mayst have
I owe no less
Being bound thereto for so
great pleasantness,
More than to other lovers
may betide;

Car voz biens sont plus qu'autres
savoreux.

Puis que m'aves toute doleur
ostée,
Et donné ce qui m'estoit
necessaire
N'est ce raison que vous soiez
rentée
D'un coeur d'amant qui vous
desire a plaire?
Ha! quel maistresse,
Qui son servant guerdonne de
largece
Des dons d'amours! tous autres
lais pour eulx,
Car voz biens sont plus qu'autres
savoreux.

De bonne heure pour moy
amours boutée
Fu en mon coeur quant recoy
tel salaire
Pour bien servir, si n'en sera
ostee
Tant quant vivray. Ha! oulce,
debonnaire
Conforterresse
De ma vigour, dame de grant
haultece
Aultre bien m'est fors cestui
doloreux
Car voz biens sont plus qu'autres
savoreux.

Doulce princcce
J'ay tout plaisir, vous en estes
l'adrece
Plus ne desir, plus ne suis

For sweeter are thy gifts
than all beside.

Thy love delivered me from
duel and teen,
All that was needful to my
soul it gave,
Is there not here in truth
good reason seen
Thy love should rule the
heart thy love did save
Ah, what mistress
So guerdoneth her servant
with largess
Of love's delight? The rest
have I denied
For sweeter are thy gifts
than all beside.

Since such a harvest of
reward I glean,
Love in my heart hath risen
like a wave;
Thy slave am I, as I thy
slave have been,
While life shall last. Ah,
damsel bright and brave,
Sweet patroness
Of spirit and strength, and
lady of noblesse
All other comfort doth my
heart deride
For sweeter are thy gifts
than all beside.

Most dear princess
Of joy thou art the fount, as
I confess,
I thirst no longer, but am

154

langoreux
Car voz biens sont plus qu'autres
savoreux.

satisfied,
For sweeter are thy gifts
than all beside.

Before I left my very sweet one, she gave me an answer to my
ballad. My ecstasy was the more perfect as my beautiful one, while
reading it, put her arms around my neck. Here it is:

Benoite soit la journee,
Le lieu, la place et demeure,

Doulz amis, qu'a ce menee
Fus, trop y os fait demeure

Que vous donnay
Toute m'amour, amis, meilleur
don n'ay
J'en lo Amours qui la commence
a faite,
Car j'en recoy joye toute
parfaitte.

Et quant je me suis donnee
A cil qui pour moy labeure

A honneur bien assennee
Seray, ce fu de bonne heure,

Dont raison ay
De lui amer, et se l'araisonney

Pour lui garir ne me suis pas
deffaitte
Car j'en recoy joye toute
parfaitte.

Si entray en bonne année

Amis, si Dieux me secueure,

Ever blessed be the day,
Be the place and be the
dwelling,
That hath ended my delay,
Shown the truth I shrank
from telling
Dear friend, behold
My love is yours, a costlier
gift than gold,
To love be praise, that first
the bond hath knit,
For I am filled with perfect
joy from it.

Since I yielded to thy sway
When thy heart with grief
was swelling,
Swiftly speeding as he may
Joy is come, my care
dispelling;
Now I am bold
To give thee love, that
guerdons manifold
May heal thee from thy
sorrow every way
For I am filled with perfect
joy from it.

So my soul, with God for
stay,
The new blissful years

Car par plaisant destinée

Tout soulas en assaveure,

Dont guerdonnay
De bonne heure le mal que
j'entonnay
Pieça on vous puis que j'en
suis refaitte,
Car j'en recoy joye toute
parfaitte.

Quant m'adonnay
A vous amer, mon coeur
abandonnay
A tous deliz sans point m'estre
meffaitte
Car j'en recoy joye toute
parfaitte.

foretelling,
Finds in thee, for whom I
pray,
Grace and gladness all
excelling
I that of old
Gave thee but sorry cheer
and comfort cold,
Am straightway turned to
serve thee, as is fit,
For I am filled with perfect
joy from it.

When I had told
My love, my heart was
yours to have and hold;
To grief I yield not, nor to
blame submit,
For I am filled with perfect
joy from it.

My path was now filled with the happiness granted me. But Fortune, as well all know, who is ever ready to harm lovers when ever she can, grievously harmed me. Within a brief time the lady who guarded our secret and helped in our affair had to leave urgently to look to matters pertaining to her inheritance which her absence might have lost her. She reluctantly left the court and I was thus in great trouble for my lady could undertake nothing without her. I could not refrain from seeing her and my lady knew this, indeed I think she felt the same impatience as myself. She remembered then one who had served her all her life, good, loyal and secret, but she lived no more at the court. My lady immediately wrote asking her:

> To my very dear and good friend
> La Dame de la Tour
> Very dear and good friend. You will be pleased to know I am in good health and I pray God that you are likewise. I write to you as I desire to see and speak with you for I have not forgotten the good and true service you always rendered me so

that I feel I can never repay you for it. Be certain that I am
your friend and shall prove it if you ever put it to the test.
Dear friend, you know in what constraint and fear I live,
forever under suspicion, controlled and treated harshly. This
life allows me but little joy, and I have no one near me to
confide in and in any case I can speak of it to no one, though,
knowing you loyal, I should not hesitate to tell you everything
just as I would to my confessor. You must understand how
hard it is for a young heart always to live without joy. I long
for you to be near me so that I can confide in you about happy
things, which I cannot for good reason write to you. I need
your help and counsel and I pray you for the love you bear me,
arrange your affairs as quickly as you can, so that within eight
days you can be by my side. I will send for you with all regard
to your comfort and honour. Do not hesitate about leaving your
household for I will make such recompense that it will be of
advantage to you. Pray do not refuse me in this and send me
your reply by the bearer of this letter. Commend me to your
daughter-in-law. Dear friend may the holy spirit guard you.
Written from my castle the eighth day of January.

The lady whom my lady thought of as a beloved friend sent this
reply, which greatly troubled me for it was against our love and this is
the letter:

My very dear lady, I send you my great respect and thank
you for your very amiable and kind letter for which I thank you
from my poor heart, as I do for the honour you do me to
remember the small services I have done for you, though they
were not worthy of your noble and honourable state. My lady I
do beseech you to excuse me, for by my faith, my daughter is
grievously sick so that it is not possible for me to leave her
side. God knows I am troubled for her and so with a painful
heart I must decline to come to you. But my dear lady I feel
bound to write and counsel you though I cannot see you, for I
have guided you from infancy and though I know I am not
worthy of this, it would be wrong if I refrained from speaking
about matters which may bring you trouble. I entreat you, dear
lady, to know that I write this as my duty and it is for love of

you. You may bear me ill will for it but your good name and honour will increase. Certain rumours have reached me, my lady, and I am deeply grieved for I am troubled lest your good name be in doubt and therefore, for it is right and fitting for every princess and noble lady, since she is greatly exalted above others in honour and estate, to exceed all others in goodness, wisdom, manners, disposition and behaviour, so that she might serve as an example by which all other ladies, and even all women, should regulate their conduct. And thus it is necessary that she should be devout towards God, and have a confident, gentle and calm disposition, and in her pursuits be restrained and without excess. She should laugh with moderation and not without cause, and have a noble manner, modest appearance and dignified carriage, with a kind reply and friendly word for everyone, her dress and attire rich but not too excessive, gracious in her welcome of strangers. When speaking, she should show restraint and not be too familiar, nor should she be hasty in judgement or fickle, never appear cruel, capricious or ill-tempered, or too difficult to serve, humane and amiable with her women and servants, not too haughty, and be generous within reason.

Further, she should know how to recognise those people who are most worthy in goodness and prudence, and her best servants, and know how to draw all these people towards her, rewarding them according to their merits, and not believing or putting faith in flatterers, but recognising them for what they are and sending them away; not given to believing gossip nor being in the habit of confiding either in strangers or close friends in any secret place, and especially not in any of her retainers or women, so that none may be able to think that he knows more than another about her secret affairs. Nor should she say anything in jest to anyone at all, in the presence of other people, which might not be understood by everyone, so that those hearing it have no reason to suppose that there is any secret between them.

Finally, she should strive not to confine herself too much to her chamber nor to herself, nor be too much in the company of other people, but be sometimes retiring and at others more sociable. Now these things and all others befitting a noble princess were in the past observed by you. It is rumoured that you have changed, become more joyful and talkative than you were before. The outward appearance is always an indication of an inner change of disposition, and you are now changeable, wanting now to be alone except for your waiting woman and a few others with whom even in public you talk to secretly and laugh together showing that you share with them affairs which only you understand together and that only their company pleases you and others are neglected in your service. This of course arouses jealousy among your servants and naturally they think you are in love. Ah! Sweet lady, remember for God's sake that your noble birth, to which God has raised you, obliges you to put away any temporary pleasure which might make you forget your honour. It would be foolish if you thought, as many young women do, that you can allow yourself to indulge in a passion if this does not lead you to commit any wrong (for I am sure you would rather die than commit one). You think it will help make your life more pleasant and that you help a man to his renown. Ah! My dear lady, for God's sake, do not pretend or be deceived. You have examples of other noble women who when only suspected of love lost their reputations. I could swear that they had never sinned, but it led to disaster. Children have been forced to hear them spoken evil of and treated without respect. Any such love in a woman, rich or poor, is dishonourable but far more so in a princess or noble lady, and the higher she stands the more harmful, and justly so, for unlike a simple woman, her reputation spreads far beyond a small circle and it is known abroad; moreover there are doubts cast on her children's birth and this is grave as they are born to rule. A suspicion that they are not the true heirs of their fathers, even if there was no wrong committed, who would believe it when it is rumoured that 'the lady is in love', though only loving glances have been exchanged. Yet malicious and evil tongues will say so and exaggerate and talk of acts which never took place and so it goes passing by word of mouth from one to another. Therefore it is the duty of a noble lady to think carefully on all her behaviour more than it is for another. The reason is that her example is commented on and all her actions noted so that she cannot secretly speak, laugh or jest without the fact being spoken of and spread abroad. And take note, therefore, my very dear lady, that it may have a very bad appearance when a noble lady, or indeed any woman, becomes gayer and more cheerful than is fitting, and more ready to listen to amorous discourse; and then, when for any reason she has a change of heart, and becomes suddenly discontented, ungracious and defensive, and no one can serve her satisfactorily and she takes no interest in her dress and attire, then, indeed, people say that she must have been in love but is no longer so. My lady, this is no way for a lady to behave herself, for whatever thoughts she may have, she should always take care to conduct herself in such a way that these and similar judgements cannot be passed on her, and although it may be difficult to maintain such moderation in one's love life, the surest way to achieve it is to eschew and shun it completely.

Dear lady, you know that a woman's fair name is the greatest jewel she can obtain, for this is passed even to her children. Very respected lady, I do understand that a young woman in her youth can allow herself to indulge in such a love. She will say to herself 'I am young and it is only just that I have some pleasure without doing any harm; is it bad when there is no evil intention? No one will know and I will help a man to be valiant. I shall by this have a loyal friend to my service.' Ah! My lady, have a thought for God's sake that you do not allow yourself to be persuaded to this illusion. In love there is a thousand times more pain, care and risk of much peril, particularly for a woman, than there is of true happiness. Then there is the continual strain of discovery and other worries which this situation brings in its train. And as for saying, 'There can be no harm in this since it will not result in sin,' alas! My lady there can be no one who is so sure of herself as to be certain that whatever good resolution she has made, she will always exercise moderation in love, or that it will not be discovered as I have suggested before. Indeed this is impossible too and there is never fire without smoke, but there is often smoke without fire. To say further that, 'I shall make a man valiant', what folly to think that you will risk ruin to help another's reputation and advancement and as for saying, 'I have a loyal friend and servant' God knows how he could ever serve a lady he would not dare champion if she be in trouble, without bringing her dishonour. How then is she served by him? And as for the renown they win in battle or otherwise for the sake of their ladies, I declare that they serve themselves, for their ladies can in no way profit from their valorous deeds. And then my lady if an excuse be made saying, 'My life is a sad one, with little joy and freedom, can I not then take pleasure with another in harmless friendship to forget my melancholy and pass the time?' But such excuses are worth nothing, for great folly it is to set fire to one's house, to destroy one's neighbours; but she who loyally supports a husband increases the honour of her name.

And as for having pleasure, for sure a noble lady and indeed every woman can, if she wishes, find without such love as this, enough lawful and honest pleasures to which she might give herself up, and with which to pass the time without melancholy. For those who have children, what more agreeable and delightful pleasure could one ask for than to see them often, and to take care that they are well fed and taught as befits their high birth and estate, and to bring up the daughters in such a way that, from childhood, they might, from the example of good company, learn to live in a good and decent manner? But, alas, if the mother is not wise in all things, what sort of example is she to the daughter? And for those who have no children, it can, indeed, be an honour for any noble lady, after she has finished her household tasks, to take up some work, in order to avoid idleness, either embroidery upon fine linen or silk, or other things of which she could make good use, and such occupations are good because they prevent vain thoughts.

In no way do I say that a young noble lady may not take pleasure, even with and in the presence of lords and knights, honour and welcome guests according to their rank, but with modesty, with restraint and with no cause for discovery in her words, looks or laugh that which will be unworthy of her or which could be wrongly interpreted. Ah, God, if all great ladies, all women, could understand how much such behaviour would enhance her she would scarcely need other jewels to adorn her. And again my very dear lady, it remains for me to speak about the perils and dangers which are inherent in such a love, and which are without number. The first and greatest is that it angers God, and then if the husband or relatives become aware of it, the woman is ruined or severely reproached, and can never be happy again. And again, even if this does not happen, let us consider the disposition of lovers. Even if all were loyal, secretive and truthful, which they are not, since it is well-known that they are usually faithless and, in order to deceive their ladies, say things which they do not mean, nevertheless it is a fact that the passion of such love does not last long, even with the most loyal.

Oh! dear lady, can you imagine what painful thoughts will torture her when this love fails her and it comes to an end? She who has been blind and has allowed this mad pleasure to develop, repents with hard thoughts when she thinks on these follies and the perils she has time and again encountered and at whatever cost she will wish that she had never passed through them so that she could not be reproached for it. She will repent it greatly and will not be able to wipe out the unpleasant thoughts which remain in her heart.

Moreover you and all other ladies can see what folly it is to put her person and her honour at the mercy of such servants. For servants they call themselves and at the end although they have sworn to keep your secrets they will not hold to these promises, and a lady in such a situation is reproached with gossip and rumour for these very people talk and in fact you are soon in bondage to them. You must realise that such people, to enhance their situation, boast that they are loved by their mistress. They lie but God grant in your case you will keep this in mind.

Your serving people whom you have to trust, naturally want it known that they are in your intimate confidence and they will so talk that your affairs are known though they may not openly speak your secrets.

Oh God, what servitude for the lady, and any other lady in the same situation, who cares not to reprove or blame her serving men or women, even if she sees them badly misbehaving because she feels herself to be in their power and because they have risen against her in such arrogance that she dares not say a word, and she is thus forced to suffer from them that which she would not suffer from anyone else, and what, do you think, do all those say who observe this, and conjecture and remark upon it? They only take notice of that which they see, and you can be sure that they whisper about it enough, and if it happens that the lady gets angry or dismisses her servant, God knows that all will be revealed and made known everywhere! And yet it often happens that it is they who are, and have been, the instigators of this love, which they have encouraged with great diligence, in order to gain for themselves either gifts or Offices, or other emoluments. Most honoured lady, what shall I say to you concerning this?

Be certain that an abyss opens before you, numerous perils await you in this amorous life, and never doubt this for it is so. My dear lady, is it for this you will risk so much. Think of it, for God's sake, and retreat before worse befall you. Better now than later and better then than never. You see already what is said about your unusual manners and if you continue this it will be commented upon in many circles. I beg you most humbly do not be displeased with me for this advice which I do entreat you to heed with all my heart. I follow what I consider my duty in writing to you in this matter, for I would rather say it and risk your anger than keep silent or advise you to your doom... very revered princess and my dear lady I pray God that He sends you love, life and paradise.

Written this 18th day of January - Your most humble servant, La Dame de la Tour.

This then was the advice the Lady of la Tour gave to my lady who was not displeased but indeed said, "If she had been with me she would have counselled me wisely, but now I will take her advice for I do see all the dangers which lie in wait for me in this love and he who is so often in my thoughts should abandon it as well." The lady sent me this letter:

Sealed Letter
My dear friend, the sincere pity I had for your pain, led me to forget that foolish love which deceives many would indeed not help me to guard my soul or my honour. I see clearly that in order to indulge your wishes and my own I have already

exposed myself to the risk that this love involves. God be thanked, no evil has come of it and never will, but who would believe it if there were some bad luck which would expose us? I see too that he who follows this path is neither master of himself nor his behaviour, so it may easily be found out, as the Dame de la Tour mentions in her letter. I send it to you so you may understand why I must stop it. I took no thought of what this love would engage me in, but she has made me see the risks and made me go deeper into all it implies. I should be ruined and this dear friend, I know you would not desire. I entreat you to cease this and you must realise I ask this of you in spite of my own love. My eyes are full of tears for truly none could be more loved than I love you. I ask you to withdraw not for lack of love: I swear to you and promise you on the hope of paradise in the future that during my life never will I love another, you alone will I love, you alone will be my friend. I do not withdraw my love, you have done nothing to deserve this, and I cannot command my heart to withdraw my love, but you will realise that we must cease to see each other, for harm will come to me through this, and you will be grieved if this does happen. I know you will be sad and my heart cannot be otherwise either. I cannot write more for what shall I say? My heart is desolate, my face wet with my tears. Farewell my dear love.

Your sorrowful lady,

When this sad letter was read I swooned and lay like one who was dead. When I recovered I could only think of the grief of not seeing her again and I felt as if my heart was broken. I cursed the lady who was the cause of this grief and reread her letter. I would have liked to drown her who had advised my lady thus. After a while I wrote to my lady bathing the letter with my tears.

To the most sovereign of ladies.

My sweet, my beloved, my sovereign love whom I serve, fear and obey, whom I worship, where can I find the words to tell you of my grief so that you will truly understand its depth? Tears have so obscured my mind and memory that I scarcely know where I am or what I do, for your cruel letter had indeed discomforted me when I know that I can never see you. Whatever the Dame de la Tour says, I am more to you than anything else you have in this world. It is true I have promised you, and I will keep to this all my life, that I will obey you in all things, as far as it is in my power. But when you tell me to withdraw my love I cannot obey for this is my very life. It is beyond my power to withdraw even if I die for it. Dear lady, as for your order that I see you no more and if you mean that this shall be so always, I must resist it for your will would either kill me or drive me mad. I cannot submit to this. But to prove to you that your honour is above all to me, more than the lady who has written about it, and to stop all rumours or suspicion that you are the cause of my death, I shall leave the country and go overseas and shall finish my days there and never return. I swear that this will be so. Alas! how could she, who is the cause of my ruin, have heard rumours of our love? She must have dreamt it, for never was anything conducted with more discretion, prudence or secrecy, and may our sweet love always be so, God willing, for He knows that I would rather die than bring you dishonour. Ah! My lady, my lady! Shall I never see you more? If so, God willing, I shall lose my sight for nothing else in the world would ever comfort me. How then can my heart remain alive when it no longer has the solace of your sweet presence, the loving delight, the tender look and the sweet words which help me to live in the hope of their renewal for they counted for more than life? My very sweet lady, as I must die without cause I ask one last favour before I leave for ever. May I take farewell of you and say adieu to all those amorous delights which you have graciously bestowed on me? Surely you will not be so cruel as to refuse your servant this favour. I had never a thought contrary to your wishes. Alas! My lady, you wrong our love by this cruel misfortune, for surely this parting is against all such desires. Dear lady, grant me this favour. I know not what I can say now except that I shall obey you unto death. Tell me what I should do. Shall I go overseas or what is your will in this? Forgive me for this letter is spoilt by my tears for on my soul I could not restrain them while I wrote this. I could not stop them. Revered lady, I recommend myself to you alone and more than I can say, pray God to grant you all that is good which can be hoped for in life. Written in great grief with tears and weeping.

Your poor lover, of all, the most unhappy.

I sent this letter to my lady, weeping bitterly while doing so. I remained silent, trembling with pain, and in my grief I said:

Ha! Mort, Mort, Mort, viens a moy, je t'appelle,
Oste moy tost de ce doloreux monde,
Car vivre plus ne vueil; puis que la belle
Me veult du tout estrangier fais que fonde
Mon povre coeur a dueil et a martire,
Car congie prens a joye et a leesce
Ne je ne vueil fors que toy, Mort, eslire,
Puis que congie me donne ma maistrece.

Ah, Death, Death, Death, to thee I make my prayer!
Come, rend me from this dolorous world apart!
Life lures no longer; since my lady fair
Would have me shun her, let my hapless heart
Be very prey to pain and sorrow's sword.
Gladness I leave and all delight for aye,
And thee alone, O Death, have implored
Because my lady hath bidden me goodbye.

Hé las! hé las! quel dolente nouvelle!
Oncques ferus de lance ne de fonde
Ne d'autre dart ne fu homs qui si telle
Nouvelle ouist com moy par qui j'abonde
En tout meschief plus que je ne say dire
Quant eslonger amour de tel haultece
Me fault, je vois a dueil mourant de tire,

Alas, alas, what doleful news is there!
Never to knight assailed with glaive or dart
Came heavier trouble than the woes I share
I, who have gathered up in shame and smart
An evil greater than I may record:
Since now my love from all adventure high
Must needs withdraw, and death be my reward

166

Puis que congie me donne ma
maistrece.

Ha! ma dame, me serex vous
si felle
Que vous souffriez qu'en si grief
dueil ja fonde
Pour vous amer, a tesmoing je
t'appelle
Amours, qui sces que ou siecle
a la ronde
On ne pourroit nul autre amant
eslire,
Plus vray servant de fait et de
promesse!
Mais tout mon fait s'en va de
mal en pire,
Puis que congie me donne ma
maistrece.

Ha! Dieux d'amours! pour quoy
souffrez, beau sire,
Que muire ainsi sans desserte en
tristece?
Car je pers tout, nul ne m'en
seroit mire,
Puis que congie me donne ma
maistrece.

Because my lady hath bidden
me goodbye.

Ah, lady of mine, canst thou
such hardness dare
And suffer me in anguish to
depart
For love of thee? Yet love
must witness bear
Who knoweth no age can
show nor any art
Servant more faithful both in
deed and word
Among all lovers that he
might espy,
But my mishaps got worse
and worse
Because my lady hath bidden
me goodbye.

Ah, god of love, why
sufferest thou, fair lord,
That thus in sorrow
undeserved I die?
All things I leave, of all to
be abhorred,
Because my lady hath bidden
me goodbye.

I was told that when my lady had opened my letter and found it so covered and blotched with tears, she in her sorrow wept so that tears ran down her face and then she wrote to me at once telling the messenger to hurry back at once and not delay on his way. He rode all night and was at the castle gates by daybreak. And indeed I had need of it for I felt I would either die or lose my mind. This is the letter which gave my heart such joy.

To the most noble, the best, the most loyal, and true friend.

My true, loyal, very sweet and dear friend, it is true that I am afraid of losing my honour, which loss I ought to fear above all things, which the Dame de la Tour advised me against. I am grateful to her for I know she counselled me for my good. I wrote to you against all my own desires in my last letter. I realise my sweet and gracious friend, I see well that our parting cannot be suffered, I regret that I told you this for I know you have been greatly pained by my letter. I beg your pardon for it and I am unhappy that our good friend your cousin is gone on a long journey for he would have comforted you. I beseech you and pray that you obey me and hold yourself in peace for I do fear the depth of your sorrow, and the fact that I cannot comfort you in time to prevent you falling into a sickness, from which God preserve you. I will have no peace till I have news of you and I write in haste, be cheerful, I beg you, for there is good news. The good lady, our friend, will return in four days and you shall come to see me, I shall send you news and we shall be as before. God help me, even if I go to my ruin I cannot part with you; by God's will may our meetings be kept secret. I rely on your preserving my honour. My sweet dear love I pray God to give you perfect joy. Written in haste,

Your true and loyal friend.

This letter relieved me of my bitter grief and I ceased weeping and thanked God for this good news. I answered her letter and thanked my sweet lady and begged for a meeting very soon so that I could tell her of the grief her letter had brought me. Perhaps I should end this now... you know that I had joy from a pure love with no evil intent, and I dare anyone to say there was dishonour in our love, which for that reason should be the more respected. It is true that I must end my story for if I went into all the details, the pleasant and the unpleasant I would weary you and go on for long. But to be brief I often saw my loved one in whom I had all trust. She gave me generously of her loving comfort and the memory of those joyful moments is still with me. This situation went on for two years, for my fair one would not let me depart out of the country, and this pleased me much and my ardour grew the stronger, for my sole desire was to be near her. This made me go to her more often than was prudent, so that evil tongues were busy and stirred up anger about us. I was greatly troubled for I could do nothing to stop it and was not able to see my lady as before, which was a grievous thing. My friends and kinsmen blamed me for leading a retired life unfit for a young noble, for I would only attend tournaments and jousts near at home. They said I would disgrace my birth if I did not seek to take up arms in other lands to bring honour to our name; I was afraid that my lady would not be pleased if I did not seek her consent and I begged her to try and see me. For the sake of her honour I thought it necessary that I journey to Spain and take up arms. It were better to do so without delay so that she would be spared slander. She could believe me, I would not forget her a single day. I had promised her to be a valiant knight for her sake and seek renown and I must try to achieve this. I talked a great deal and she scarcely spoke. She had come to our meeting place at great peril and could stay only a short time. She wept and so did I, she could hardly be reconciled to my going to the war. My tears bathed her face and neck and kissing her I commended her to God, a thousand times I commended myself to her will. I promised that where ever I was I would send her news, and she would send back to me also.

I departed from my beloved, weeping and in great sorrow. I joined the army in Spain and was absent from my fair one for a whole year when longing to see her overcame me and I returned. She met me secretly and with great joy and our union was happy. But there was such peril in our meetings that she was always trembling with fear of discovery which spoilt our pleasure. When I saw that she was so distressed it spoilt my pleasure too for I saw how much she risked for my sake. So I left again and went on many journeys sailing over the sea, and ten years went by in this way. I often returned and when I could I saw my dear lady. In our battle I was made prisoner of war which deeply upset my lady. Many trials awaited me during these ten years and even my love brought me trouble. Though she had never given me cause I became mad with jealousy for at one return I thought that her heart had changed towards me and had become that of a stranger. This made me rage with jealous anger. My happiness for a long time was gone, for nothing could appease my sorely troubled heart and this displeased my lady. And then another time I saw her jealous of me and this troubled me for I could not see the cause of it. God was my witness that neither in thought nor action was I false to her, nor did I ever look at another lady. But I realised that those who are passionately in love will become jealous at some moment and cannot avoid this. If then love is great, it bears the seed of jealousy with it. Many songs were made on our love, some sad some joyful. I composed various ballads, lays, complaints and other ditties which had one joyful one out of ten. It is the way of a heart full of love. My lady sent me some whenever she could do so and they helped to ease our anguish when we were so far apart. It kept hope alive within us of some better time to come however long. So for ten years with painful thoughts our love persisted and is not ended yet, nor indeed will it do so till our bodies pass away. Because of my love slanders were spoken about her and many gossiped about her so that I almost hated my life. I saw that I had brought her trouble and I desisted from seeing her whom I loved so dearly, and I grieved that she was blamed for me. All my goods, my body, everything I possessed were hers and I would die for her; this is no fable. I pray God to bring her peace, honour and a happy life with joy without end.

And now my story is ended.

Note: The translations of the poems in *'Le Livre du Duc des Vrais Amants'* is by Laurence Binyon, published with thanks to Chatto and Windus from The Duke of True Lovers trs: by Laurence Binyon and R.D. Maclagan - London.

One ballad has been omitted from this text, the poem sent by the Dame de la Tour with her letter advising women to guard their reputations.

This is the only complete short story written by Christine and there are only two manuscript copies of it in contrast to her other books of which there are several.

Few stories portray the Medieval idea of chivalry so well as this one, an extraordinary true story of princely lovers. The description of the fête given by Jean de Bourbon, at which Marie de Berry was a guest, is not exaggerated. There are various accounts of such occasions, one such being the tournament held during the knighting of the two sons of the Duke d'Anjou, uncle of King Charles VI.

Jean de Bourbon always helped Christine and was a real friend to her. She tells us: **this good Duke was a comfort to poor gentle women, helping them by his words, sustaining them in their rights and this I can speak of by personal experience for I had his aid in my need...**

Christine had also known Marie from her childhood and the Dame de la Tour of the story was perhaps Christine herself, writing to Marie advising prudence.

Marie de Berry had been married three times; as a child to Louis de Chatillon, Count Dunois who died in 1391; to Philippe d'Artois, Constable of France, who died in 1397; and to Jean de Bourbon in 1400. It was at this time that Christine's poem was written.

An interesting sidelight on Marie's history is that in 1398 Henry of Bolingbroke, when exiled by Richard II, went directly to Paris where he was a great favourite with the French *Fleur de Lys*. Charles VI and the Duke de Berry arranged a marriage between Henry and Marie. Richard II, however, sent the Count of Salisbury to Paris in order to forbid the match. Marie was therefore free to marry Jean de Bourbon, the man she loved.

When Jean was captured at the Battle of Agincourt, although he was a brave soldier, the thought of captivity was too much for him and he tried to transfer his allegiance to Henry V proposing to leave two of his sons as hostages and offering an enormous ransom for his release. The results of the Battle of Agincourt were terrible for Marie. Though she may not have known the details of her husband's behaviour she had to try and find the money he was offering for his ransom. Jean died in captivity soon afterwards.

Marie also lost her son by Philippe d'Artois at Agincourt; her father, Jean de Berry died in 1416, also several of her cousins either died or were taken prisoner. These were all friends and patrons of Christine. Christine, writing to Marie after Agincourt, wrote her consolation in the form of *'L'Epistre de la Prison de Vie Humaine'* (The Prison of Human Life), where she says that those who were killed at Agincourt escaped an earthly existence of degradation and old age, and as they died fighting for their country they were sure of paradise, and probably in reference to her husband's behaviour, she says she knows that there are difficulties for the **loyal and loving heart** to accept.

...In this world what could be more precious than to posses beautiful children, you have cause to be joyful for you still have children, though I in truth know too well that a heart that loves deeply is always in anguish at the thought of the danger that lies in wait for those one loves; God by his grace has saved you from this (losing all your children)... this must be reason enough to console you for the death of your great friends and other tribulations... I come back then to my first words; those who died there (at Agincourt) at least died in a state of grace...

Christine's true story *'Le Duc des Vrais Amants'* follows the rules governing courtly love. The lover had always to be obedient to his lady's wishes; he was in her service, he was her vassal, and even went through a ritual to take the vows of 'bondage' to his love. Thus the whole relationship was viewed in feudal terms; it was the 'feudalization of love'. In almost all cases it was also an illicit love because, in general, marriages were arranged by parents and had as their objective the accumulation of power and property. However, secrecy was essential. As the poet says,

"Quan entre vos bra les tense,

E les accolez et baisiez,
Taisiez, taisiez, taisiez, taisiez,
Pensez de vos langues tenis,

When you hold her in your arms,
Welcome her and kiss her,
Secret, secret, secret, secret,
Think to hold your tongues,

Car rien n'en peu a chief venir	*For nothing good can come*
Guan des secrez sont pascouieres.	*Of sharing secrets. "*

Courtesy and humility on the part of the lover were also necessary besides faithfulness; his faithfulness must indeed have help from the god of love, for it would be this quality, above all, which might eventually wring consent from his lady.

In 1402, a decisive year for Christine, she wrote her *'L'Epistre au Dieu d'Amour'* (Epistle to the god of Love) and *'Le Dit de la Rose'*, both of which were dedicated to Louis d'Orléans. These years were to see the emergence of Christine not only as a poet able to sustain long works but also as a defendant of women, an almost unknown creature in her day. She was to become the first champion of feminism, the precursor of the women scholars of the Renaissance and the modern feminists. The target which inspired her views, and to which she directed her attacks was a famous poem called *'Le Roman de la Rose'*.

'Le Roman de la Rose' (The Romance of the Rose) was written by Guillaume de Lorris who was born in 1210 and died between 1237 and 1240 leaving his book unfinished. He was influenced by Ovid's *'Art of Love'*. He had lived at the court of Aquitaine and was reputed to be *"as pure as men but met in dreams where all is fair and nought is wrong..."*

Forty years after his death a second part had been added by Jean de Meung or Jean Clopinel, who was born c.1250 and died c.1305. Although Jean de Meung was a writer of great talent, this second part of the book is neither passionate nor chivalric and differs strikingly in spirit from Guillaume de Lorris. Where Lorris is courtly, passionate and sensual, Jean de Meung adds a cynical and mocking treatise on women from a highly prejudiced point of view quite devoid of ideas of romantic love.

'Le Roman de la Rose' is an allegorical work in which the beloved is represented as a rose which grows and flowers in a well-guarded garden belonging to the god of Love. The Dreamer whose dream the poem relates, describes how he enters the garden in order to pluck the fairest rose of all *"for whatever one may say, it is paradise in this world to possess the lady one loves."* He is admitted into the garden by Idleness, and inside, finds Mirth holding court. Nightingales and larks sing; fair ladies greet him, while Courtesy and Gladness attend him. As the god of Love's arrow strikes the Dreamer's heart he learns the rules he must obey as Love's vassal. Above all he must avoid discourtesy, dress neatly, wash frequently, be kind in return for evil, honour his lady and keep his love secret. He is forced to suffer the agony of love, the *"sickness of love"* which is compared to the physical pain of a toothache and which can even incapacitate the lover. The Dreamer has Fair Welcome to guide him, while the guardians are Fear, Shame and Danger; there are also Ladies Reluctance, Reason and Jealousy too. These barriers have to be overcome before he can enjoy the Rose: *"The most marvellous, the most noble girl that my eyes in a dream could imagine. A small laughing red mouth, her forehead smooth and glowing, the eyebrows designed like an arc, the blond shining hair a gold casque glistening in the sun... These splendours maddened my senses. I gazed in ecstasy..."*

In the first part of *'Le Roman de la Rose'* Guillaume de Lorris touches the flowers, the fruit, the trees with magic and his eroticism is thinly disguised. *"I could never tire of the rose carnation of this face, this fine skin without blemish, white breasts like the morning snow, a delicate throat, a small delicious nose and sweet savorous breath, a dear dimple on her chin, all this was an enchantment for me... with a body like a goddess, sveite and slim, never had I seen in all my life so gracious and lovely a girl..."* In the end the Lover cries; *"What is this wondrous malady that fills me with fire and ice and ice and fire and kills me?"*

He clearly sets out codes and conventions of courtly love.

"C'est le beau roman de la rose	The beautiful Romance of the Rose
On l'art d'amors tote enclose	Encloses within it all the Art of Love. "*

It was Christine's objection to the second part, added by Jean de Meung, that started the controversy which created disbelief and shock amongst the intellectuals of Paris.

Jean de Meung's opinions on life, love, art, morality and women are hardly equivocal. He writes against marriage and advocates free sexual relations between men and women to prevent "perversion". Marriage he says is an outdated institution and the important object is the sexual imperative for the continuation of the race. The contempt that he feels for women is evident in his verses:

"Beau Seigneur, gardez-vous des femmes	Good Seigneur, protect yourself from women.
Fuiez, fuiez, fuiez, fuiez,	Fly, fly, fly, fly,
Fuiez enfants, fuiez cette beste	Fly children, fly from this beast
Je vous conseille et amoneste...	I advise you and admonish you..."*

Jean de Meung's defenders were numerous. One of them was Jean de Montreuil, Provost of Lille. Among Christine's contemporaries and intimate friends there are two who should be mentioned, Guillaume de Trigonville and Jean Gerson, the Chancellor of the University of Paris, who took her part in the debate of *'Le Roman de la Rose'* for theological reasons. In this debate Christine, the woman, was defending the honour of her sex, while Gerson, the man of the church, attacked the *'Rose'* because sensual pleasures were compared to paradise and Christian mysteries. Although Christine's view of marriage was dramatically opposed to de Meung's advocacy of free love, she admits that there are good things in de Meung's poem but this makes it all the more damaging.

When Jean de Montreuil heard from Christine that Jean Gerson supported her against de Meung, he sent a *petit treatise* on the matter to Gerson. This letter is lost but Christine's reply is long and she answers his arguments.

Chapter Twelve

Le Debat sur Le Roman de la Rose

> "What is this wondrous malady that fills me with fire and ice and ice and fire and kills me?"
>
> *Guillaume de Lorris*
> *"Le Roman de la Rose"*

o Master Jean , Secretary to the King, our master, and Provost of Lille.

I respect, honour and recommend myself to you dear master of wisdom, lover of science, versed in theology and expert in rhetoric, forgive the weakness and feebleness of my perception. Do not despise the unimportance of my reasons but I beg you to acknowledge the feebleness of my sex.

As it pleased you to send me, for which I thank you, a *petit treatise* where beautiful rhetoric disputes the value of your argument (which treaty is a collection of opinions and criticisms of 'Le Roman de la Rose', but above all, the partisans of those who approve these authors and their work), I have read and considered your prose... though it does not answer my questions, nevertheless I am of an opinion contrary to yours, particularly a certain point that has been raised, proclaimed and publicly sustained. With great respect to you I must say that I think you are very wrong to praise this work without reason. It

174

could in my opinion, be more appropriately qualified a work of pure vanity rather than of real worth... do not tax me with presumption to examine and take to task an author so solemn and so subtle, but on the contrary please note the strong and definite opinion which animates me against certain aspects of this work. Of course opinion is not law if you can reply without prejudice.

Though I am not well versed in science nor subtle language, (which would permit me to use beautiful phrases and words expressing my ideas more brilliantly) I will nonetheless express them simply in common language, not able to express them in elegant words...

It is true that the subject is not to my taste and pains me as a cock over fire, that is to say that it completely displeases me, and I ask myself if I have really read it correctly. Nevertheless certain things remain in my memory, that my judgement utterly condemns and I cannot change them. Certainly my feeble understanding appreciates that at certain points there is a grand eloquence in the solemn manner and that a number of beautiful terms and gracious verses are very sweet. But in certain parts that which he treats without restraint could be expressed with more subtlety and in terms more carefully chosen. For example when the person named Reason openly mentions by their names secret members, on this point you may sustain his opinion and adhere to the idea that this is the most reasonable way to do it, and you may allege that in all things created by God there is nothing vulgar, and that consequently the name should not be hidden. I confess in truth God originally created all things pure and clean. In a state of innocence there is no harm in naming them. But by man's sins they have become polluted and so it comes about that we rest in a state of sin and pride, the Holy Scriptures tell us so.

For example God made Lucifer more beautiful than all the angels and gave him a beautiful name but consequently by his sin his name has a horrible aspect. So that a name which was in itself beautiful, gives a false impression to those who hear it... To the affirmation that all that is shameful is not so when these things are spoken of openly in public, things which by their nature are shameful, I reply that, except for reference to your author, you commit a great error against the noble virtue of shame, which by its nature restrains evil behaviour and dishonour in speech and acts. Great acts of vice are strangers to all honesty and good lives, and this is apparent in many places of the Holy Scriptures... I confess the name is not dishonest in itself, but is made dishonest by its use.

For this reason, in my humble opinion, one must use these terms with discernment and not without absolute necessity – apart from certain particular cases such as illness and other honest purposes...

And again later, when de Montreuil admonishes her for her stance against 'Le Roman de la Rose': "The more I think about the gravité des mystéres and the mystére de la gravité of this profound and celebrated work I am astonished at your opposition." Christine replied:

What a beautiful doctrine! Have you gained a great deal by deceiving women? Where are those women? Who are they? Are they serpents, wolves, lions, dragons or horrible devouring beasts that you must make an art of deceiving them to possess them? Learn then to make war machines to bring down these women, to press them, hurry, vilify them, assail this castle between you men, take care that none escape and the fort be given up to shame!

And, by God, who are these women? Your mothers, your sisters, your daughters, your wives and your friends; they are yourselves and you yourselves are them...

Christine had done what no other person had dared to do – She had attacked this universally acknowledged work publicly. Challenging the morality of its author's attitudes, she had propelled herself into the centre of public consciousness. Above all, quite aside from this denigration of women, she was totally against promiscuity between men and women which Jean de Meung advocated

Christine's letter in answer to Jean de Montreuil prompted the two brothers, Gontier and Pierre Col, to enter the controversy and oppose Christine in this debate. In 1380 Gontier Col had become secretary to the King and after 1395 he was sent on several foreign missions which gave him the reputation of being a subtle diplomat. He carried out negotiations with the King of England and no doubt met Chaucer, who on several occasions was entrusted with diplomatic missions for the King, particularly in France. Gontier Col was in the administration at the same time as Christine's husband Etienne. Pierre Col was his brother and the canon of Paris. These three men defended Jean de Meung, and their letters to Christine and her answers make up a large part of the debate.

It was to be expected that the Cols would be opposed to her stance but what is surprising is the arrogant attitude of both the brothers towards Christine. With deliberate irony Gontier Col starts his letter with praise for Christine.

"To the prudent, honoured and scholarly demoiselle Christine.

Woman of high and notable understanding deserving of all honour and great esteem. I speak on behalf of several notable clerics who have among other studies looked into works which are much recommended... you have again written against my master Jean de Meung, the very catholic and profound mentor, doctor in theology, a philosopher with a knowledge of all that human understanding can know... I beg you to send me a copy of your letter to Jean de Montreuil so that I may be able to answer it in detail... I am sure that being a woman you have been used by others to propagate their views..."

Christine answered Gontier Col by sending him a copy of her reply to Montreuil.

Pierre Col, now entered the debate and wrote an answer to both Christine and Gerson. In his reply he does not address himself to the essential question but becomes abusive and arrogant, very anti-woman, in fact insults Christine and is full of malice towards her and indicates that she is presumptuous to try and attack de Meung. He says:

"What conceit and loose words spoken by a woman against a man of such knowledge... you should be content with the reputation you have won of your high understanding but now you try to aim at the moon... you must not resemble the crow who, praised for his voice, opens his mouth too wide and loses his meal..."

Christine's reply is dated October 2nd 1402:

And do you believe, that I think all those who are in love long to sleep with their ladies as the only felicity? I believe rather that those who love loyally and perfectly do not need to make love with their beloved and are never disillusioned. And further, for you know that though it is never said, the act may perhaps be called saintly, but it is turned into derision, to attract and excite passion.

If you want to read a better description of paradise and hell, in terms far more subtle, more profoundly theological, more poetic and far more effective, read Dante's work... where you will find better founded and more subtle ideas... and you can profit from it far more than from *'Le Roman de la Rose'*... Why should I be jealous of this work? My feelings towards it are neither hot nor cold: it causes neither good nor evil in me, nor does away with either; it does not give me offence by touching on my personal condition, for I am not married, nor do I wish to be, nor am I a nun: nothing it says concerns me directly at all...

Indeed I am a lover of good, fine books and good treatises, searching them out to see if my rude understanding can master them. If I do not like the book of the *'Rose'*, the cause is simply and solely because it is an incitement to wickedness and a work with no integrity, and to delve deeply into it is a cause of evil rather than good: according to my judgement, it could lead to damnation and a corruption of the life of those who enjoy it, a temptation to immoral behaviour. I swear on my soul and by my faith that I have no other reason for such sentiments...

I have no high opinion of my deeds and my knowledge... I like the solitary life of the scholar; and by frequent visits to this lovely garden (of learning) it may be that I have picked some of the flowers in the beds without succeeding in climbing up the tall trees to seek out that sweet-scented fruit, not for want of appetite, but for lack of adequate knowledge, yet even on account of the fragrance of the little flowers from which I had made slender garlands, there were those who marvelled at my work and desired to have it, not for its magnificence, but for its sheer novelty; they did not by any means refrain from speaking about it.

I, on the other hand, had concealed it for a long time, and it was certainly not publicised at my request... For my part, I am not going to write any more on this subject whatever may be written to me about it, for I have not undertaken to drink the River Seine dry: what I have written, I have written. I am not holding my peace for fear of being misunderstood, however much my lack of knowledge may detract from a good style, but because I would rather devote myself to something more to my taste.

I do not know why you take me to task more than any other person. There is no honour in attacking one less gifted than oneself; there are plenty of scholars and great princes of this kingdom, knights, nobles and others who are of the same opinion as myself and who think that it is not worth reading 'Le Roman de la Rose'. Why don't you set your lance against them rather than a nobody like me?... I am beginning to be weary of my own writing on this subject. What must it be for those who read me? And as for other points in your letter they make me laugh...

To all knowledgeable poets, the woman who composed this poem would like to point out that in every line she has included a rhyme either leonine or free, and that this is her scheme throughout the work. In truth it is hard to forge such material; I do not know if anyone has noticed this except myself that there does not exist in any of these lines a rhyme so weak – I am not exaggerating – that a vowel placed before it would sound stronger than the final rhyming syllable. I wanted to carry out such a scheme to show its essence; for it needs a lot of work and knowledge to accomplish this, while covering such varied subjects, some of a delicate nature and some not. Whoever is not convinced by the experiment should try it, unless the tale he wants to tell is a long one, which would make his task very difficult.

I ask all those who may see my poems to make up for the deficiencies in my knowledge by considering my person, my honest intention and good aim – if you did not do this I would not publish anything more... Written and completed by myself, Christine de Pisan, on the 2nd day of October, 1402.

Christine herself sought support first from her dear *Seigneur* Lord Albret:

Take my part, my dear Lord. I am under attack from several people, since I have dared to reproach both old and young for their vain dishonest words and their inaccurate calumnies; and now to criticise that tit-bit for the curious, *'Le Roman de la Rose'* – which ought to be burnt! For such words many would poke out my eyes.

My dear lord, take my part! The allies of *'Le Roman de la Rose'* have declared war on me and launched their attack, since I have not gone over to their side. The battle has been fought so fiercely that they were justified in thinking they had already surrounded me; my dear lord, take my part! Despite their assault I will not be swayed from my intention – he who dares defend the truth must get used to being under attack; but I am not well versed in intellectual matters, so take my part, my dear lord!

Jean Gerson was to complain, *"Would to God this rose had never been planted in the garden of Christianity!"*

A collection of the controversy was dedicated to the Queen.

I cannot understand why men wrote against all women when they owe their existence to them. Did they not love their mothers, wives, sisters or daughters? Had they never met virtuous women? Had they passed their lives only among immoral women? Indeed did they really know any women at all?

Where Guillaume praised and painted a picture of true love and reproved false lovers Jean (de Meung) talks of reason which he says is the sole arbiter.

Love which was defended by Guillaume has Jean deploying gross words. He justifies all this, cynically, in theory and practice.

Love in the first part of the poem commands respect for women. In the second part women receive the most cruel insults ever hurled at them.

The allegory of the rose, delicate and gracious in Guillaume becomes coarse in Jean's poem.

As a work of art Jean de Meung's *'Le Roman de la Rose'* is a great deception. What a tedious process; what a difficult thing; what an obscure science; what a great adventure, to assault this feeble sex, what a number of people humiliated and ill treated, and nothing but unpleasant incidents encountered. All this only to deceive a virgin up to the end by ruse and fraud. Does a feeble place need such a great assault!...

In olden days in the city of Athens, scholarship flourished, but in spite of their great judgement a grievous error misled their scholars. Various gods were rivals and some people preached that there was only one God. This was not favourably received. One is often beaten for speaking the truth.

Aristotle, that wise and clever sage in the sciences, was chased out of this city, so full of errors. He suffered greatly. Socrates, that fountain of wisdom, was also banished from this city: many others were killed by the envious for speaking the truth. Everyone can see that under the heavens one can often be beaten for speaking the truth. So goes the judgement of this world...

The polemic called *'Le Debat de Roman de la Rose'* (The Debate on the Romance of the Rose), is the most celebrated of literary discussions of the Middle Ages. This debate produced about twenty treatises and letters in three years. The main protagonist against Christine, Jean de Montreuil, Provost of Lille, was a humanist and one of the leading intellectuals of his time. He was in fact with Christine's husband, Etienne, in the administration. Christine says it all started when one day in 1401 she had a discussion on books with her friend Jean de Montreuil. Gontier and Pierre Col, both eminent men, also entered the debate.

To understand Christine's courage in attacking the second part of *'Le Roman de la Rose'* one must realise the importance that this poem held in the intellectual life of the period. By 1350, every cultured and educated man or woman could recognise a quotation from *'Le Roman de la Rose'*. This book had known an incomparable vogue for nearly two centuries, and no other, except Chretien de Troyes's *'Lancelot'*, had so captured the minds of medieval men and women. At that time, the main subject of nearly every poem was love: in *'Troilus and Criseyde'* the poet Geoffrey Chaucer wrote one of the most beautiful poems in the English language, which embodies all the passionate, lyrical, sensual emotions of romantic love enshrined in Guillaume de Lorris' *'Le Roman de la Rose'* which indeed inspired Chaucer, who translated it into English. There are still extant three hundred manuscript copies of *'Le Roman de la Rose'* and many translations. For centuries, generations of poets and writers were to be influenced by it.

The importance attached to artistic life at court was clearly shown by the elaborate libraries, the permanent troupes of minstrels and players and by the constant entertainments of one kind or another held by the princes. We can gauge the esteem in which poets were held at the time by the fact that they were sometimes entrusted with affairs of state, apparently by virtue of their talents; thus it was that Chaucer was twice sent to France on secret missions during the last part of the fourteenth century.

Literary suppers given by princes and nobles formed a central part of the artistic life of the time and poetry was their mainstay. Poets attached to a court were expected to write for the various entertainments put on in the household, and maintain a high standard of writing. They were often asked to devise courtly pleasures for feasts, weddings and festivals of various kinds, and they also accompanied their lord on journeys to provide recreation. The quality of a court was judged by the lavishness and excellence of its artistic life, and no court dazzled as much as that of Louis d'Orléans. The style of life enjoyed by Louis was so costly that many kings could not live on that scale. Inventories of their jewels, *objets d'art*, silver and gold vessels, clothes, tapestries, paintings and books defy the imagination; the accounts of the Orléans' household read like a fairy tale. Among these lists are many items of money paid by his treasurer to the duke *pour fais sa volonté*, an euphemism for payment to his women. Less dubious are payments to painters, writers, poets and musicians.

Social comment or criticism was often a feature at these court gatherings, though satire was not yet a current form; such social comment was generally in the form of allegorical dialogues between gods and goddesses.

Andreas, a thirteenth century poet from Aquitaine, said that: allegory which *"represents what is immaterial in pictorial terms"*, was ideally suited to the expression of courtly love. It served as a wonderful vehicle for the *"profound moral revolution occurring in the later days of paganism"*. Love was above all, in this concept, a power for good over evil, for *"it is agreed among all men that there is no good thing in the world and no courtesy which is not derived from love as from its fountain."*

Petitions even for financial help, presented in the poetic form were the general custom and many of those sent to Henry IV and Louis d'Orléans survive. Chaucer's Lament to his purse, directed to the King, is well known; Henry answered almost immediately only four days after he took possession of the throne and gave the old poet a pension. Louis received poetic petitions from both Eustace Deschamps and Christine. In a ballad, Eustace asks permission, because of his age, to wear his hat upon his head in winter in the presence of his royal Duke:

"A vous monseigneur d'Orliens,	To you Monseigneur d'Orléans
Très humblement supplie Eustace	Eustace very humbly begs you
Que, comme il soit des anciens	That as your ancient
Vos serviteurs, par longue espace	Servant since many years
De temps, que de vostre humble grace,	By your humble grace,
Actendu la débilité	Knowing the debility
De son chief et fragilité,	And fragility of his head
Son estat, sa poure nature,	In this state, and his poor health
Qu'il ait par vostre autorité	That he will wear by your order,
Chaperon, tant comme yver dure,...	His hat upon his head as long as the winter lasts...

...Prince, la poure humanité
Pour honeur ne pour vanité

Qui ne lui vault, n'ait de ce cure,
Puis qu'autre en est débilité
Laissiez moy, par humilité
Chaperon, tant comme yver dure.

Prince, my poor humanity only,
Neither success nor honour nor vanity
Makes this request,
Nothing but my debility
Leave me, by grace,
The hat upon my head as long as the winter lasts..."

Louis' witty answer is also in the form of a ballad:

"Nous Loys, filz de roy de France,

Duc d'Orliens, de Valoys, conte
De Bloys, de Beaumont, cognoissance

Soit à ceuls que pité surmonte
Et qui tous frans coeurs vaint et dompte:
Qu'attendu la fragilité

D'Eustace et l'ancienneté,
Avec sa piteuse requeste,

Nous plaist qu'en yver et esté

Nous serve chaperon en teste.

Pour pité et pour remembrance
Des services que droit raconte

Que fait nous a en nostre enfance,

Dont nostre grace lui est prompte,

Sanz ce que nulz pour ce l'a honte,
Voulons, pour garder sa santé,
Qu'il n'ait ja chaperons osté,
Mais en jours communs et en feste
Nous plaist qu'en yver et esté

Nous serve chaperon en teste.

Chambellans, gens de nostre hoste,
Ne soit nulz de faire ahurté

We, Louis, son of the King of France,
Duke d'Orléans, of Valois,
Count De Blois, of Beaumont, makes known
To whom pity has overcome
The vain rule of the noble
Who taking count of the fragility
Of Eustace and his great age,
And in answer to his pitiful request,
It pleases us that in winter and in summer
He serves us with his hat upon his head...

In pity and in remembrance
Of the service he rightly recounts
That he rendered us from childhood,
By our grace we have replied promptly
Without any sense of shame,
He need never be uncovered

On ordinary days or days of festival
It pleases us that in winter and in summer
He serves us with his hat upon his head.

Chamberlains and others of our house,
None shall hurt by speech

Chose villaine ou deshonneste	That is malicious or dishonest
Au dit Eustace, oultre son gré,	Against his will – the said Eustace,
Ce que nous avons acordé	That right which we have accorded him
Soit tenu: car sans arresté	Be kept without limit
Voulons qu'en yver et esté	We insist that in winter and in summer
Nous serve chaperon en teste.	He serves us with his hat upon his head."

The interchange of ideas and the intermingling of all those who loved poetry, the *conteurs* and the *bon diseurs* was far greater than we imagine. The elite of England read French and some were still French-speaking.

The Courts of Love were a popular form of entertainment. This tradition had numerous cults and rituals and many "orders". In her poem *'Le Dit de La Rose'* Christine describes one of these literary suppers, held at the house of Louis d'Orléans. Here she created The Order of the Rose, the insignia of which was a rose worn or embroidered on their clothes, and the members of the Order were sworn to protect women wherever they were slandered.

Chapter Thirteen

Le Dit de La Rose (1402)

> To all wise, courageous and agreeable women... I tell now of marvellous news good knights... swear to defend the honour of women.

Sages et bons, gracieux courtois
Doivent être par doit tous chevaliers;
Lages et francs, doulz, paisaioles et cois
Pour acquerrir honneur grans voyagiers
En fais d'armes entreprenans et fiers,
Droit soustenir et deffendre l'Eglise,
D'armes porter doit estre leur mestiers
Qui maintenir veult l'ordre a droite guise
Hanter les cours des princes et des roys,
Les fais des bons recorder voulentiers

Wise and good, gracious and courteous
Must all knights rightfully be

Generous and open, gentle, reserved and calm
To win honour, great crusaders
In deeds of arms, proud and daring,
To uphold the right to defend the Church
And to bear arms must be their practice
Who rightful order would maintain.
Frequent the courts of princes and knights,
Eager to recount deeds of the brave

Estre doivent d'orphelins et des
lois
Et des femmes deffendre
coustumiers
Accompagnier les nobles
estrangiers
Preux et hardis et sanz
recreandise
Et voir disans, fermes, vrais
et entiers
Qui maintenir veult l'ordre a
droite guise.

Et noblece dont il es si grant
voix
Les doit tenir loyaulx et droituriers

Pour le renom qu'il est des bons
françois
Leur doit estre tous pesans fais
legers,

Ne orgueilleux, vanteurs ne
losengiers
Ne soient pas, car chacun trop
desprise
Si fais mahains, bourdeurs et
noveliers
Qui maintenir veult l'ordre a
droite guise.

Telz chevaliers doit on avoir
moult chers;
Dieu et les sains et le monde
les prise.
Or suive donc toudis si fais
sentiers,
Qui maintenir veult l'ordre a
droite guise.

Ever ready to protect
orphans and the law
Accustomed to defend
women,
Accompany noble strangers

Valiant, bold, unafraid,

Truthful in speech, steadfast
faithful pure in heart
Who rightful order would
maintain.

nobility which is of so great
acclaim
Must hold them loyal and
just
For the reason of all good
Frenchmen
Heavy burdens carried
lightly

To be not proud, boastful,
nor fawning
For everyone despises

Such deceivers, liars and
chatterers
Who rightful order would
maintain.

Such knights are beyond
price
God, the Saints and the
world hold them dear.
So let them follow these
paths always
Who rightful order would
maintain.

186

It was St. Valentine's Day, the day when lovers from early morning choose their beloveds for the year to come... in honour of Valentine Duchess of Orléans... this dictée is dated in the year fourteen hundred and one when the month of February is more than half done...

To all amorous princes and chivalrous nobles and to all those who love all goodness for its reward; and to all well taught lovers in this kingdom and abroad, in fact, everywhere that the light of valour shines; to all celebrated ladies and beloved maidens and to all wise, courageous and agreeable women, here is a humble recommendation for a faithful and true intention I would make known to all valiant folk striving to attain an honour... I tell now of marvellous news, gracious and not fraught with danger...

In January 1400 over a fortnight before this poem was composed, more than twenty noble people arrived in Paris, happy and carefree, for a social gathering of their own kind... it was in the palace of the noble Duke d'Orléans, a secluded house in fine surroundings, amid much revelry. There were famous knights and squires of good repute. I shall not recall their names but suffice it to say that each of them was renowned in some way, some of the best loved and most highly thought of belonging to the household of the most noble Duke d'Orléans, whom God preserve from all evil. What had brought them together was courtesy, the constant companion of people of discernment.

And, I believe, there was not a single person there who did not love all good deeds; there were enough of these here. They gathered together in the house and, with them, the retainers who are always attached to those who are of gentle birth.

The door was made fast, for we wished to be quite private in this place, free of the presence of strangers, so that we could talk at our ease. Then supper was prepared at leisure; they were shown to their places, all joyful, gay and without care. They were well served at the table with delicious food created to please. For, as far as I can judge, there was no greater pleasure for them than dining in company nourished by good and true love.

They were merry and rejoicing, gay and mirthful, singing throughout the whole of this supper, as folk do who are, one and all, amongst true friends. Nought was discussed at this feast but that which touched on chivalry and honour, homage being done to both great and small; the subjects being beautiful books and poems and ballads, all of which diverted everyone in increasing measure and love, which made its appearance there with gracious entreaties. The most delicious meats were served, as I believe, to suit everyone's tastes, no cost was spared and there was sweet bread too...

Yet I daresay their real pleasure lay not in eating, but in the good and loving company around them, like people who are one in their friendship and in no respect strangers to one another. The conversation was of nothing but courtesy and honour, without any slander of anyone in high or low state. More than ten ballads were composed by them in attempts to outdo one another, and subjected to criticism; tales of love were told... They could not have had any meat more to their taste; but their food was not extravagant... Thus this gracious assembly continued for some time... But at this point the god of Love, to whose rule we submit, sent to us his messenger, a lady who came forward and desired to visit those loyal friends of hers who had dedicated themselves to virtue; for all at once, though the doors were barred and the windows made secure, a most noble lady appeared, the goddess called Lady Loyalty, who was of great beauty. She came down in an aura of light, filling the whole hall with radiance. All the other beautiful women paled beside the grace of her body and face and her dignified bearing, richly adorned and sumptuously dressed. She was surrounded by nymphs and young girls, decked with garlands of flowers, all with great celebration singing out a new motet; so sweetly, in all truth, that it seemed we were in paradise... There was not one of us who did not strain to hear all that she wished to make known to us...

"On behalf of the god of Love, who can put an end to the suffering of true lovers, I bring you gracious news:

"Here are the roses, which the god of Love in his pleasure, presents to you through me; they were gathered with his permission, in the lovely gardens of which I am keeper. I ask you to accept this gift most joyously, but on one condition, that from now on you will uphold the honour of women.

"He wishes that none should accept this beautiful and precious rose, should he not consent never to gossip or spread rumours about a woman who holds her honour dear. It is for this that he sends me now; so come, give me your true word that you will defend the

188

honour of women, that we form the Order of the Rose in defence of women and its insignia is to be a rose worn or embroidered on our clothes...

"Good knights, and all of noble birth, you lovers all, your duty is to submit your hearts to this vow: love wants it so. He makes it a covenant that is not to be taken lightly, for your renown will suffer if you do. Come, swear that you will defend the honour of women to the grave."

And we swore:

"To perfect Love I make this promise,
and with the flower – the rose
to the valiant goddess Loyalty,
by whom we are asked,
always to guard ladies of good reputation in all things,
and never defame a lady of virtue,
and I take this oath to the Order of the Rose."

While Christine became immersed through her studies with the difficult position of women, she must have been encouraged in this support from an unexpected source. The Marshall of France, Jean de Meingne, known as Boucicault, for whom Louis d'Orléans had composed a ballad, was a distinguished soldier. He had been taken captive in the crusades against the Turks at Nicopolis in 1396 and eight months later a ransom was paid and he was freed. On his release, Boucicault became a champion of women and founded an Order of Chivalry whose members were pledged to *"succour all ladies of noble lineage because powerful men had robbed them of their land"*. He named his Order "L'Ecu Vert de la Dame Blanche". The date was 11th April 1399, and Christine, just three weeks away from finishing her response to *'Le Roman de la Rose'*, must surely have been encouraged as she completed her poem, *'L'Epistre au Dieu d'Amour'*. Exactly a year later, to the day, Christine herself was to found the "Order of The Rose".

A second order was created at the Burgundian court to honour women and to make judgements at the Courts of Love. Perhaps it was significant that there was a predominance of women in these entertainments. One of the more famous of these 'orders', created in England, was the order of the "Floure and the Leafe" of which Phillippa of Lancaster, John of Gaunt's daughter, was the leader.

Christine's "Order of the Rose" however was in defence of all women of whatever rank who were wronged; it was also an attempt to change the general attitude towards them.

In the following year, 1403, Christine followed up *'Le Dit de la Rose'* with two important books – *'Le Livre de la Mutacion de Fortune'* (The Mutation of Fortune) and *'Le Livre du Chemin de Longue Etude'* (The Path towards Long Studies).

In *'Le Livre du Chemin de Longue Etude'*, Christine is influenced by Dante's *'Divine Comedy'* and *'The Travels of Sir John Mandeville'* written first in 1356 in French. Christine, in the true allegorical spirit of the age, dreams that Sybil appears to her and takes her on a journey through this world and the other world. There is no difficulty about the journey as she is taken through the air and they stop at every place which is worth seeing: Constantinople, Jerusalem, Judea, The Holy Sepulchre, the City of Troy *de si grant renon*, Cairo and the Nile and Babylon. They journey to the East, meeting crocodiles, dragons, bears, lions, unicorns and elephants; they come to the *riche Isle de Cathay ou vi moult, mais riens nachetay de soie, dor, d'argent, despices...*

In India, she not only sees the pepper-bearing vine (pepper being one of the most sought after spices) but also the body of St. Thomas: *En Inde vi en bian moustier le corps Saint Thomas tout entier...* (in India a beautiful church and the entire body of Saint Thomas), the four rivers which flow out of the Terrestrial Paradise, first the Ganges: *grant pais et terre foison le noble fleuve de Phison* (Ganges) *court par Inde, en lui sont trouvés precieuses et esporouvées pierres* – (great country and fertile earth the noble river of Phison runs by India, in which are found many precious stones).

In Ethiopia, the land of Prester John, she sees **the trees of the sun and the moon** of which Alexander spoke. When she leaves the terrestrial world for that of the heavens she looks down at the earth and sees it rather like one of our astronauts *comme une petite pilote, ronde qu'une balate* (like a little bundle, and as round as a ball). She also makes a journey to the House of Reason where she is given a message to take back to the French princes; this was in the form of a discussion held there on universal peace; in this part of *'Le Chemin de Longue Etude'* she is preoccupied not only with the fate of France but of Christendom as a whole. The Battle of Nicopolis (1386) against the Turks which was a disastrous defeat for Christendom, must have left its mark upon her. Her longing for peace, her dream of harmony among nations and her horror of war has already developed.

Christine's assiduous work eventually bore fruit of a more tangible sort and brought to an end her chronic financial plight, for in 1404 Philippe of Burgundy, possibly impressed by *'La Mutacion de Fortune'*, commissioned her to write a life of his brother Charles V and subsequently appointed her Official Chronicler to the court.

Chapter Fourteen

The Court Biographer

> "If it be a vice to pardon
> too lightly I had rather be
> weak in this than too strict."
> *Charles V, King of France*

The most high son of the King, Philippe the Good, of the Burgundians, who holds wisdom dear and has no trace of pride... keeps a most attractive household... a court resplendent with nobles: noble in deed and manner, so handsome, so courteous... without affecting pride, and so gracious that it is a joy to see them...

I had gained the affection of Philippe, Duke of Burgundy, the respected and powerful prince who was the King's brother, and who had been reading my works of which I had made a gift to him shortly before, realising in his benign clemency what it had cost me to produce them, rather than seeing any great subtlety in my work. But I think he must have found them to his liking, for he praised me for them, and gave me kind and considerable help, as well as to my son, who was now a well-beloved servant in his pay.

In this present year of 1403, after I had with good intention presented to my lord of Burgundy on the first day of January a work of mine called '*La Mutacion de Fortune*', which in his humility he had gladly received, he sent a message to me by Monbertant, his treasurer, that he would be pleased if I should compile a treatise touching certain matters which the prince himself would explain to me. For my part, wishing to accomplish his wishes so far as lay within my power, I went accompanied by my servants to the Palace of

Christine: "La Solitude Volontaire" (La Cité des Dames").
Bibliothèque Nationale, Paris.

Christine teaching her son ("Oeuvres Poetiques").
British Library, London.

The Ride to Poissy.
British Library, London.

Offering of the Heart.
Early XVI century tapestry, Arras.
Musée de Cluny, Paris.
Photo: RMN.

Christine presenting her Book to Queen Isabeau of France.
British Library, London.

Christine presenting her Book to Duke Louis d'Orléans
("Epistre d'Othea").
Bibliothèque Nationale, Paris.

La Cité des Dames.
Bibliothèque Nationale, Paris.

Christine dreams – Apparition of "Reason", "Justice" and "Rectitude"
("La Cité des Dames").
Bibliothèque Nationale, Paris.

the Louvre in Paris. His Grace, having been informed of my arrival, summoned me into his presence, escorted with all courtesy by two of his esquires.

There I found him in quiet retreat, in the company of his noble son, my lord Antoine, Count of Rethel. Having made a respectful bow to him, I asked his Highness in what manner I might serve and please him, and my desire to be informed of the nature of the work he wanted me to undertake. So he, most benignly, having given me more gracious thanks than I deserved, informed me of the task he had in mind. It pleased the very redoubtable prince to ask me to use my *petite engin* to bring to mind the memory of the history and virtues of that most Serene Prince, the Wise King Charles.

He deigned to spread my reputation, in addition to all his other kindnesses, to the extent... that from his own mouth he commissioned me to set down in a special volume the good life of the Wise King, and to list his notable deeds, so that there should remain a perpetual memory of his noble name to serve as an example to the world...

To help me in this task I could be informed by Chronicles and by many people still alive, who had been his servants. They could inform me of the conditions, the customs and habits, the style and order of his life and other particular facts about him... And his Highness after many expressions of his good will took leave of me. I went away with his agreeable command with which I was honoured and I hoped I was sufficiently able to accomplish this task.

At the beginning, the mid-point and the end of my life, may all I do be to your glory, O sovereign power, immeasurable and incomprehensible dignity! What is expedient and considered necessary for the edification of virtuous and praiseworthy behaviour has been recorded by wise men in their writings and brought to mind for our instruction in goodly living; if it is true that good and noble examples may be given as evidence of the matters they consider, for which they furnish strongly-founded proofs, then I, Christine de Pisan, following the style of these early writers, the edifying men from whose work we derive our morals, will now by the grace of God, and with careful thought, undertake a new work in prose that is rather different from those works I have already completed.

My understanding is darkened by ignorance, but God and nature have given me the gift of a love of scholarship; and I have been moved to begin this work by the knowledge that it would please my lord Philippe, Duke of Burgundy, son of Jean, formerly, by the grace of God, King of France. At his command I have taken on myself this task, begging him to make allowances in his virtuous humility for the inadequacies of my experience, seeing as I have no adequate insight into the sciences that might give me guidance in this work... May I now present this little work, insufficiently researched, to all nobles and lovers of wisdom, announcing my present intention to treat the virtues and properties of nobility, and the good that comes of them...

And so that I may be well informed of his life I could, I thought, divide the book into three distinct parts. I would write of his courage, his chivalry and his wisdom, and include other additional virtues, like a precious stone which has many facets and to bring it into greater prominence is encased in gold or enamel and worn against silk. This would illuminate his virtues so that his noble life may serve as a profitable example to others...

...The critics may accuse me of ignorance: "This woman says nothing original in her book, but composes her treatise on the basis of what other authors have written" to which I can reply that in the same way that the architect or stonemason has not made his building materials... yet nonetheless assembles them together, every one in its appointed place according to his intention, so I have treated my subjects. Like an embroiderer working on different designs according to the power of her imagination, who may not be reproached with not having fabricated her silks, gold thread, or materials herself, so it is sufficient that I should know how to use my materials relevantly, in the service of the conception I am seeking to execute.

I pray almighty God to help me to explain events held in my memory, so that this my work will find the way to praise him, a sovereign, powerful and with incomparable dignity, with a humanity which was exceptional... I, Christine de Pisan, am a woman who is full of ignorance, which I regret because it impedes my clear understanding...

I pray almighty God that he may grant me strength to bring this present work to its conclusion, in a way that may be to the praise and perpetual glory of him who is its principal subject and to the increase of virtue and destruction of vice. Amen. Here ends the first part of *'Le Livre des Faits et Bonnes Moeurs du Sage Roy Charles V'*, completed on the 28th day of April in the year of grace 1404...

Praise and thanks be to God, who has granted me the understanding, health, time and place to conclude this small work, my own intelligence alone being inadequate to treat such an elevated subject. I humbly beseech all the excellent princes of this noble royal line who are mentioned in this history, together with their descendants to whom it will be shown in times to come, that they will bear in mind more my intention to give them the praise due to their names than what my limited understanding may have achieved in this aim. After my life, I recommend my soul to them, for although this work was commissioned, I have found it a very pleasant task to work on material concerning such a cultured prince as King Charles. Among several reasons for this, the two main ones have been the excellence of his virtues and the fact that as I was nourished at his table in my childhood with my parents, I hold myself obliged to him.

But the prince, who had commissioned this work, never saw it. On April 27th 1404, Philippe, Duke of Burgundy, died suddenly and unexpectedly. Christine poured out her grief:

I must make mention of my greatest loss since the time of King Charles, the death of the great prince Philippe... Just as he was becoming ever more favourably disposed towards me, disloyal Fortune robbed me of him by his death; this was yet another heart-rending misfortune for me, as well as a great loss to the kingdom, as I record in deep regret in this very book that he commissioned... Is this not sure evidence of Fortune's perverse hatred of me?

My ballad on his death on 27th April 1404 (extolled the nation):

Weep Frenchmen, weep great and small, weep for your terrible loss... weep good King... weep Berry... weep Duke d'Orléans... weep O Queen... weep commoners... weep royal princes, weep for the good Duke... for by his good sense and his very presence he protected you and overcame many faults... pray for the good Duke...

It is not surprising that Christine's *Le Livre des Faits et Bonnes Moeurs du Sage Roi Charles V'* (Life of King Charles the Wise) is a eulogy rather than an impartial biography; one reason for emphasising the late King's virtues rather than his faults may have been that the biography was commissioned not so much for general reading, as for the Dauphin Louis, Duke de Guyenne and son of Charles VI, as a model of proper kingly conduct for the young man to follow. This is quite possible from what we know of Christine's interest in the behaviour of those of noble birth and high office, and her special interest in the Dauphin himself, whom she saw as being the key to France's well-being. This view of the work is reinforced by its nature, for it pays scant attention to historical fact, and much of the chronology in it is wrong, while the emphasis is clearly on Charles' characteristics as a king and not on the details of his politics or his diplomacy.

Christine evokes Charles V's adolescence, his accession to responsibility at a young age while his father Jean le Bon was imprisoned in England, his taste for letters and philosophy, his attitude towards his queen. Here Christine abandons the role of historian and gives her personal opinions. She glorifies the attitude of the King towards his wife, Jeanne de Bourbon, and she sings the praises of the virtues of the Queen.

The chronicler, Jean Juvenal des Ursins tells us: *"there was a great hatred, envy and division between Philippe Duke of Burgundy and Orléans, brother of the King"*.

There were many reasons for this; the main one being that Louis d'Orléans, as brother of the King, was the natural heir to the throne after the Dauphin. An ordinance of Charles V in 1374 had stipulated that the elder son of the King on inheriting the throne would become independent of regents at the age of thirteen. In case of the death of Charles VI, Louis d'Orléans, the King's brother and therefore uncle to the Dauphin, would assume the Regency.

The Duke of Burgundy was indeed awesome, with his experience, enormous wealth and powerful personality. He was ruthless in his ambition to rule to his own personal advantage whenever his nephew the King was incapacitated. But he was always opposed in this by Louis d'Orléans. According to his rights as head of the blood royal, he was second only to the monarch.

The scandal of the two popes, one in Avignon and the other in Rome, created a schism in the Church and bedevilled the political scene in Europe. When royal marriages were arranged, realignment in loyalties was inevitable, and countries and kings were constantly switching their support from one pope to the other.

Charles V had supported Pope Clement VII in Avignon, whereas England, the Italian states and the Holy Roman Empire supported Pope Urbain VI in Rome. There were differences of opinion between Burgundy and Orléans about where France's loyalty should be placed. The King had given his brother the right to guard the Pope, an honour greatly resented by Burgundy.

On 18th April 1402 the King named his brother as leader of his council *"as it is necessary and needful that one of our blood should be closest to us, wise and with great authority and pre-eminence, I therefore designate my brother Louis d'Orléans, whose great sense and loyalty and true love he shows to my royal person..."*

But this was overturned on 24th May 1402 by the pressure put upon him by the old Duke of Burgundy as the president of the council. However admirable Philippe of Burgundy had been in many ways, he was determined that the House of Burgundy should rule France. To this end he consolidated his power by arranging a double alliance between the Dauphin, Louis Duke de Guyenne and his granddaughter Marguerite, and between Princess Michelle of France and his grandson, the Count de Charrolais. This arrangement was his political triumph over the House of Orléans.

In the Kingdom of France, disorder and lawlessness was growing amongst the people who were suffering greatly under a weak King whose bouts of madness made him unfit to rule. Queen Isabeau during this period favoured Burgundy, and the Duke made her Regent during the King's illness in 1403. With the death of Philippe, Duke of Burgundy, Louis d'Orléans, as the brother of the King, felt that he should be the rightful regent of France. In fact, while Philippe was alive, Louis d'Orléans had been no match for him. One of the most able and intelligent princes at the court of France, he had unfortunately several passions that mitigated his talent, and allowed his enemy to use this against him. Now that the old Duke was dead, Louis found himself no match, either, for his son and successor, Jean Sans Peur (The Fearless) for whom the death of his father was the signal to challenge Louis d'Orléans' authority.

Philippe of Burgundy died in 1404. In August 1405 Louis d'Orléans and Queen Isabeau planned to remove the Dauphin from an increasingly turbulent Paris but Jean Sans Peur prevented this and the tension created by the attempt aggravated an already deteriorating situation.

Jean Sans Peur must have hated Louis for personal reasons as well as political ones. Jean was the opposite of the handsome seductive Louis; ugly, small, thin-lipped, with a protruding chin. He was cynical and ruthless like his father had been before him, but lacking his father's sense of honour. He was feared but not loved.

He started and sustained a brilliant campaign against Louis d'Orléans, using satirical mysteries, poems, ballads and pamphlets to spread hatred against the King's brother – and he succeeded.

Christine must have heard from her own son, Jean, who resided in the Burgundian household, much that was hidden about the envy and hatred for Louis d'Orléans in the Burgundian family, for Christine expresses her fear for him. **If he lives to a great age,** she writes and warns him, **his enemies are on the watch.**

When Christine mourned the death of Philippe of Burgundy she knew that in spite of his ambition and age, his experience and power were an overwhelming factor in the overall stability of France. She must also have known the character of his successor, Jean Sans Peur, and with her political instincts knew of the dangers he would bring.

The Duke of Burgundy, Philippe le Hardi, died before Christine had finished her biography of Charles V, so she presented it to his brother, the Duke de Berry. A copy was given also to Jean Sans Peur. There is a reference to this in his accounts: *"To demoiselle Christine de Pisan, widow of the late Master Étienne du Castel, hundred écus in reward for two books which she presented to our Seigneur, the late Duke of Burgundy, whom God pardon, a short time before he died:* and again: *She has finished and given our Seigneur another book which Monseigneur wanted to have; which book*

196

and others of her Epistles and dictées Monseigneur had found very agreeable and also in compassion, and... to use for the marriage of her poor niece."

On November 17, 1407, the Duke gave Christine fifty francs in gold for several books in parchment containing many notable and beautiful teachings which she had presented a short time before his death to Monseigneur. Two other payments, one in June 1408 and another in December 1412 were made to her from the Duke's treasury. A copy of *'Lavision'* presented between 1406 and 1412 was mentioned in the Burgundian inventory taken in 1420 and again in 1467 and 1487.

Christine dares to talk a great deal against war at a period when honour, chivalry and feats of arms made great masculine prestige possible. She believed that women, while guarding the honour of their lords, should prevent war and help to bring about accord between barons and the King.

It may well have been that it was a year earlier while she was writing the official biography of King Charles V that Christine's mind, full of the great qualities of the King, began to dwell on the decline of France and its people under the present regime. Even before she had finished this work she had written to her friend and fellow poet, Eustace Deschamps, voicing her fears for the prosperity of the people of her adopted country.

Her epistle is in the form of a poem, full of extremely skilful wordplay and scholarly virtuosity: an impressive intellectual exercise which must have delighted contemporary readers, especially Eustace himself – and which belies her plea of humility in presuming to address him. Christine recognises perfectly her own worth, as is indicated in her somewhat tongue-in-cheek opening lines. Although she calls Eustace "Master", she also calls him brother and friend – as between equals! Eustace replies to this, calling her his dear sister *"eloquent muse in the midst of nine, Christine, today without equal..."*

Perhaps, due to her privileged position among the nobility but also, because of her courage, Christine was never afraid to voice moral opinions and uphold standards. She had no hesitation in taking to task her social superiors when they were lacking in the qualities she felt they ought to posses as leaders.

Only a year after the death of Philippe of Burgundy dangerous tensions were already becoming apparent. In 1405, she wrote a letter to Queen Isabeau begging her on behalf of the poor people of France to use her influence and intercede in the conflict between the Burgundians and the Orléanists.

It could be said that Christine started her career as a political figure with these two letters: one to her friend Eustace Deschamps and the other her letter to the Queen.

Chapter Fifteen

The Politician

What grief for so noble a
kingdom to see all its chivalry
perish...

o the learned and notable Bailiff of Senlis, author of
many renowned verses, Eustace Mourel Deschamps:

Your great reputation, dear friend and master, has prompted
me to address myself directly to you, notwithstanding my
unworthiness so to do. If I allow myself to take this liberty it is
because, as is well known, the wise instruct their disciples to
seek their friends among the wise...

Thus, because I am certain that I can rely on your good
sense and judgement, I will here share with you my concern
about the way in which we are presently being governed. What
most troubles me, and weighs upon my spirit, is that everything
continues to go from bad to worse. Surely, everyone who
wishes that right may prevail must be aghast at the lies and
stupidity which are everywhere the order of the day in our
cities, our castles, even at the court of our princes. Whether
among nobles or commoners, or the clergy, as well as in
every court of law, the disregard for truth runs rife; while out
of greed and envy each rivals the other in malicious and
fraudulent deceit. No one has the least desire for practising
virtuous conduct. All is mundanity, leading to vice. Everyone
strives to acquire vain goods, thinking only of himself and of
how best to reap all benefits to his own account...

... So little respect remains nowadays for the public good that all horrors are performed quite openly and without shame. This is even true in personal relations between men and women. Couples go about quite openly, fondling and embracing each other in public with the greatest permissiveness, which no one seems either to notice or to tire of – until Nature herself is put to shame. Any virtuous conduct is utterly disregarded, even despised – as is the learning and knowledge by which once we were governed...

Once upon a time our princes were educated. They were the pillars sustaining our justice, keeping the people in order with their good sense. Our nobles acted for the betterment of society, and were solicitous in maintaining good morals and lawful behaviour. This may not have been easy, but was worth it for virtue's sake, and what a noble example it furnished!

Whereas nowadays, the great have become haughty and proud, parading a superfluity of ill-gotten riches. I consider that such a state of affairs has gone on long enough, and that it is high time the people were once more given a proper example of right behaviour by those in power. How does it seem to you? Do you not agree?

At the moment I can take no comfort from the situation. Everywhere the ordinary people are being deceived and widows and orphans cheated of their worldly goods. It is time that highly placed functionaries like yourself intervene, in order to ensure that justice is properly carried out.

All this weighs on me more heavily than I can describe... Wishing you courage in your undertakings, and in the hope that God will give us all the requisite patience to survive the times and to live a long life hereafter, I am your devoted and valiant disciple, Christine de Pisan, writing from the solitude of her study, on the 10th day of February, 1403.

****

To the Most High Lady, greatly to be respected, (Queen Isabeau of France):

Although you are well informed of those matters which it befits you to know, it is nonetheless true that seated on your royal throne, crowned with honours, you cannot be aware of the everyday needs of your subjects, expressed in word and deed, unless someone reports them to you. For this reason, noble lady, do not be indifferent to one who brings to your attention the pitiful woes of your aggrieved and suppliant French people, at present burdened with afflictions and treachery, who are crying out to you with humble, tear-choked voices... Do not hesitate to open your heart in humble pity to their desolation and misery; who desire you to secure peace at once between those two high princes, blood-relatives and naturally friends, but lately by a stroke of ill fortune moved to strife...

Alas, what mother would be so hard as to bear the sight of her children killing each other, see their blood soak the land, unless her heart were of stone?... I have no doubt that this kingdom's enemies will rejoice at the present state of affairs and come over the seas with a large army to humiliate and persecute us all and to pillage our goods. Ah God! What grief for so noble a kingdom to see all its chivalry perish! Poor little children, some not yet weaned, will cry for their widowed mothers... dying of hunger; but they will have nothing with which to comfort them, stripped of their goods...

Then, very exalted dame, you can be certain what will come of this persecution... Is it normal that the poor people must support the result of a sin of which they are innocent? The voices of martyred children and babies cry out, and as it is said in the Bible, will pierce the heavens reaching God and calling for vengeance on them that call.

I will bring my letter to a close, beseeching your worthy majesty to receive it well and to favour this pathetic request I have written on behalf of your poor subjects, loyal Frenchmen...

Christine's letter to Queen Isabeau had little effect.

In the year 1405, Christine was still recovering from shock over the death of Philippe, Duke of Burgundy, and the treacherous character of his son, Jean Sans Peur, was becoming increasingly manifest.

'Lavision Christine' (Christine's Vision), written that year, is perhaps one of the most interesting of her books. It is a poem in three parts. The first part is an image of the world and its wonders. The second part talks of Dame Opinion and her Shadow, and the third part tells us of the comfort given Christine by Dame Philosophy. *'Lavision'* is a revealing poem for what it tells us of her personal life, and it includes the only account of her husband's death and of her subsequent struggle to survive. In this important work, much of it autobiographical, Christine also gives us an allegorical account of the bloody history of France depicted as *La Dame Couronnée* and describes Christine's journey from Bologna to Paris, **this second Athens**.

'Lavision' starts with Christine resting on the way to a pilgrimage and dreaming a strange and fanciful dream, in which she meets a Giant Shade, Dame Nature. In this image Christine evokes Nature and Chaos which represent the creative power of God. Christine herself emerges from this, fashioned as a *petit corps de sexe feminine*.

La Dame Couronnée recounts to Christine the vicissitudes that France has gone through, and tells her of the wounds inflicted upon her body.

From the blood of innocents shed throughout the centuries grew a Golden Tree in the garden which is France. From this Golden Tree grew a seed *un pepin*, which refers to Charlemagne, a descendent of Pepin le Bref. *La Dame Couronnée* talks to Christine, relating her history and the good and bad gardeners who tended the garden that is France. Charlemagne was the good gardener who constructed the Empire of the West.

Dame Opinion and Dame Philosophy are also present and when Christine complains to Dame Philosophy of her ill-fortune, she is reminded of the joys she has experienced which should balance out her sorrows.

There are two manuscript copies of *'Lavision'*, both of which belonged to the Duke of Burgundy and were included in his libraries. At present one is in the Bibliothèque Nationale in Paris and the other in the Bibliothèque Royale in Brussels. Both manuscripts contain miniatures of Christine sitting in her study and there are illuminated borders of flowers and leaves which decorate the first folios of both.

The text of the following chapter is a translation from the French version by Sister Mary Louise Tournier. It is a short adaptation of those parts of *'Lavision'* which are allegorical rather than autobiographical.

Chapter Sixteen

Lavision Christine (1405)

> Dame Philosophy is the
> voice of my conscience and
> brings me her consolation.

I was half way through my pilgrimage when I felt tired and wanted to rest and in my sleep I had a strange dream. The colossal monster, Chaos, appeared to me. I felt as if my spirit left my body and I was transported into a tenebrous country. The monster Chaos had hovering over it a giant Shadow with a feminine form. She was busy mixing a concoction, continually stirring and pouring it into various moulds. Without taking any rest she diligently filled them, and when they were ready she fed the monster Chaos.

My spirit too was moulded by Dame Nature and I emerged into the world in my small human body in the form of the 'feminine sex'. My small body was swallowed like the others into the stomach of the giant until I met Earth who was the chamberlain of the nurse Chaos. Earth gave me a sweet liqueur which refreshed me and gave me strength to embark on a journey. My body became stronger and I was transported through the diverse entrails of the stomach which showed me the stones and rocks, the mountains, woods, valleys and brilliant rivers of my native country.

I heard of a beautiful princess, whose sceptre was of an ancient lineage. This royal princess was France and I was taken into the service of this crowned princess whose great authority and beauty was renowned throughout the whole world.

I was impatient to know her but I was still too young and I had to apply myself to learn a new language different from that of my parents. However I learnt the language and informed myself of all the manners and condition of this princess, and I was rewarded for my patience when the princess, the *Dame Couronnée*, appointed me to relate her history and adventures.

And so the same *Dame Couronnée* began her story of France, her garden, her Golden Tree, and the good and bad gardeners that tended her. I thanked God that this princess gave me her grace and favour and recounted to me the secrets of her heart.

She told me that the Golden Tree was planted in a fruitful soil and grew in beauty and took the name of Liberia – Francia – Freedom. The young shoot spread its branches. The invaders who devastated the soil were the weeds that retarded the growth of the Golden Tree. "Look upon the horrors inflicted on my body," said the *Dame Couronnée*, "my bruised limbs. Contemplate what it has cost me and look upon the ugly wounds. I was threatened with destruction. Ignorance was stunting my growth when it was stopped by the wise counsel of the first Merovingian kings, although it was the horrors of the last Merovingian king that inflicted these tragic wounds which I show you..."

The *Dame Couronnée* goes through the history of France and tells me of the devastation and ruin which at the present moment has brought great peril to the garden. This had been arrested by King Charles V, the wise gardener, who reconstructed the garden by his judicious and careful laws. He rid the garden of its invaders till they only occupied Calais, Bordeaux and Bayonne. But the wise gardener was struck down at an early age.

From his limbs two little golden butterflies emerged, very gracious and of great beauty. They grew in strength until they were like the Phoenix who rose from the ashes; they developed until they were transformed into the most beautiful and noble birds of prey. One of them had a crest over his head (Charles VI, who was crowned).

The falcon who flew high was fast winning the love of his people, and was beginning to be feared by his enemies when he fell into his grave illness.

"Ah, my sweet friend, I have related to you the great part of my adventures but I cannot tell you all. However, dear friend, in anguished language I must tell of my present tenebrous period.

"What greater tragedy can hurt the heart of a mother when her children come to fight against each other? A poisonous wind has struck her children – the children of three beautiful women, Truth, Justice and Chivalry, lie in confusion in a prison cell. Chivalry is fast asleep... Voluptuousness, Fraud and Avarice have taken over in the house of the *Dame Couronnée*... Indolence, Greed, Cruelty and Vapidity reign unchecked... Fraud and Ambition bring about the wickedness that will ultimately ruin the children of the *Dame Couronnée*... But she fears that like Cassandra's prophecies final disaster will not be averted... but a second Samson will come and restore France to its true and rightful heirs...

"Dear friend, I have now told you my story, my adventures, good and bad, in particular the origin of my name and the piteous afflictions which beset me. But I cannot go on because it will become too lengthy. But what pleasure it is to have discovered a loyal friend and tell her my thoughts – for sometimes a stranger may appreciate more than one who is too close. God in His grace will find a remedy but, alas, how can remedies sent from heaven hope to help my own, when they do not deserve it? And still my grief makes me suffer; but I thank you, my good friend, that at the end of my story your loyal love and company did not fail me..."

Here ended the words of the *Dame Couronnée*, and I have done the best I could to comfort her, and I pray that she will return from humiliation and shame, for God has mercy and will help her recover her honour.

After the *Dame Couronnée* had told me her history, full of bloody intrigue and moral degradation, I thanked her for the honour she had bestowed on me by confiding her story; I pledged her that my fidelity to France would never waver.

But now my dream took me to the second Athens where a noble University of Students profitably discussed together various questions and put forward different arguments. A great Shade with a feminine form hovered over them all and smaller shadows of different colours symbolised the various sciences and differentiated one from the other. In the great hall they each discussed their points of view. The Shade spoke to me and told me of her numerous activities and asked me if I knew who she was. However, contradictory reasons made me uncertain and I hesitated to answer. But she did tell me of spiritual things of a strange nature. The great Shade, however, is not immortal.

Dame Opinion is a daughter of Ignorance. She has the character of Good and Evil. Even the worst of men can be in error through Dame Opinion, though she arouses men to seek after truth... but in fact Dame Opinion and her daughters do not exist where Truth is found because she is both soul and body, and Truth is hampered by the body. All concepts conceived by the human mind are under the governance of Dame Opinion. But Reason and Common sense might and should prevail. When these are disregarded, disaster follows, and Dame Opinion has power over us and has often led men astray.

Dame Opinion is the cause of all dissension and desires for domination that fill the hearts of men, throughout history. It was she who pushed Alexander to conquer the world. I too am subject to the good and evil of Dame Opinion. Remember the polemic of the debate of '*Le Roman de la Rose...*'

In the end, when I, Christine, complain of the misfortunes of my life, it is Dame Philosophy who says I am blind when I attribute to Fortune the trials of my life. Dame Philosophy shows me my ingratitude to God for the good things I have written. My sorrows are blessings in disguise for it is not Fortune that brings to me ill luck. All things are disposed of by God, who ordained all this in my life. Dame Philosophy is the voice of my conscience and brings me her consolation.

'*Lavision*' is one of the most revealing books of an extraordinary woman; it also presents the first translation into French of Greek philosophic thought as Christine incorporates fragments of the '*First Book of Metaphysics*' by Aristotle into '*Lavision*'.

Christine for one last time returned to a subject which had preoccupied her since the debate on '*Le Roman de la Rose*'; the position of women in medieval France and the low esteem in which eminent men and many writers held them. In her next book, '*La Cité des Dames*' (The City of Ladies), she wrote an attack on a treatise, '*Lamentations*', by Matheolus, which described married life as unbearable.

'*La Cité des Dames*' represents the summation of Christine's feminist views. It is an exhortation to women to uphold their dignity and honour and to defend the rights of their sex. Christine expresses the view that women everywhere have been sadly underrated (something which might be said to be still the case today) and that they are capable, in their own way, of achievements equal to those of men. She illustrates this not only from the past history of France and women from countries such as Arabia, Egypt and Ethiopia but also with examples of her contemporary friends and patrons – women who dominated their circumstances even when they were left widowed. They not only brought up their children but governed their states with good sense. Christine herself was one of these, who had shown tremendous courage and purpose of will in the greatest adversity.

Christine followed up *'La Cité des Dames'* with *'Le Livre des Trois Vertus'* or *'Le Tresor de la Cité des Dames'* (The Book of Three Virtues or The Treasure of the City of Ladies). This book is quite different in tone to *'La Cité des Dames'*, for here there is no polemic against the male writers and philosophers who wrote against women. In the first part of *'Le Livre des Trois Vertus'* she talks directly to the high born princess and warns against overweening pride; talks of prudence above all; her charitable deeds; wisdom in promoting peace; the upbringing of her children; the ordering of her finances; the distribution of her largesse; her behaviour if she is widowed; advice to a young princess who wants to plunge into a love affair.

The second part of the book is directed to all women. Four points are advocated; two points which they should follow and two which they should avoid. Above all they are warned against envy. It goes on to advise all women; those in court; the wives of merchants; young and elderly widows; young girls; the wives of artisans; servant women; prostitutes; the wives of labourers and the poor.

Some of the advice comes directly from her own experience such as when she talks of widows and remarriage. But above all she talks of peace; peace in the domestic sphere; peace between barons and their followers; peace between nobles. We must remember that in 1405 civil unrest and the antagonism between Orléanists and Burgundians had already caused much tension. When civil war broke out Christine continued her advocacy for peace.

Chapter Seventeen

La Cité des Dames (1405)

and

Le Livre des Trois Vertus (1406)

> I came to the conclusion that God created a vile creature when he formed a woman... an abominable vessel, which they say was the refuge of all evil and all vice.

La Cité des Dames

One day as I sat in my study as was my custom, surrounded by my books on various subjects and pursuing my studies, I put aside my serious books and looked for some light poetry to help me to relax. I wanted some small pleasant book. By chance I came across a strange book. It was not one of my own but it had been given to me with some others.

When I opened *'Lamentations'* I found it was by Matheolus. I was amused because I had not read him before and I had often heard that he discussed respect for women. I thought I would 'visit' him but I had not read for long when my good mother called to me that the hour had come for supper. I put it aside and decided that I would look at it again next morning. The next day as was usual, I sat once more in my study, I had not forgotten that I had intended to visit Matheolus again.

But soon I found that it was unpleasant to those who did not like lies. It was useless to those who would like to develop virtue, seeing that the contents lacked all honesty and integrity. *"Were it not better to have a faithful and devoted servant than a wife,"* he wrote. *"A wife costs a great deal, is unfaithful and will abandon her husband when he is ill, while when she is ill her husband is forced to wait on her and dare not leave her side."*

I put the book away and turned my attention to other more worthy subjects. But the very sight of this book, though not authoritative, made me uneasy. How could it be that so many different men, scholars and others, in their writings expressed such disdain and had such wicked and slanderous thoughts about the behaviour of women?

It was not only this Matheolus (who in any case had no great reputation and whose work was supposed to be satire) but in general in all the treatises of philosophers, poets and orators – it would take too long to name them all – who seemed to speak with one voice from one mouth. They all came to the same conclusion: that women's behaviour was inclined to every vice.

Thinking deeply on this matter I began to examine myself and my character and behaviour as a natural woman. I thought of other women whose company I kept, as well as princesses and great ladies and those gentle women of the middle and low status who by their graciousness had confided in me, told me their private and intimate thoughts. I wanted to judge without favour if what so many notable men said was true. Yet though I thought and searched for hours I could not perceive that such judgements could be true against the natural behaviour of women.

I argued strongly against women saying that it would be an impossible thing that so many famous men, solemn scholars with such great understanding in many matters as it seemed, should write lies in so many places so that I could find no book, even before I had finished it, that did not have a chapter or sections   no matter who the author was – that did not blame or castigate women. This was the reason, I concluded, that in my simplicity and ignorance I could find great faults in my own nature and those of other women, and so that

208

this may be truly so, I gave way more to the judgement of others than to my own and what I felt.

Thus it was that I was half out of my mind. In this stupor the various sayings of different authors (ditties, proverbs and poems) on this subject rose like a spring gushing through my mind. I came to the conclusion that God created a vile creature when he formed a woman. I marvelled that such a wonderful craftsman could have deigned to make such an abominable vessel, which they say was the refuge of all evil and all vice.

While I was in this mood I felt great unhappiness, and in sadness I disparaged myself and all womankind as though we were monsters in nature. I made this complaint:

"Ah Lord, how may it be that if I err in my faith I ought not to doubt that in Thy infinite wisdom and infinite goodness Thou hast created nothing but what was good? Didst not Thou, Thyself, create woman in a singular manner and then gavest her all such inclinations that it pleased Thee she should possess? How is it then, Lord, that Thou shouldst fail in anything? But always there are so many accusations brought against women and I cannot understand this repugnance. And yet, Lord, if it be true that womankind abounds in so many abominations, as many writers and Thou Thyself sayest, then I doubt not it is true.

"Alas, dear Lord, why didst Thou not let me be born into this world a man so that all my inclinations would be to serve Thee better and I should not err in anything and I might have been of such perfection as they say men can be? Yet as it is so and Thy goodness did not extend to me, then forgive my negligence in Thy service, good Lord, and be not displeased. For the servant that receives the least rewards from his lord is least bound to leave his service."

In my lament I spoke these words and many more and in my folly I thought it an evil day that I was born a woman into this world.

I was in this sorrowful mood, my head cast down like a shameful person, with tears in my eyes, holding a hand under my cheek, resting on the pommel of my chair, when suddenly I saw a ray of light fall onto my lap like the sun. I was sitting in a dark corner where the sun could not have penetrated. Then as though in a dream I raised my head to see where this light came from. I saw standing before me three crowned ladies, their radiant, bright faces shining on me and on the whole room. No one could ask whether I was surprised for my doors were shut and I thought a phantom had come to tempt me and I was very frightened and made The Sign of the Cross on my forehead.

Then the first of these ladies smiled and said, "'Dear daughter, do not be afraid for we come to comfort you for we have pity on your distress. You have blinded your intellect by avoiding what you know for certain and accepting what you do not know because of strange opinions – dear daughter, where is your common sense?"

The three goddesses were Reason, Rectitude and Justice. Reason held a mirror, Rectitude a ruler, and Justice a golden vase. In turn the ladies answered my thoughts:

"It is my office as a daughter of God to redirect men and women when they have lost their way and to direct them again on to the straight path. I show people how to right their errors and how to mend their ways."

Reason held a bright mirror instead of a sceptre in her right hand – "This mirror reveals to people what they really are. It is very precious and only used in good causes. Your compassion, understanding and devotion to study, which you do in solitude and away from the world deserves help. You need to be comforted in your trouble and sorrow, as a dear friend.

"Also there is greater reason for coming – that worshipful women might have, from now on, some place of refuge to come to, to be protected against all that would assail them. Ladies have had no champion, and men who ought to defend them, do not do so. Where is there a city to protect ladies?

"We have come to tell you of a certain abode made in the manner of a city, cloistered and strongly built – we want you to build it and people it with our help, with ladies of good fame and worthy women, – for to the unworthy the walls of our city shall be shut...

"Not all opinions of men are based on reason. As for Matheolus and his ideas of marriage and the martyrdom of men in a marriage – where are they, these men who suffer more than women? There are many marriages that are happy and which are filled with peace, love and loyalty. You yourself have known such a marriage and the sorrow of that death will remain forever in your heart.

"Descriptions of married life have not yet been written by women, and anyone making an impartial enquiry would have to report differently... Alas, dear friend, how many women, as you well know, waste their sad lives in marriage to hard husbands, their penance is as great as if they were slaves of the Saracens! Oh Lord, how many cruel blows, struck by their husbands for no good reason, how many insults, how much servitude, how many injuries and humiliations are suffered by many good women. Ah! How many dutiful women care for their husbands and cherish them in their sickness or health as though they were gods... When you speak of husbands that are put upon when their wives are ill, I pray you, my friend, where are they? Fortune, whom women must endure, my nature and my pity force me to weep for their martyrdom. Ye gods! What a sad destiny to be a woman, how hard it is to be sold by Fate to a bad husband who wants to beat her.

"There is given to each sex inclinations and aptitudes which fulfil their particular mission in life... and incapacity to be like men has nothing to do with a woman's intellect, which is as sharp as that of a man's... Because men were physically stronger than women they thought her also inferior in intelligence and moral force. The intellectual inferiority of women came from their education, or the lack of it. If it had been the custom to put little girls to school and teach them the sciences as was done with boys, they would have learnt just as perfectly. Though their bodies were weaker, their understanding was sharper where they applied it... Not all men share the opinion that it is bad for women to be educated. Your father, a natural philosopher, did not have the opinion that a woman should not learn her letters. As he saw your inclination to learn he had great pleasure in it. Yet because of the common opinion of women and of your mother you were prevented in your youth from entering more profoundly into the sciences.

"Medea, who has had so much written about her, was also a scholar in the arts and sciences... She was the daughter of Hecate and Aeetes, King of Colchis. She was a beautiful woman, tall and elegant, with a most agreeable face; but in knowledge she was far above the rest. She knew of the virtues of plants and all the possibilities of different potions that could be concocted. From these she ignored nothing that could extend her knowledge. She wove her spells and her incantations could change the air to cloudy or dark; she could move the winds into tempests and stop the course of rivers; she could concoct poison; spontaneously create fires which burnt all she wished to burn; and many more prodigious acts. It was thanks to her enchantment that Jason won the Golden Fleece."

Then I, Christine, spoke as follows, "My Lady, I am troubled and grieved when men argue that many women enjoy being raped."

She answered, "Women of honour find the crime of rape greatly repulsive. It is the greatest anguish for them and many noble women have taken their own lives after being raped to show their abhorrence and to prove their chastity of spirit. Some claim, that after the death of Lucretia following her rape by Tarquin the Proud, a law was passed whereby a man could be executed for committing rape – a law which is fitting, just and holy."

And I, Christine, said, "My Lady, you have given me a remarkable account of the marvellous constancy, strength, endurance and virtue of women."

Look ladies, how men accuse you from every side of so many vices, make their words into lies by showing your qualities and virtues. Accuse them of lying when they blame you and speak ill of you. Turn away those who falsely flatter you by devious ways. Try and choose carefully those you keep by your side.

Realise it is your honour that brings beauty into your life. Oh my ladies, fly, fly from the *fol amour* that they counsel you... fly, fly... Remember, dear ladies, how men think of you, despise you as light and weak, with heads that are easily turned, they search by all despicable means and with great pains to possess you if you resist them... and the greatness or pettiness of men is not found in their physique or in their sex but in the perfection of their life and in their virtues...

******

At her request Christine sent a copy of *'La Cité des Dames'* to Queen Isabeau.

Most noble Queen of France, I come to present you this volume which contains no history or literature that did not originate in my own pure thoughts and feelings and take shape in my own style, although many others have greater gifts than those I have received from God and nature. It includes several works in which I use different styles, for the reader derives more learning from hearing a variety of subjects, some weighty, some light, from whoever delights in undertaking to write of them elegantly. For this reason books should be held dear and not despised. For, as the wise testify in their works, those who trouble to read books cannot fail to banish ignorance in following the paths of wisdom.

Those who do not feel the burden of learning are worth much less; there is no worthier pursuit, nor one which makes men so complete, however much fools may grumble at the idea. So I have completed this work, my lady... to the best of my ability, and I have had it well copied and illuminated, having received your commission... so that it may be seen how I labour to achieve your wishes. May you accept it willingly. Do not dwell on the defects of this book that I am putting into your keeping: it is the product of much hard work, even if there may in places be shortcomings due to my lack of knowledge; but rather consider the end to which I work, that I may achieve something praiseworthy in my freely-given labours.

We cannot judge Christine in a 20th century context. Today we are free to speak frankly and are able to come to conclusions quite impartially. Christine in her day and for her time could not afford to do so, for women were only vilified in all the books which mentioned them. She simply tried to redress the balance in the only way she could. Thus, when she mentions Medea, she describes her knowledge and beauty and ignores her terrible deeds of murdering her children to spite her husband.

The whole work is remarkably modern in its outlook, and if, today, Christine's work is enjoying a resurgence of interest, it is partly because of the views she expresses in this book, which coincides with those expressed in the current debate on the 'liberation' of women. Unfortunately, as a result, her other works, no less important, are sometimes not given the attention they deserve.

Christine followed *'La Cité des Dames'* with *'Le Livre des Trois Vertus'* which she dedicated and presented to Princess Marguerite of Burgundy, wife of the Dauphin Louis.

To the most high... Princess Marguerite of Burgundy...
I, Christine, your humble servant, desiring to please you in
so far as it lies within my power, have composed in your
name and specifically for you this present book. It is for the
teaching of good and dutiful living to princesses, and
generally to all women who may read it... My honest
intention has been the increase of the goodness and honour
of every lady, be she high or low, and not the thought that
you yourself stand in need of such teaching, who are already
perfectly taught in these matters, thanks be to God...

****

Le Livre des Trois Vertus

When I had built with God's help the *'City of Ladies'*, at the
command of those three virtuous ladies, Reason, Rectitude and
Justice... and declared its form and content, I was tired after such a
long piece of work, like a workman who had just discharged a heavy
load he had been bearing, and I felt lazy and in need only for a time of
rest, but the three reappeared without delay and told me: "Get up and
stop festering in your inactivity... Take up your pen and write...
Why have you let your ink dry and turned aside from the labours of
your pen? Do you not take as much pleasure in it? Do you think you
can now atrophy in your maturity? Is laziness now to be your path?

"You must not give up the good work, you cannot stop in the
middle of it. The knight who deserts the field of battle before victory
is deeply ashamed for he does not deserve the laurel wreath which is
the prize of those who have fought to the end.

"Listen to our lectures and you will want to continue the good
work. We do not wish to overwork you... but our City of Ladies is
blessed and useful and known throughout the world. This same work
will be also further known..."

Then I, Christine, hearing their counsel, filled with joy and knelt
before them and offered my obedience. "Take up your pen and write,
so that to those blessed inhabitants of our city will be added all the
feminine community; first from the queens, princesses and great ladies
and then on down to the most humble. We will sing our good counsel

to all ladies and all classes of women so that our lessons will be of value to all women. Amen."

This is the book that I, Dame Christine de Pisan, write for all ladies. From the three goddesses named Reason, Rectitude and Justice, I bring loving greetings to all women. Love motivates the desire to increase the honour and spiritual development of women in general... to those who desire riches in this world nothing could be more pleasant than gold and jewels, yet can these endure for ever as virtues do? Virtues enhance the soul, and those ladies who are of the highest state should aspire to this noble aim; and above all others the foundation of virtue is the love of our Lord... Our sermons and lessons should be known to all women from the highest princess down the social scale to all classes of women to help them in their lives.

From pride spring many other vices... I can see this in myself for, because of pride, I fell into revengeful rage. The lady, who, because her husband is powerful, is full of pride, wakes of a morning lying in bed with soft sheets... and her ladies-in-waiting attending to her every wish or whim, could well think that she is the greatest lady... and not because of her husband's position.

O woman, are you blind that the great danger of pride, that is beyond all reason, does not strike you as a temptation?... God hates this so much that he exiled Lucifer from Heaven to Hell for his sin of pride...

Women should be dignified and defend the honour and respect due to their sex. As for widows who think of remarriage it is not always a happier solution than remaining a widow and independent. If one is not constrained by necessity, there is a good deal to be said for caution.

If marriage was always a felicitous state, peace and love prevailing, it would certainly be a good thing to re-enter into the married state. But we know that this is not so. For a young woman it is a different matter, and there may be no alternative. But for widows or those of mature years who have independent means it is a great deception. Some say that it is no life for a woman living alone. But widows with experience must use their own judgement and not simply give in and say that they cannot manage their lives alone. Widows are particularly open to every sort of swindle. My advice to them, when they are faced with the law, is to get an experienced lawyer, and to be wary that the legal expenses are included within the sum in question.

There are two paths to choose from to serve God, namely the active life in the world and the contemplative life; the two paths, the scriptures tell us, that lead to Heaven... The contemplative life is for the person who would forget everything in her desire to serve God... I can only describe this indirectly for those who experience the joy that is like no other, try to explain the comfort this life brings to them...

But the active life is, if she follows the charitable way, another way of serving God... both the active life and the contemplative life are pleasing to God, and when our Lord Jesus Christ chided Martha, saying that Mary also served him though she did not help in the preparations, he must have meant that a life spent serving only God leaving the world behind was the highest path towards serving our Lord...

The wise princess will have habits of charity that pities the unfortunate... and above all she will follow the path that Prudence will teach her. Prudence will instruct her that she must love her good reputation and her honour. Truth, good manners and her thoughtful behaviour to all... Prudence will teach her how to order her life, how to treat her husband's relations and friends... how to protect and guide the welfare and upbringing of her children... Prudence will teach her to behave so that she has the goodwill of all classes of her subjects... Prudence will teach her how to live carefully within the limits of her finances and order the expenditure of her court accordingly... Prudence will help the widowed princess, for married life is not always a life of repose... quite the contrary, and women should think carefully before marrying again...

This long piece of writing exhausted me, but I rejoiced to see the beautiful product of the lessons of the three ladies which I had recorded and revised, and which seemed to me increasingly to be profitable for a virtuous way of life, and to the honour of the whole community of ladies, present and future, wherever this book may be seen. As their servant... it is my continual hope that this noble work will be multiplied into many copies that will be dispersed all over the world, whatever the cost, and be presented to the queens, princesses and noble ladies of many countries, and that these will in turn be distributed to other women, so that its reputation increases. May this desire be put into effect, and these thoughts be spread abroad and published in all countries, in the French language. Since that language is more widely used in the world than any other, our work will not be left ineffective, but in its various copies will outlast this century. May those valiant ladies and wives in authority who see and hear of it, in the present and the future, pray God for their servant Christine...

'*Le Livre des Trois Vertus*' is strictly a moral and social guide for all women written for the first time by a woman, to help them in their conduct of various aspects of their lives and the problems they faced. Through these descriptions Christine gives us wonderful evocative pictures of Medieval life.

After '*La Cité des Dames*' and '*Le Livre des Trois Vertus*' Christine is silent. The following years saw France in a state of civil war and a period of unrest, which may have affected Christine's literary output.

Christine had an abiding interest in the Dauphin, Louis, Duke de Guyenne, and she firmly believed that peace and stability in France could be restored through him. Louis was born in the Hôtel St. Pol in January 1397, five years after his father's madness had set in, and he was only twelve when he started acting in his father's place. Though Shakespeare gives an unflattering picture of him in '*King Henry V*', and although Christine takes him severely to task for his unrestrained temper, loose living, sloth and lack of eloquence, he seems to have been a remarkable young man. We know that he once paid Christine fifty gold écus for one of her books.

In 1409, two books were written particularly with the Dauphin in mind and dedicated to him. For the good of France, Christine lay great store by the correct education of princes, the bourgeoisie, merchants and labourers.

The first of these books was '*Le Livre du Corps de Policie*' (The Book of the Body Politic) which was inspired by John of Salisbury Salisbury was a leading scholar of his time and an intimate friend of Thomas Beckett, and was in fact present in Canterbury Cathedral at the time of Beckett's assassination. He was one of the first to write a life of Thomas Beckett.

In her book, Christine examines French society and compares the body politic to the human body, the various limbs corresponding to the different classes of society. Once again she calls attention to social abuses in France, the jealousy at court, corrupt clergy, plundering soldiers, the barbarous treatment meted out to the population of captured towns during the civil war.

The second book, '*Le Livre des Faits d'Armes et de Chevalérie*' (The Book of Feats of Arms and Chivalry), divided into four parts, is such a shrewd and detailed analysis of war that, although written by a woman, it came to be recognised as the definitive work on war of its time.

Christine writes about the reason for war; the siege of castles and cities; fording rivers; provision of food, water and medicine; wages; the behaviour of a commander in defeat and victory; the choosing of a site to set up camp; loyalty to one's oath; arms and strategy; the order and manner of fighting;

discipline; examples from Greece and Rome – Alexander, Caesar, Hannibal and many others; the lists and tournaments; arms; standards; heraldry.

In it she argues the Christian concept of just and unjust war, defining war as being just only when it is one of liberation, regaining territory captured by an invader, or to correct a flagrant wrong. Both of these ideas are still debated today, and belong more to modern analysis of war than to the views held in medieval Europe, and in this she is remarkably ahead of her time.

She also took the opportunity to include a condemnation of the growing practice of duelling to the death, a practice she considered as being against divine, canonical and civil law. The entire book represents an effort to uphold the ideals of chivalry which had become decadent and debased at this time of civil conflict.

In fact there is no aspect of war that she did not deal with and she acknowledges her sources such as the authors Vegetius and Honoré Bonet to which she added her own ideas. It is a remarkable achievement for one who was so much against war, but she wanted true chivalric behaviour to be re-established so that it was available to all men.

Chapter Eighteen

Le Livre du Corps de Policie (1406)

and

Le Livre des Faits d'Armes et de Chevalerie (1409)

> And the wise teacher should also instruct them on the difference between good and evil and teach them and show them the path to follow in order to achieve good manners and virtues...

Le Livre du Corps de Policie

Here begins *'Le Livre du Corps de Policie'*, whose subject is virtue and etiquette. It is divided into three parts. The first part is addressed to the princes, the second to the knights and nobles, and the third to the generality of people...

Concerning the early education of the children of princes...
The teacher should attempt to please him by giving him

those trifles which children like, and by telling him sometimes, in a suitable way, some amusing children's stories to make him laugh, and all this in order that he should have as much study in the state of his graciousness and love as the teacher himself. The teacher should arrange a suitable hour and regulate a certain period of time in which the child can attend and continue with his schooling, and then give him some time for playing before his meal, the which should also be regulated. It ought not to contain too many delicious or dainty meats and wines, which are sometimes the cause of corruption or illness. And, when the child comes to his grammar, then the teacher should begin by using only a few subtle words and doctrines, so that the child is able to comprehend them, and then introduce more of them little by little, as does the nurse who is in charge of the child's nourishment at the beginning of his life.

Now, I suppose that the prince might wish that his child be introduced to letters, such as the knowledge of the rules of grammar and the learning of Latin, which things are pleasing to God, for this was the usual custom for all children of princes both present and past. For I suppose that great prosperity follows as a result, both to them and to their subjects, and they will acquire thereby so much more virtue. Such an education have had the children of the present Duke d'Orléans, a very prudent prince, and they still continue to do so, at the instance of the very wise, good and virtuous duchess, his wife, who, like those who prize and honour the possession of knowledge and science, is diligent and a prudent mother and her children have learnt all virtues well...

And the wise teacher should also instruct them on the difference between good and evil, and teach them and show them the path to follow in order to achieve good manners and virtues, as those valiant, renowned princes have done, their predecessors. And, further, he should show them the great rewards which are to be gained from living a goodly life and which follow those who are righteous and govern well, and, on the opposite side, the bad things which dog those who are evil or vicious. And if he sees in them any inclination towards science (knowledge/study/wisdom/*scientia*) he should, in order to encourage them, show them and tell them of the great happiness which is to be derived from knowledge, and introduce to them the field of philosophy; that is, make known to them and open their eyes to all learning. And, thus, with such a teacher at the beginning of his life, the son of a prince can, if he continues to adhere to this doctrine as he grows older, come to attain the excellence of virtue and a great reputation.

Here I begin the section dealing with the three estates of people. The community of people is comprised of three estates, which is especially the case in the city of Paris and thus in other cities – the clergy, the bourgeoisie and merchants, and then the common folk such as artisans and labourers. I would advise that the things which I shall say are profitable as an example of good living to each of these three estates in a distinct way, as much as they are different from each other.

Concerning the first estate of the people, that is to say the clergy.

Since the estate of the clergy is, among the others, the most noble and worthy of honour, I shall first address myself to them. This is my address to the theology students and scholars, whether they be of the university of Paris or of some other place.

To you people both well-advised and learned, I would address myself, to you disciples of knowledge, who by the grace of God and good fortune or by nature, are applying yourselves to the search for the nobility of the clear joyful star that is science (wisdom) – guard carefully this treasure, drink of this clear and pure fountain, gorge yourselves on this pleasing confection which can be of so much value to you. For what thing is more worthy of man than science and the nobility of knowledge? Indeed, those of you who desire it and use it, you have chosen a glorious life!

Concerning the second estate of people, that is to say the bourgeoisie and merchants.

I have already said that the second estate of people is the bourgeoisie and merchants of the cities. The bourgeoisie are those who are of ancient lineage in the cities and who have a proper name, surname and are the bearers of ancient family arms. They are furthermore the principal residents and inhabitants of the towns, the landlords and inheritors of houses and manors, from which they live purely and simply. In books dealing with them they are called citizens, and such folk should be honourable, wise and of fair appearance, dress in honest clothes, without disguise or frivolity. They should further be truly wise and upright men, people of faith and of discreet language; for this estate of citizens is both good and profitable. And in some places they are said to be of ancient stock, some of them nobles, for they have been for a long time folk of good estate and renown. People everywhere should praise the good bourgeois and the citizens of the towns. And it is a very good and honourable thing when there is a notable bourgeoisie in a city, bringing much honour to the country and great wealth to the prince. It is these folk who should occupy themselves with the deeds and the needs of the cities in which they live, so that all things appertaining to commerce and to the life of the community might be well-governed. And because the lower classes have, generally speaking, not great prudence in speech, especially in that which touches on politics, they ought not to meddle in those laws made by the princes; and so the bourgeoisie and the upper classes should take care to see that the commune does not impede the course of policy, and that they are able to prevent the people from bringing about any serious conspiracy against the prince or the council. The reason for this is that such conspiracies and machinations of the commune always recur and prejudice the interests of those who have something to lose. Let it never come about that one day they gain the upper hand, for the outcome is always bad and prejudicial; and, therefore, should it happen sometime that the community seems to bear some grievance against any policy, the bourgeoisie should assemble amongst them the wisest and most discreet in words and deeds, and approach the princes or the council to air these grievances in a humble manner and present their case in a debonair way, and not allow the entire community a voice themselves, for this would mean the destruction of the towns and of the peace. They should use their authority to appease the murmurings of the people to avoid all turmoil which could arise. They especially should guard themselves against this. And if it happens that at any time, according to their judgement, they consider the orders of the princes and their council to be in any way wrong, they should again humbly present their case.

Concerning the merchants, this estate of the people is very necessary and without them the estate of kings and princes and even the policy of the cities and countries would be unable to function. For without their industry, all classes of people, working in any way towards prosperity, would be much poorer, because these merchants bring from afar all the necessities and luxuries of life for the body of men, and anyone can buy them if he has money. And it is a necessary and well-appointed class which can deal with these worldly matters, for then the rest of the men can attend to other business. For if it were otherwise, everyone would be too involved with the buying of life's necessities to be able to indulge in other occupations, we see how well God reasons. And for the advantages they bring to each of us in this way, we must recognise the loyal merchants who, by buying and selling for money, or in another honest way by exchanging goods, are much admired by other peoples and recognised as indispensable in several countries, where they are held in high esteem. And, indeed, in some cities, the merchants have become such reputable citizens that they are considered to be on a par with the nobility, such as in Venice or Genoa and other places where there are many rich and powerful merchants who travel to all lands to fetch goods of all kinds which they then dispense to the people. Thus is the community provided with all these diverse things by those who loyally acquire them. I maintain that, by dint of this commercial traffic, the office of merchant is one most worthy of merit and is accepted, permitted and approved by both God and the law.

Concerning the third estate of the people, that is to say the artisans and labourers.

Afterwards comes the third estate of people, who are the artisans and labourers of the field, and which we may regard as the last part of the body politic. They are as the legs and feet to the body, says Plutarch, and one should take care to see that they are not hindered in any way, because a blow received by them could cause a very serious upset to the whole body. Thus, it is most necessary to guard them and provide for them well, since it is vital for the well-being of the body that they do not cease to walk; that is to say, the artisans are necessary to the body politic for the diverse labours which they perform and things would not function without them, just as a human body could not function without feet, but would tread clumsily and trail along uselessly, causing very great strain on the hands and the rest of the body. Similarly, he says, public affairs could not support themselves without the labourers and artisans...

And, taking into consideration the other services which they perform, there is still more to praise because, among the other worldly estates, it is they who most closely approach the sciences. For they put into action what the sciences prepare for them, as Aristotle says in his 'Metaphysics', for their work is the result of science, like geometry, which is the science of measure and of proportions, without which no occupation could proceed; and similarly with other things. And to bear witness to this, there is a commentator who says that the people of Athens wished to make a marvellous altar to the goddess of wisdom, Minerva, and because they wanted it to be a fine and beautiful work of art, they sought the advice of the great masters. They went to Plato, who was the supreme master of all sciences, but he sent them to Euclid, the supreme master in the art of measuring, for he devised a geometry which one reads every day and which is generally studied. And, by this example, one can see that the trades follow the sciences. For masons, carpenters and all the other workers of some trade work according to the teachings of science. And as for art, which is also recognised as a craft, Valerius says that it should reflect nature. When a workman copies exactly what nature has produced, it is like a painter who is such a good craftsman that he makes the figure of a man so alive and in such good proportion that everyone recognises it as such, or a bird, or some other beast, or a sculptor who does the same, and similarly others. And, therefore, some people say that art is rather like the monkey in nature, for just as the monkey imitates many of the gestures of man, so art should reflect many of the works of nature...

But to talk a little about their manners, I would wish that they would please God and not themselves, for it would please God if they were to lead sober and fastidious lives, which they do not appear to do. For the lechery of the taverns and eating houses which they frequent in Paris can lead to many downfalls. Aristotle talks of the voluptuous lives led by such people and others like them, and says that several seem to be quite bestial, for they choose lechery for all their pleasures. And as for the false opinion which these gluttons hold, and of which the holy scripture speaks in the second chapter of the Book of Wisdom, and the gist of which is that the period of our lifetime is short and full of ennui and at the end has no rest, so we should use our youth to follow our desires and gorge ourselves on wine and meat, and in all ways make evident our delight, without doubt, such words are foolish and vain, though one can often hear them spoken, not only by those folk who are simple but by others who are held to be wise by their estate...

As for the estate of simple labourers of the field, and what is said of them, not forgetting that many people are contemptuous of them and do them down, they are of all estates the most necessary, just as those who are cultivators of property, for they feed and nourish all human creatures, and without them the world would fail in very little time. And, indeed, those who cause them so much harm do not take care enough to recognise what service they perform, for anyone who regards himself as a sensible person should hold himself obliged to them. It is sinful to be ungrateful for all the services which they perform for us. And, indeed, those people are truly pious who sustain the body politic, for they sustain by dint of their labour the body of all men.

When Christine describes the various classes of society and their functions, we must remember that it is within a background of strong feudal resistance to the rise of the bourgeois and the merchant class. There was active hostility to the politics of Charles VI and his brother Louis d'Orléans, who had brought these classes into the royal councils as their father had done before them. They were called the *Marmousets*. When Charles' illness left Louis to try and carry on these policies, the uncles of the King, the royal Dukes of Burgundy, Berry and Bourbon, dismissed the *Marmousets* from the Council and ruled by themselves. Whenever the King recovered his senses during the first years of his illness, before he was too debilitated by repeated bouts of madness, he always brought them back.

One copy of *'Le Livre du Corps de Policie'* is in the Cambridge University Library and also an anonymous translation of it, which seems to have been done late in the fifteenth Century: *"Here begyneth the Boke which is called the Body of Policye and it speketh of virtues and good manners..."*

Le Livre des Faits d'Armes et de Chevalerie

Here beginneth *'Le Livre des Faits d'Armes et de Chevalerie'*, which book is divided into four parts.

The first part describes the manner in which kings and princes ought to conduct themselves in their wars and battles. They should do so after books and stories and examples of the most noble conquerors of the world, and emulate the manner in which they ought to behave in their office of arms.

The second part speaks, after Frontinus, of stratagems to use, the order and manner in which to fight and defend castles and cities, after the author Vegetius and others, and how to make war and give battle in rivers and in the sea.

The third part speaks of the duties and rights of arms after the written laws.

The fourth part speaks of the duties of armies in the case of safe conduct, of truces, and on the field of battle and of fighting in the lists.

Because boldness is necessary for the enterprise of high things, without which nothing would be undertaken, the same would apply to me in this present work to bring it out without other considerations, seeing the smallness of my person, who I know is not worthy to treat this high matter. You must not think that I am foolish for I am not moved by arrogance or misguided presumption, but I have a great desire to show my affection and a good motive to help noble men in the office of arms...

I have assembled matters that have been treated in various books to produce mine own in this present volume. But this matter had to be treated with diligence and wit rather than with polished words. The art of chivalry is not commonly instructed in plain and understandable language and I, with the help of God, declare that this present book may be clear to all men.

This matter is not one habitually clear to women who learn to spin on the distaff and occupy themselves in matters of their households. But I humbly come to treat the noble state of chivalry in homage to the lady Minerva, born of the country of Greece. The ancients treated her as a goddess and the poet Boethius mentioned her in his book of learned and noble women...

I, though a woman, charge myself to treat of such a matter... therefore I propose to address a prayer to the lady.

O Minerva, goddess of arms and of chivalry, by virtue of your deep understanding above all other women... be thou not displeased that I, a simple woman who compared to your great renown is as nothing, dare present this present volume... and it may please you to be favourable to me... I too was born in a country beyond the Alps which is now Italy... I am an Italian woman.

Cato the valiant combatant and fighter whose force and strength of arms achieved many fair victories and who was never discomfited in battle, said that there was more profit to the common good in the writing down of rules, teachings and discipline of arms he had composed in a book, than anything he had ever done with his body, for that endureth but one age; but that which is written endureth to the common profit evermore...

It appears manifest that wars undertaken for a just cause are permitted and suffered by God... for war undertaken for a just quarrel is none other but the execution of justice... and war may be waged lawfully only by a sovereign king or prince. Though it appertains to all men to guard their rights, it is the duty of the King to protect his subjects, who may be oppressed. He must be like a good shepherd who risks his life for his sheep...

There are five causes that lead to wars and battles, lawful and unlawful wars, upon which they are founded. The first of these is for justice, the second is to withstand oppression and grievous harm to the country and the people... the next is against usurpation; there is also the war of revenge and the war of aggression.

A prince may also in justice fight for the Church, or to help an ally whose cause is just and for the cause of the needy and oppressed... It is contrary to the laws of God to fight for revenge or fight an aggressive war, for man should not take revenge thereby usurping the right due to God... Though the prince may take arms to obtain justice for himself he should do so only after advice from his wise men in parliament...

A prince should look to ancient history and not rashly undertake a war. He must have wise counsellors and take heed to his finance and money, the two principal things without which it would be folly to undertake a war.

If it is not expedient for a king to lead his troops into battle, his deputy should have experience rather than lineage, he must be courteous and wise, he must not be hasty but be assured of the justice of the cause he is fighting for...

As I waited to enter into the third part of this present book and as my wits were almost weary of the weight of the labour concerning the other preceding parts, I was surprised, when lying on my bed asleep, I saw appear before me the semblance of a creature having the form of a stately man in the robes of a clerk with the appearance of a wise judge who said to me, "Dear praiseworthy Christine, while in deed and in thought you exercise the labour of studying more and increasingly... in the exhortation of all noble works and virtuous conduct, I am come to help you in the achievement of this present book of knighthood and feats of arms whereby with great diligence and good will you have occupied yourself.

"Therefore, I come to encourage and advise in the good service that you give to the cause of all knights and noble men that shall now read this work and employ themselves to those deeds which are required by the nobleness of conduct in the exercise of arms in both the labour of the body as well as by the laws written down...

"It is good that you take and use the Tree of Battles which grows in my garden and pick some of its fruits which you should use. Your vigour and strength will grow within yourself and will help you to finish this present work... You have been inspired and borrowed the works of other authors to build up your book. So you must cut asunder some of the branches of this tree. Take the best and upon that same timber you shall build the foundations of your edifice.

"For this I, as master, shall be there to aid you, as disciple ...

And I said to him, "O worthy master, I know that thou art upon that same study which I love and have loved so much that I remember nothing more than the practice and virtue of this work for which I have already thanked God, and which helped me to finish many a fair enterprise. Certainly I am right glad of your company but would it not displease the master if a disciple uses his learning? I pray you to tell me of any rebuke that shall be cast on my work for you have counselled me to use the said fruit."

"Dear Christine, to this I answer that the more a work is used and approved of by many folk, the more it will become known... It is common among my disciples to give and take one to another the diverse flowers out of my garden... Did not Master Jean de Meung help himself in his Book of the Rose with the sayings of Lorris? It is then no rebuke but it is laudable and praiseworthy when it is well and properly applied.... Do so then boldly and doubt not that thy work is good and I tell you that many a wise man shall yet commend and praise it..."

Concerning the colours to be used in arms, banners and standards.

Because we have entered into this matter and you have reminded me of the banners and arms of great lords, I shall tell you of the colours that men take for the most rich and most noble. For among them there is a difference of honour... So hold the masters of the law of arms that the colour of gold is the most rich... and the law says that there is nothing more aristocratic... and ancient laws did order that no man should have gold but that he were a prince... The second colour is purple that we call red which represents fire... The next in order of quality is the colour azure which represents air which after fire is the most noble of all the elements... The next colour is white which in armorial terms men call silver. The colour white is the most gentle of colours that follow after, because it is next to the shining colours and this signifies innocence and cleanliness, and the scriptures say that the vestments of Jesus Christ did seem to the apostles white as snow and the colour white represents water which after air is most noble... The other colour is black which in armorial terms men call sable. It represents the earth and betokens sorrow for it is further from the light than any other... So it is the most low and humble colour that there is and therefore it was ordained that religious persons should clothe themselves in the same. The next colour in armoury is green, that men call *verte*, which betokens woods, fields and meadows, and because it is not represented by the four elements it should be taken as the least noble.

All these colours are used in all manner of arms, pennants and banners by diverse persons from very ancient times.

'Le Livre des Faits d'Armes et de Chevalerie' was Christine's most popular book and was considered in England to be the best medieval manual of military tactics and international law. Henry VII had it translated and printed by Caxton in 1489 *"so that every gentleman born to arms should know it..."*

Caxton, in his translation, concluded: *"Here endeth this book of which Christine de Pisan made and used out of the book by Vegetius and the 'Tree of Battles' by Honoré Bonet with many other things set in it which was delivered to me, William Caxton, by the most Christian King and my Sovereign Lord...*

"I received the volume containing four books and according to his desire, which to me is a command, I was very glad to obey and with the little understanding that God had lent me I have endeavoured to accomplish his desire and command... so that it may come to the knowledge of every gentleman and soldier...

"I humbly beseech his most excellent and bounteous sovereign to pardon me this simple and rude translation where there is no strange or gay term of rhetoric. But I hope to almighty God that it shall be available to and understood by every man and also that it shall not be too unintelligible in comparison to the copy I received from my Sovereign Lord... I am glad to think my labour was well employed as a little servant of the most highest and Christian King in the world and I beseech almighty God to preserve and keep him to continue his noble work... This translation is finished on the 8th day of July of the said year (1489) and printed the 13th day of July in 1490.

"I beseech almighty God that my Sovereign Lord will always be victorious and daily increase in virtue to his glory and honour in this present life that is short and transitory and that he may attain everlasting life in heaven, which God grant to him and all his people. Amen – Caxton."

A manuscript containing *'Le Livre des Faits d'Armes et de Chevalerie'* was presented by John Talbot, Earl of Shrewsbury, to Queen Margaret. This magnificent book, evidently a wedding gift for her marriage to Henry VI in 1445, contains one hundred and forty-four exquisite miniatures, and is now in the British Library. A second copy is in the Bodleian at Oxford.

William Worcester, secretary to Sir John Falstaff, translated several passages of *'Le Livre des Faits d'Armes et de Chevalerie'* in his *'Boke of Noblesse'*, and acknowledges his debt to "Dame Christyn".

* * * * *

On November 23rd 1407 at eight o'clock at night the Duke d'Orléans rode out of the Hôtel Barbette, where the Queen of France lodged at that time. While he rode playing with his gloves and singing, he was ambushed by about a dozen masked men. He was hacked to death, his brains spilling out onto the pavement.

The murder of the Duke d'Orléans affected generations of Frenchmen and is in effect one of the most important events in the history of France.

He was assassinated by the hired killers of Jean Duke of Burgundy. If Jean had repented of his crime and the King had been able to pardon him, peace could have been restored. But on the contrary he justified his act. This was all the more cold blooded because four days earlier there had been a formal reconciliation between Louis and Jean, and the two cousins attended Mass and took Holy Communion together to cement vows of their "good friendship and fraternity". Burgundy, however, had already laid his plans to assassinate his cousin and only brother of the King of France.

Christine could never have willingly accepted Jean Sans Peur as the leader of France. He had murdered Louis d'Orléans, her friend and patron; he held the sick, mad King and his wife Isabeau practically prisoners, and favoured the English. In fact, she seems to have had very few contacts with him after this assassination, even though he twice paid her for books; this perhaps could not be avoided particularly as she would have had to present to him the book that his father had commissioned if he had expressed a desire to have it. Everyone was terrified of this violent man and Christine's son was probably still in the Burgundian household, making it difficult for her openly to express her true feelings.

The King could do nothing to bring to justice the murderers of his brother, to whom he had been devoted. The civil war in France had begun with this assassination. The following year, Valentine, Louis' wife, died, leaving their son Charles, aged fourteen, to take up his responsibilities as Duke d'Orléans.

Queen Isabeau, distraught by the barbaric murder of her brother-in-law, turned against his murderers, and for a short period the Orléanists had the support of the Queen.

Christine's relationship with the handsome and charismatic Louis d'Orléans was a complex one. Widowed at an early age, Christine was still young, a passionate, sensual woman susceptible to physical beauty, male or female. Her work is full of detailed voluptuous descriptions even of her husband whose physical appearance she mentions.

In order to understand Christine's feelings towards Louis we must look upon the whole of her work. It was so inextricably woven into her admiration for this prince that though her strict code of discipline and morals would have made it unthinkable to break through the ritual formality of accepted behaviour towards a prince, reading through her work one begins to get a picture of a deep unspoken love and devotion. Apart from work especially dedicated to him and manuscripts rewritten for him, she mentions him in several of her books. *'La Cité des Dames'*, *'Le Dit de la Pastoure'*, *'Le Livre des Faits et Bonnes Moeurs du Sage Roi Charles V'*, *'Le Livre du Corps de Policie'*, *'Le Livre des Faits d'Armes et de Chevalerie'*, *'La Prod'homme de l'homme'*. There are several ballads dedicated to him which praise him.

Louis also must have held Christine in high regard and felt a deep friendship and admiration for her. He permitted her to stage her "Order of the Rose" in his palace; he tells her about his experience which Christine then writes about in *'Le Dit de la Pastoure'*; he sends his wife Valentine a copy of Christine's *'La Prod'homme de l'homme'* no doubt to show her that Christine praised the serious side of his character; for Christine had by then earned the respect of many and was an influential figure. On New Year's Day, a ballad written by Christine for him reveals joy, love and devotion.

When Louis refused to take Christine's son, Jean, into his household, was it because he did not want her to know details of his life of which she would not have approved? Louis d'Orléans loved his wife Valentine but this did not impede him from being unfaithful to her.

Valentine and Louis had in fact lost several children in infancy. Apart from this sadness she had to face the fact of Louis' infidelities. We are told in effect that the Duchess loved her husband, *"loved him too much"*. Her exile away from her beloved Louis must have been all the more painful because she was fully aware of his disloyalty.

What Christine thought about Louis' affair with the Queen is, of course, unknown. It appears to have become serious after 1402. She was fearful for him, fearful of what Fortune would bring him – Fortune which is blind, inconsistent, cruel and deceiving. Louis, a brilliant prince, a political force, physically very attractive to women, could not leave Christine unaffected. His liberal ideas, his charm, his love and respect for women, his acceptance and encouragement of her work would bring this about. We are told by a historian, writing the life of his grandson, Louis XII, that Christine was the brightest attraction in Louis d'Orléans' literary salon.

The French have many expressions which describe love which do not necessarily have sexual connotations. *Ami du coeur* and *amitié amoureuse* are two such descriptions of that type of love. Perhaps there was more of an *ami du coeur* in Christine's feelings for Louis. As we know from one of her letters in the debate on *'Le Roman de la Rose'* she did not believe that those who loved inevitably desired to sleep with their loved ones.

Chapter Nineteen

Christine and Louis d'Orléans

> And do you think that all
> those who love want to sleep
> with their loved ones?

A ballad, sent by Christine to Louis for a New Year's Day greeting:

To Louis of France, Duke d'Orléans:

De tous honneurs et de
toutes querelles,
De tout boneur et de
bonne aventure,
De tous plaisirs, de toutes
choses belles,
Et de cellui qui creé a nature,
De quanque ou ciel et en
terre a mesure,
Et de tout ce plus propre a
homme né,
Mon redoubté seigneur plein
de droiture,
Ce jour de l'an vous soiez
estrené. .

All honour to you in all your
quarrels,
All happiness and lucky
adventures
All pleasure and all things
beautiful
All things created by Nature
All that is in heaven and
earth
All that is right for man that
is born
My redoubtable Seigneur,
full of rectitude
May this New Year's gift
bring you joy

Trés noble duc d'Orliens, de nouvelles	Very noble Duke d'Orléans, I renew
A vo souhaid et d'amour vraie et pure,	My wish that you have love that is true and pure
De ris, de jeux de notes nouvelles	Laughter, games, new music
Res jouyssanz, d'union sanz murmure	Rejoice in union without pain
Et de tout ce de quoy tous bons ont cure,	All that is good of itself
De tout le bien qu'en corps bien ordenneé	All that is good for a body well kept
Il doit avoir, de paix qui tousjours dure	To possess lasting peace
Ce jour de l'an vous soiez estrené...	May this New Year's gift bring you joy...

The first son of King Charles V was Charles (later Charles VI) who was sovereignly beautiful in face and body, better than most men... the other son of the King was Louis Duke d'Orléans, at present living and flourishing by God's grace. Louis added to the joy of his father born three years after the elder son Charles. There were other children including three beautiful girls who died young.

Great rejoicing marked their birth. The King was happy to have male heirs and this was celebrated by all the churches ringing out their melodies in praise of Our Lord. Great feasts were held by the barons and the people who made bonfires in all the streets of Paris. The King, his father, took measures necessary for his well being and appointed a wise and good lady as his governess, Madame de Roussel. She took great pains to nurse him, and the first words she taught him were to say an Ave Maria. It was a sweet sight to see him kneeling with his small hands joined in prayer before the image of Our Lady, and he learned at an early age to serve God. He continued his devotions and his orisons to the church and he rendered great service. He frequently made long visits to the Church of the Celestins, a convent where pious men gave service to God. He gave largely to the poor each day with his own hands. Particular devotion was given during the time of the Passion of Our Lord. He regularly visited the hospital (L'ostel Dieu) and the poor sick patients to whom he gave alms.

He was of middle height, rather tall and slim, very elegant; he had
a very gentle and good physiognomy, full faced, a large forehead and
a rather long nose... He was infinitely amiable to women and adored
their company; he laughed and joked with them but did not care to
hear women spoken ill of; his qualities of heart and spirit and
physique formed an ensemble...

He was a most handsome and cultivated Prince who continued to
study all his life. He was seductive and charming and had a most
fastidious appearance... Among the graces which he possessed was
the natural ability to speak beautifully. Rhetoric came to him
naturally and no one surpassed him.

Frequently he had before him large congregations of wise doctors
of science, and other solemn scholars and clerks, and on other
occasions at the council where a variety of subjects were proposed and
discussed, he was often asked many questions about various problems
and had to respond to these diverse and difficult opinions. It was
marvellous to hear how he answered them all point by point. His
memory was remarkable. He answered them all in good order, so
well and in a lively manner, sometimes in Latin and other times in
French. It seemed as if he had studied each subject in great detail. If
he lives until old age he will be a prince of great excellence and will
do many good things...

This prince had a natural sense which was advanced for his years,
and he loved all that was good. His speech was benign, reassuring
and moderate. He was devoid of cruelty, and his replies were amiable
to all persons who had need of his help. I saw this with my own eyes.

One day I went to his palace to present the copy of *'L'Epistre
d'Othéa'* dedicated to him. I stayed for more than an hour in his
presence. I was pleased to see his countenance so moderate and
poised, dictating his letters and orders to his secretaries, dealing with
each person in turn, and when it came to mine I was called by him
and he granted me my request (to accept *'Othéa'*).

******

La Prod'homme de l'homme

Here begins the description and definition of nobility of character
according to the opinion of Monseigneur d'Orléans written by me,

Christine de Pisan. I have dedicated this epistle to the brother of the King.

On a previous occasion I had spoken of your learning and of your virtue and I rejoice to have the opportunity of once again praising you and the noble understanding and justice of your laws. To bring them to people's notice sets an example of good breeding and of virtuous living. It is not flattery to speak the truth about what one sees before one's eyes. To praise the quality of your bounty is a cause of rejoicing and a way of ensuring that your good works continue.

Why praise emperors and sovereigns of antiquity like Caesar and Trajan when we may quote from examples in our own lifetime, such as the fitting and beautiful words which issued from your lips, most noble Duke... such as I heard with my own ears. I was much honoured by your benign grace, when I came to present you a small epistle addressed to your worship, who received me so kindly.

At which time you vouchsafed to reply to me a mere woman and unworthy as I am – but nonetheless admitted into the presence of your assembled barons and knights – giving me of your time and speaking to me at great length, having made me a very beautiful speech substantial and full of meaning.

Then issued from your lips such precious words, as of gold and of silver, that hearing them I was transfixed before you by a joyful wonder and admiration. Beholding your person, who those who do not know you imagine to be some ordinary prince – versed only in matters pertaining to the court or to everyday matters – I listened to you discoursing so well and pertinently, not only in French but in Latin too, quoting saintly authority to demonstrate how the proof of nobility and virtue resides in three places, the heart, the lips and the hands and is by them revealed.

These words I shall hereafter set down, not perhaps exactly as you spoke them... but as they revealed themselves to me upon reflection and, as far as I am able, measuring by the Holy Scriptures your powers of judgement.

Thus this little work is written... in praise of God, and in your honour, most noble Prince, who gave it birth.

I have used your quite beautiful and exceptional words.

While you were speaking I thought of taking them down. But when I had parted from you and was alone to ponder on them and think about them more deeply, I began to reflect and consider more clearly. Unable to write of anything more worthy myself I decided to enlarge in greater detail on the said matter, taken from various authors of whom the most appropriate seems to be Seneca (in this case a pseudo-Seneca-Martin de Brage) and passages from the Bible, the Fathers of the Church and Dante.

Concerning science (wisdom) which resides in the hearts of the wise and reveals itself as such both in words and deeds. These virtues fortitude, temperance, prudence and justice are, according to the men of the Church, virtues necessary for illuminating the understanding and thus achieving wisdom.

Language which issues from the mouth is the wisdom which is in the heart.

This version of the Book of Prudence I beg noble Duke to be pleased to accept, for it has been accomplished by you and for you. I therefore attribute to you whatever honour is due.

Prenez engré s'il vous plaist cest escript	Graciously accept, if it please you, this manuscript
De ma main fait aprés minuit une heure,	Written by my own hand one hour after midnight
Noble seigneur, pour qui je l'escript	Noble seigneur, take it not amiss that I have written it for you
Prenez engré quant vous plaira	Graciously accept, if it please you.
mieux vous sera escript;	It can be rewritten at your pleasure
Mais m'avoye nul autre direr a l'eure	But at this hour there was no other clerk to be had
Prenez engré s'il vous plaist cest escript	Graciously accept , if it please you, this manuscript.

Never did he say anything to dishonour women and he had a very wise policy. *"When I am told"*, he said, *"something detrimental about a person, I consider whether he who told me this did not have a particular hatred against the person he spoke of and if there were not other good qualities about him."*

He had pity on those he saw were confused, and an example of this was given one day. A hot-headed young man came to blows with another and feloniously menaced the other with his fists in the presence of the prince (thus committing *lèse majesté*). The good duke seeing that the situation was getting serious said to his people in a low voice: *"Tell him to stop and let him go."*

This prince is of a noble courage and has a great desire to bring confusion to our enemies.

He sent *chevauchées* to England; for his niece, married to Richard II had, on his death been left a widow. He offered to meet Henry of Lancaster, now King of England, in personal combat with him and dared Henry to accept this challenge...

The noble court of this prince was a refuge for the chivalry of France and many young sons of the nobility and gentry from all parts of the country were accepted into his court, and every beautiful youth who wanted to shine in public longed and hoped for this opportunity...

****

Oroyson de Notre Dame

A prayer to our Lady, for France, for the King, for the Dauphin and for Louis d'Orléans.

O Vierge pure, incomparable,	O Virgin pure and incomparable
Pleine de grace inextimable	Full of inestimable grace
De Dieu mere trés glorieuse,	The glorious Mother of God
A qui te requiert secourable	I implore your succour
Ma priere soit acceptable	Accept my prayer.
Devant toy, Vierge precieuse!	Before you, precious Virgin
Doulce dame, si te requier	Sweet Lady, if I pray to you
Que m'ottroies ce que je quier:	To grant that which I require:
C'est pour toute crestienté	It is for all Christianity

A qui paix et grant joye acquier

Devant ton Filz et tant enquier

Que tout bien soit en nous enté.
   AVE MARIA

Trés pure, qu'on ne puer louer
Souffisement,
Tant a louer s'y sache nul, dit
saint Jerosme

De la science de parlair
Et d'onnesté le mirouer,
Le pilier de foy et la cosme:

Pour le noble duc d'Orliens

Te pry que gardes des chaines

De l'enemi qui tousjours veille;

Prie ton Filz que de tous biens

Il remplisse lui et les siens,

Et l'ame en paradis recueille.
   AVE MARIA.

To obtain peace and great
faith
Before your Son, in constant
prayer
That all be well with us.
   AVE MARIA.

Very pure, who, one cannot
Sufficiently praise
Blessed by St. Jerome who
has gifted him above all
others with
The science of rhetoric
Honesty clear as a mirror
A pillar and ornament of the
Faith
For the noble Duke
d'Orléans.
I pray to you, guard him
from the chains
Of his enemies, constantly
on the watch.
Pray to your Son that all
good
Will bless him and his loved
ones
And accept his soul in
Paradise.
   AVE MARIA.

'La Prod'homme de l'homme' has been translated by Deborah Chattaway.

The story of 'Le Dit de la Pastoure' (A Pastoral Poem), written for Louis in 1403, is told through the words of a pretty shepherdess, who wore a green surcoat and was always singing, happy and laughing. So happy that she never wanted to change her life.

One day as she rested near a fountain, guarding her sheep and singing to herself, a party of nobles rode into the wood. Frightened, she stopped her singing. But they took her to Monseigneur who made her sing for them, and, before they left, he made her laugh by calling her sheep for her.

Of course the little shepherdess fell in love with the noble lord. Her friend, however, told her that no good could come of this as the lord was bound to marry a noble lady. She pined for him and in her sadness she quite changed.

He came again and they spent a happy hour laughing and singing. He returned several times and she fell more and more in love with him. He then did not come for over a year and the beautiful dream evaporated as it had to do. The chevalier's visits became increasingly rare and eventually he stopped altogether, leaving the young girl inconsolable. The descriptions of a simple life, the honest and innocent feelings, the peasants' love for their work and the animals, the meals eaten under a tree, all this is in deliberate contrast to the court, where, says the peasant, that one cannot be sure that poison does not lie in the extravagant meals, and where intrigue and envy dodges one's steps...

I have written this (says Christine) **at the request of a noble lord with a worldwide reputation, who is well able to command me. It describes an incident in Monseigneur's own life.**

This short synopsis of *'Le Dit de la Pastoure'* shows Louis at his most lively and flirtatious. He does not seduce the little shepherdess but treats her with sympathy and his calling her sheep for her must demonstrate how playful he could be in real life.

After this poem, Christine, who was still working on her long poem *'La Mutacion de Fortune'*, wrote three religious poems; the first *'Les XV Joyes de Nostre Dame'*, asking Our Lady to pray for her because of the fifteen joys she had on earth; the second is *'Une Oroyson de Notre Seigneur'* which relates with deep feeling Christ's suffering; the third was *'Une Oroyson de Notre Dame.'*

There was a copy of a variant of *'La Prod'homme de l'homme'* in the library of Charles d'Orléans and his mother Valentine. It must have been written after the 30th November 1404 but before *'Le Livre du Corps de Policie'*, perhaps even as late as the end of 1405 or the beginning of 1406. There are three variants of this manuscript in the Bibliothéque Nationale in Paris.

'L'Epistre d'Othéa a Hector' (The Epistle of Othéa to Hector) was written in verse. At least four manuscript copies of this work exist, the one dedicated to Louis d'Orléans, is the most richly illuminated, and the frontispiece is a picture of Christine offering a copy to the Duke. This beautiful manuscript which contains one hundred and one paintings seems to have been prepared under Christine's supervision and carefully directed by her; the miniatures by various artists are very lovely.

The domains of the English King in the south-west of France created a very confused situation. Charles V had persuaded many French or Gascon nobles to adhere to him while they were situated in the territory held by the English King. One day seven English noblemen informed the French authorities that they would like to challenge seven French knights for the love of their ladies. Part of Louis d'Orléans' lands were in that region, and seven members of his court took up the challenge. The combat took place on May 18, 1402 near Bordeaux. But the joust, which started light-heartedly, became serious when the French team was asked by the English to fight for the French King's quarrel with them. Christine no doubt asked by Louis wrote three ballads on this combat, the first of which was in praise of Louis.

In this society, of which both Louis and Christine were an integral part, the hierarchies were strictly defined. Every genuflexion, every inclination of the head, and the folding of hands denoted the position of the person who received a greeting. The equally strict injunction allowed no familiarity with the princes which formed one more barrier between the King, his close relatives and his subjects. The King was supreme in this structure. Next came those of his blood, his children, his brothers, all of them sons and daughters of a king. In this respect in England when Edward III died there were many who thought that John of Gaunt, the King's son, should inherit the throne instead of Richard II who was not the son of a king but only the grandson of a king.

One has to understand the enormity of the indiscretion if there was the slightest deviation from the strict rituals that surrounded the princes of the blood. It limited Christine's expression of her feelings for Louis to her writing. If as some people thought that in her writing she flattered him unduly, one must remember that this was the only accepted manner in which she was able to express her emotions.

After the death of Louis d'Orléans in 1407, his son Charles became the Duke d'Orléans. The new Duke was no warrior. He was a poet and a thinker – a fact which would become evident later when, taken prisoner by the English at the Battle of Agincourt, he would spend the twenty-five years of his imprisonment writing poetry. As a prisoner in The Tower of London, his longing for France never diminished. He wrote:

"Looking out towards the coast of France, it happened one day, at Dover by the sea, that I recalled the sweet delight which I was accustomed to find in that land. Then, from my heart, I began to sigh, indeed, what great good it would do me to see France, which my heart should love.

"I warned myself that my mind should know how to guard against such sights which appeared in my heart. I longed to see even the merest glimmer which would light the way to a fair peace. This could bring with it so many good things. For that, I turned to my thoughts for comfort: but all the same, my heart never grows tired of the thought of seeing France, which my heart should love.

"Then, I loaded in the ship of Hope all my desires, begging them to cross the sea without delay, and to take me to France. May God not tarry in bringing us peace! Then I would have the leisure, however it may be, to see France, which my heart should love.

"Peace is a treasure which one cannot praise enough. I hate war; it is deserving of no praise. I have been long disturbed, be it right or be it wrong, by the thought of seeing France, which my heart should love."

In the Tower of London there is a well known painting of Charles d'Orléans looking out of the window of his prison.

It was customary that at seven years of age the education of a prince or noble passed into the hands of tutors. In 1402, Louis d'Orléans had appointed a chaplain as tutor for his son, Charles, who was expected to teach the boy the manly attributes of a chivalrous education. At the same time the King gave his nephew a pension of twelve thousand livres a year. It was an expression of his affection towards his brother, Louis.

In exile, Charles' mother, Valentine, Duchess d'Orléans, had administered her husband's lands with wisdom and skill and away from the corruption of the court in Paris, brought up her sons.

Under the influence of this Italian princess, whose superior spirit was imbued with the enlightened influence of the Italian Renaissance, Charles was inspired. He expressed the happiness of his childhood in later poems:

"Ou temps passé, quant nature le fist	*In times past when nature*
En ce monde venir, elle le mist,	*Had brought me into this world, I was*
Premiérement, tout en la gouvernance	*First put into the charge of*
De une dame qu'on appeloit Enfance;	*A lady called Infancy;*
Enluy faisant estroit commandement	*And she commanded me*
De le nourrir et garder tendrement,	*She fed me and guarded me tenderly*
Sens point souffrir soing ou mérencolie	*Without any suffering or melancholy*
Aununement lui tenir compaignie,	*In all she kept me company*
Dont elle fist loyaument son devoir:	*And loyally did she do her duty:*
Remercier l'en doy, pour dire voir.	*I thank her."*

After being liberated for a heavy ransom, Charles retired to the family castle at Blois aged only thirty-four and continued to write, becoming one of the most important poets of his century. His library contained several of Christine's manuscripts and he acknowledged that his own writing had been influenced by Christine and Guillaume de Machault.

By 1409, the civil war, apart from the massacres, seemed to have achieved nothing. It had no direction or resolution, and Frenchmen were being driven to exhaustion. On the one side was a ruthless and ambitious Duke of Burgundy, and on the other side the Orléanists who now, led by Charles d'Orléans' father-in-law, Bernard Armagnac, called themselves the Armagnacs.

In the same year Jean Sans Peur proposed a peace treaty with the Orléanists, which Charles VI signed at Chartres. The debris and destruction of the civil war was all around Christine and in 1410 she wrote her powerful appeal *'Lamentations sur les Maux de France'* (Lamentations on the Sorrows of France). This was one of Christine's political poems. It is a lament of the devastation left in France by the civil war. The problems of war and peace continued to trouble her and in this poem she foresees the country becoming so weakened as to be in danger of being enslaved by foreign enemies. She makes the point that France could not survive divided, and needs a strong and virtuous ruler, supported by a moderate, non-factional party. France could then again grow strong. Christine felt deeply about this and had, as early as 1404, on the death of Philippe of Burgundy, foreseen the splits that would develop under his violent son, Jean sans Peur.

Chapter Twenty

Lamentations sur les Maux de France (1410)

> A kingdom divided within
> itself will be desolate from all
> sides; a house divided against
> its own good cannot endure.

hough quite alone, and scarcely able to restrain the bitter tears which fill my eyes and flow down my cheeks to blur my words – yet while I have space to write, and out of very compassion for its appalling evil, will I here record my grievous lament.

Oh, how is it that this curious creature the human heart can bring man down to a level of cruel and rapacious beast? How account for this contradiction in his usually reasonable nature? How can it be in Fortune's power to transform man into a serpent, an enemy of the human race?

For mercy's sake, reflect on this, you noble French princes. Do not be offended if I ask what has become of your erstwhile gentle blood, of the courteous conduct you were wont to show one another, and which was unequalled the world over: of which since antiquity our legends and history have been filled, and the songs of fame universally known?

What has become of the clear vision of your noble understanding, which by nature and long tradition you had put at the service of men of valour and of upright conscience? Is this now blinded? It would seem so.

You fathers of the French race, whose ancestors protected, defended and nourished generations of the children of this land – which will now be reduced to desolation unless your pity tends it – how you wrong those entrusted to you by God, you who once carried abroad our honour and our renown. You, who blinded by your quarrels, now treat even your sons as mortal enemies, fighting them in grievous wars.

For the love of God, most high princes, open your eyes with that understanding which once seemed yours by nature, and see where this strife is leading. For you will find nothing but cities in ruin, towns and castles destroyed, fortresses razed to the ground. And where is this? Here, right in the heart of France!

For our noble knights and our young men, who normally defend together, as one, the crown and the body politic, are now ranged shamefully one against the other – father against son, brother against brother, families against each other – their mortal sword-thrusts covering our sad earth with blood, the dead, and dismembered corpses. Oh, what a very dishonourable victory is this! What fame can be given to such glory! Will the victors be crowned with laurels? Oh, woe is me, they should be crowned with the blackest of thorns, shamefully entwined, and regarded not as conquerors but as the murderers of their own flesh and blood. They should all be wearing mourning, as for the death of those most dear.

And you, knight, returning from such a battle, tell me, I beg, what honour you bring home? Will your deeds be called more valorous because you happened to be on the winning side? May these perils from which you escaped be charged against our fine deeds, for no praise can belong to a day of such shame and retribution. Oh, if only it might please men, as it would certainly have pleased God, that neither side had shown courage! For what was the outcome, in God's name? Famine, caused by the decimation and laying waste of our land. And from this stems the rebellion of those oppressed and pillaged by foreign soldiers, and the subversion of our hard pressed cities – constrained by necessity to impose heavy taxes on their inhabitants. And, as if that is not enough, there are the English – who side with the winners of this game of chess whenever it suits them. Until all that remains is the dissension, mortal hatred and betrayal rooted in numberless hearts.

Was this intended? Indeed it was! Weep therefore. Weep and
wring your hands and make great noise, women of France. For the
swords are already sharpened by which you will be widowed, and
your children and families taken from you. Oh, Sabine women, we
have need of you in our task! You who, braving all dangers,
attempted to make peace among your warring brethren. Who, taking
your little ones in your arms, your hair dishevelled, advanced onto the
very field of battle, crying aloud: "Have mercy on our beloved
families and friends! Make Peace!"

And what of you, our reigning Queen of France? Do you sleep?
Can you not put your hand to their horses' bridles, and arrest their
mortal enterprise? Do you not realise that the heritage of your noble
children hangs in the balance? You, redoubtable princess, as mother
of France's noble inheritance, would any dare disobey your sovereign
authority were you to make a stand for peace? Come, all you wise
men of this kingdom, and range yourself behind our Queen. Of what
use are you, the king's advisors, if each one of you does not lend his
weight in this endeavour, rather than busy himself with petty affairs?
How can France pride herself on her wisdom, when this can no longer
be guaranteed? When not even our churchmen will save us from
peril, what will become of their undertakings and their good counsel?
Oh, priesthood of France, you are letting your influence fly on the
wings of chance, when you should be offering up prayers for us all in
devout procession! Do you not feel the need? For I believe God has
condemned us to destruction as he did Nineveh, and that his anger has
been so roused by the abundance of our most grievous sins that it is
doubtful whether even the intercession of devout prayer can revoke
this sentence.

Assuredly, my people, our devout womenfolk, must we beg for
God's mercy in this grievous storm. Oh, France, France! Once
glorious realm! Alas, what more can I say? For such bitter tears
stream onto my paper that there is no place left whereon to continue
my sorrowing lament. My heart is so overflowing with pity for you
that I wish I could wrench it from my breast. My hands are weary for
pain of the words I am writing, and my eyes blinded by my tears,
when I consider what will henceforth be our reputation. For shall we
not be compared to other former nations, whose brothers, cousins and
families set upon one another like dogs, from false envy and greed?
Will they not reproach us thus: "Come, come, you Frenchmen, you

who boasted that your princes were no tyrants, but of gentle manners; you who disapproved so strongly of the warring factions of Guelphs and Ghibellines. Now it is you behaving like this, though it once seemed impossible. So bow your heads, for your glory is in decline."

Alas, most gentle France, you are weary. Do you realise the peril you are in? Yes, indeed. Yet there is a remedy. God is merciful. Not all is lost, although the danger is so great.

Oh, Duke de Berry, noble prince, excellent stock of royal children, son of a French king, brother, uncle and father to the ancient lineage of our *Fleur de Lys*! How is it possible that your kindly heart can bear this day to assemble in mortal battle, and take up arms against your own nephews? I cannot believe that the memory of the great love between their fathers and mothers, of their most beloved brothers and sisters since dead, does not cause the tears to stream down your cheeks, nor that your noble heart will not melt for sorrow at what is happening. Alas, how painful it is to witness today, noble uncle of kings, dukes and counts, the gathering of your troops in mortal combat against your own flesh and blood. Likewise, to see your nephews, who in turn should revere their noble uncle as a father, ranged against him in battle! Oh noble and irreproachable blood of France! How can you bear the coming of such a day? That such shame should fall on us! How can it be that those who were the main pillars of our Christian faith and supporters of the church, whose virtue, strength and learning sustained and held it together, and who by all nations were known as the defenders of peace and friends of concord, how can they now be brought to such a pass as this?

So come then, noble Duke de Berry, most excellent prince, and follow the divine law which commands us to be the peacemakers. Wrench the bridles from the hands of the dissenting parties, and halt this dishonourable army. Force them to the conference table. Come to Paris, the city of your birth, where your father, imploring you with his sighs and tears, is begging, commanding you to stop. Come soon to comfort this dear city, and – like a good father – chastise its children with your words if you see them doing wrong, then console and take them to you again as it behoves your right and your duty. Bring both sides to reason, reminding them that, however great their discord, it is they who should be the mainstay, the defenders and supporters of our noble crown and the boast of our realm: that it is not for them to bring about its destruction through the antagonism of their several demands.

What is more, noble Duke, for the love of God I beg you to warn them all that, although at present they are divided by their differences, each hoping for his own victory in battle, they should not be too certain of it. For boastfulness is folly, and the strange ways of chance cannot be ignored! No man can foretell how a battle may end. He may propose, but Fortune disposes. What did it avail the ancient King of Thebes to leave the battlefield a victor, when so many of his knights and his soldiers were left lying there dead among the ranks of his enemies, decimated by the swords of his princes and his own kin? Oh God, what a doleful victory that was – the King of Athens mortally undone! Of what good to him was his victory? Of what profit to these multitudes? They covered hill and valley, yet Xerxes remained unmoved. No quarrel can justify such a state of affairs. Our saintly King Louis, who won so many great victories, did not look with disfavour on the miscreants at Thunes. There is no better example of the marvellous disposition of God, who allowed the battle to rage on, seemingly lost, and as if its final happy outcome were in doubt. Above all, though warfare is always dangerous and full of risk, there is no question that when between such close kindred, who should be linked together naturally by love, it becomes altogether perverse and dishonourable – meriting excommunication – if the discord cannot be brought to a peaceful conclusion. Alas, if such dissension must be the cause of fighting and bloodshed, then the greater the reason for bringing it to an end and establishing peace.

Let us vanquish vice by virtue. Let us find a way to bring peace among those who are friends by nature and enemies by accident. Alas! that it would please God to guide all our energies towards such an achievement, instead of towards the contrary! I believe that, at great cost, we shall manage it, if by common consent and true unity this army be directed against your natural enemies, instead of employed in killing our own French people. Oh God, what joy that would be! What honour forever to this kingdom!

Oh, most honoured prince, noble Duke de Berry, I beg you heed what I say, for there is no undertaking that the human heart cannot accomplish, if performed with good intent. Thus, if you will make peace by your endeavour, you will be acclaimed as founder of this reign, custodian of the crown and its most high and noble lineage; as

248

he who ended the strife between the nobles, as comforter of the ordinary people, as protector of the highborn ladies and of widows and orphans. To which end may the Blessed Holy Spirit, from whom stems all peace, give you the heart and the courage to bring these troubles to a happy conclusion. Amen.

May I too, your servant Christine, a humble voice crying aloud in our realm, desirous of peace and of the general good, and moved by most righteous intention, live to see this great day. Amen.

Written on the 23rd day of August, in the year of grace 1410.

'Lamentations sur les Maux de France' has been translated by Deborah Chattaway.

The struggle continued fitfully, interrupted by occasional truces, until the bloody battle of 1411 in and around Paris, in which the Armagnacs were defeated. The battle itself had made life in the city intolerable. Paris was in the grip of terror. Savage massacres periodically rocked the capital and famine and disease were rampant. Wolves roamed the streets at night eating the corpses of the victims. Incensed by a situation which held no respite for the poor, the tradesmen of Paris, mostly butchers, gave themselves over to the ransack of Paris which the King could do nothing to prevent. The defeated Armagnacs retreated to Bourges pursued by Burgundy who had the support of the King and the Dauphin. But in the middle of a fierce and bloody battle, the fifteen year old Dauphin, Louis, suddenly took charge and proposed an immediate truce. The Peace of Auxerre was signed on 22nd August 1412. Christine was inspired to begin another book, *'Le Livre de la Paix'*, again directed at and dedicated to the Dauphin. Then, when the peace was broken, she stopped writing, ***pour cause de paix defaillie*** – because of the failure of peace.

Meanwhile, the Paris tradesmen, having had a taste of power, and now fully aware of their strength, began again to flex their muscles. They had expected civil peace; instead the nobility was again up to its destructive quarrels. Earlier, the tradesmen had extracted promises of reform from the Armagnacs on the understanding that each would help the other, but Burgundy had quickly isolated his opponents and won the support of the population by promising more. The cynical tactic of using the Paris crowds as pawns in a civil war was to be repeated up to and beyond the French Revolution. Evidently, Burgundy had no more intention of implementing the demands for reform than had the Armagnacs. Pawns had no value in the game of power. The butchers, led by their leader, Caboche, thought differently. The very men who had led the uprising against the Armagnacs now launched the attack against Burgundy.

Eventually the entire city fell under the control of the *Cabochiens*. Old scores were settled. Many nobles were forced to flee while others were killed on the spot. Christine says she trembles to think of it. Among those who left Paris was Jean Gerson, Christine's friend, who fled disguised as a monk. He had originally supported the *Cabochiens*, as had the University as a whole, but this support dwindled as *Cabochien* excesses increased. With a threat of invasion from England, there subsequently emerged a call for a moderate "party of conciliation", to bring about peace between the two factions. Christine expressed the views of this party in *'Le Livre de la Paix'*:

A kingdom divided within itself will be desolate from all sides; a house divided against its own good cannot endure, for holy writ gives testimony to this and there are several examples known to us from Troy, Rome and other cities wrote Christine.

In March 1413, King Henry IV of England died and was succeeded by Henry V, a brilliant soldier and military strategist, whose ambition was to have a devastating effect on an already war-torn France. In that same year, the Burgundians and Armagnacs negotiated an agreement, and signed a treaty at Pontoise. Paris was saved for the moment.

For Christine, the main consideration was the achievement of peace. She resumed writing *'Le Livre de la Paix'*.

Chapter Twenty-One

Le Livre de la Paix (1412-13)

> As the soul governs and maintains the body, so also an honest prince is the health of his kingdom, and as the body weakens when deprived of a soul, so too does a kingdom fall apart when governed by a weak or dishonest prince.

lory, honour and reverence... be yours, most excellent Prince Louis... Duke de Guyenne... Most excellent lord, the great joy at present welling up in my heart because of the recent peace of which you, by divine ordination, were the author, compels me to take up my pen in order to compose a new work filled with your glorious praises... Your servant is occupied by nothing but the solitary work of scholarship, with the purpose of making happiness you have created more durable, by having you clothed in a fitting royal garment... for which I have gathered some beautiful flowers in the fields of literature. From these I can make you a garland to adorn your youthful features, for they have grown from other plants with the main roots of virtue, the first of which is called Wisdom, from which the others stem. Their names are Justice, Magnanimity, which comes from great courage, strength, clemency, liberality and truth...

Noble prince, if you knew what good inheres in it, for sure you would desire no other treasure so greatly, since it alone can make you great, strong, powerful, rich, renowned, feared and loved. And know you what this virtue is? To describe it briefly – to be sure it is to keep one's behaviour subordinate to one's will, to shun all stain that is ugly or brings reproach, and to take delight in all good doing and good speaking, to love good counsel and act according to it. Virtue is nothing but right reason; prudence the source of riches and nobility.

It behoves no one more than a prince to know much and what is best, since his prudent and well-ordered life can be of profit to all his subjects... Rather than hold up Caesar, Pompey or Scipio as examples... it will suffice to present as a model your forebear Charles V, who exemplified prudence and perfection from his youth.... He dismissed those whom he thought might make him swerve from his good intent, and surrounded himself with the wise and the worthy, taking their advice and doing them honour...

Imagine, if you would, what an extraordinary difference there is to be seen between the royal state as it was then (i.e. in the time of Charles V) and as it is now. Oh! what order there was in everything, what punctuality, what sense, what government... what eloquence – and what a redoubtable, revered person he was to behold, who passed no moment except in performing good works.

Doubt not the truth of this, for many, and myself among them, have witnessed it with our own eyes.

Qualities of good officers at court and how such men are to be chosen.

The prime quality a good tongue, i.e. always to speak truly, loyally and encouragingly to one's lord; to know when to keep silent, even on pain of death; and never to blame another falsely, out of envy or malice, so as to put them out of favour or so as to usurp their position. Also, diligence and readiness to serve one's lord at all times. Such a one always says the right thing, brings peace where there is discord, blames no one and is ready to excuse.

I shall never to able to describe the joy with which my heart is filled on account of this glorious peace once more affirmed between the French princes, who, by an evil spirit jealous of the happiness of this kingdom, had been fighting together for a long time. This strife turned the whole of France to ruin... Who would not feel joy at seeing the end of these killings, atrocities, ruins, rebellions, the arrogance of evil and pathetic people, the senseless government of a lowly and brutish population, the prince apparently a slave to others, the nobles scorning him – in short, the infinite number of evils and detestable barbarities which have been current this year to a greater extent than ever before?... Oh God! Where is the heart that would not quake to contemplate how this piteous war placed our kingdom in danger of total annihilation? I recall this in my writing only in order that the present example be held always before the eyes of the wise men of today and of the ages to come...

For God's sake, noble and excellent French princes, knights and all other noblemen of our age and ages to come, may this mortal danger never be absent from your memories, out of pity for yourselves... May you not forget or make light of the ruin, destruction, outpourings of blood, horrible cruelties, populations made destitute, the people's lack of respect for their sovereign lord and for ladies and maidens made widows and orphans by these evils... I was evidently saved from this not by my own presence of mind, but only by a divine miracle, for which God be praised.

What joy to be able to take up my pen again and continue my book after the interruptions of war. Calm sea after tempest, clear sky after storm and cloud are insufficient similes for peace after war, and all its attendant joys. So I must continue my praise of you (the Dauphin) to whom we owe this good.

It is essential that peace should be preserved. To which end you should always be mindful of the evil that comes from strife, and how many a kingdom has come to destruction through its long continuance. You should show benevolence to the princes of the realm and cultivate their friendship, extinguishing any spark of animosity that might appear. Let Charles V be your mirror and lesson in this, who not only earned the love of his people through gifts and good deeds, but equally earned the friendship of his foes by such means, and thereby demonstrated his great wisdom and prudence.

Cruelty in a King only multiplies his enemies and causes war.

Justice is the second cardinal virtue (prudence being the first).

Justice consists in favouring neither the rich nor the poor, friend nor foe. One is not to be intimidated in its practice. By justice the bad must be punished and the innocent protected. Justice prevents ill doing; it does not merely punish ill deeds. And justice demands that the good be remunerated for their good deeds. The prince alone is not enough to put this into effect: he must appoint ministers who are wise, clear-sighted, god-fearing, upright, gentle, humane. By his servants is the master known.

<u>The evil that comes of not punishing malefactors with justice</u>.

Covetousness is the root of all ills and vices.

Envy and covetousness above all other sins bring their own hell with them.

One of Charles V's chamberlains struck a sergeant at court. Despite his pleas and those of his brothers and others of royal blood, he had his hand cut off in accordance with law, nor was he ever again in the King's good grace.

One day, as Charles V was going out to hunt, a woman fell at his feet and complained that one of his servants, who had lodged with her, had molested her daughter. Charles, having heard the man's confession, immediately ordered him to be hanged from a tree in sight of all, so that others might learn from his example.

<u>The good should be rewarded according to their deserts</u>.

The Romans elected to public office only those of proven worth, whose good deeds were officially recorded. The greatness of the Romans was founded on their personal discipline and simplicity of living. As soon as their rulers became proud and greedy their empire declined. Their success in the arts of war and peace was due to the high value they put on the worthy, which then inspired others to emulate them. Charles V did likewise, that is, when or wherever he heard good spoken of a person, he would seek him out and promote him to some appropriate office, and hold him of great account. The populace are as unruly and worthless as they are for lack of example from their superiors.

Magnanimity is the third virtue of a prince. Its effect is to make him peaceable, calm, gentle, self-contained and impervious to injury and offence. This in turn lends a certain splendour to his deeds, makes him talked about, and both feared and loved.

<u>Exhortation to the Dauphin to cultivate magnanimity</u>.

Magnanimity exalts and exhibits the other virtues. It is the quality most prized in a prince by his subjects. As Aristotle said to the boy Alexander: *"Take upon yourself courage and magnanimity, and if there is in you the stuff of virtue, put it into practice, that is, demonstrate it by your works."* These words, most noble prince, could be addressed to you as to Alexander. For, as St. Augustine says, he can know little of what virtue is who does not put it into practice. Heigh! noble youth, may it please you to consider how fine a thing it is to behold a prince, even in his early years and ever growing in goodness, adorned with the fine upbringing and demeanour inherent in the said virtue, that is, despising vice in all things and desirous of acquiring every good habit and demeanour – such, in effect, is the wise prince, moderate, eloquent, discreet, dutiful towards God, attentive to the opinions of the wise men who give him counsel, gracious towards strangers, according each the respect due to his degree, showing great love to those of his own blood, both in outward manner and in speech, as though nothing were more agreeable than to honour the valiant and the good, gladly to hear tell of their deeds, to reward the deserving, to be gentle, humane, gracious, amenable, joyous, ready at all times and places, courteous when disporting himself, measured, and fearless at all times.

A prince should not be too solitary.

As Aristotle says, those of high courage and good understanding are the natural leaders of others. Also, nothing gives his subjects greater pleasure than to see and to have access to him. Besides, as Aristotle further says, man is by nature a social animal. Furthermore, a prince ought to be in touch with his people and aware of everything that is going on around him, which he cannot do in solitude. Charles V never failed to show high courage and magnanimity from the moment he was crowned at an early age. He could not abide the fact that the English had control of such large portions of France and that his successors should in such wise be impoverished in their honour and their heritage. Accordingly, with great courage as well as sober sense, he put his hand to the task – no mean one – of recovering what was his but had been lost by long-drawn-out war.

The virtue of strength which grows out of magnanimity.

By which I do not mean physical strength, but purely moral, enabling one, in the words of Virgil, *"to pardon the defeated and disarm the proud"*.

Charles V showed his moral ascendancy in the wisdom with which he conducted his wars, and his ability to inspire loyal service both in his nobles and in those of his own blood.

How the commons should be governed in accordance with clemency, liberality and truth.

In praise of the virtues of clemency and benignity in a prince – of which Jesus Christ himself is an example. Clemency is the virtue which most attracts friends to a great lord. Witness your good father, King Charles VI. Thanks to the impression he gives to everyone of great benignity and gentleness, and the way he would be a friend to all and harm none, his people desire nothing more than his noble presence. Such benignity inspires so great a love in a man that he would die for him if need be. And this virtue of benignity was no less apparent in your grandfather Charles V.

Despite the violence and wrong lately perpetrated by the populace, now that peace is restored the time is ripe to act with mercy towards them and to soften the rigour of their punishment. The stars' movements are ordered by just proportion, concord and peace; likewise the elements and the lower creation.

France is powerful when united and at peace within itself.

Already Julius Caesar said that against a united France the whole world could not prevail. O noble son of the King, whom the crown awaits, when foreigners attest to such vigour among the French as long as they are united, you, whom this matter touches more than anyone else alive excepting your father – you must be at pains that this accident, this civil war that keeps France from attaining such excellence, should be completely wiped out and eradicated, for it is prejudicial to everything. If there is a greater ill it is that its prolongation can turn into a state of perpetual warfare that then becomes the norm, as we see happen in Italy.

A prince is held in honour for treating each estate of society according to its deserts.

May God grant that you, Louis of France, noble youth, may shun all trace of the ill doing of wicked princes which we have mentioned above, as I firmly believe you will... The prince who can maintain sovereignty without creating discord among his subjects, is clearly wise and very virtuous... The sign of a city being in good state, large, rich and well governed, is when one sees in it a multitude of distinguished citizens. These statements serve to illustrate that when a prince governs well and keeps his people in peace, he achieves and maintains the common weal... The noble realm, above all other countries in the world, is splendidly adorned with four excellent things: the first is the grandeur of its noble princes, all of the same royal blood and lineage: the second is its valiant knights, the noble estate: the third is the solemn clergy: the fourth is the rich and distinguished burghers in its many cities, but especially here in Paris. And all the estates, with all the countless people they comprise, ever and naturally, loyally and lovingly, recognise, in all obedience and reverence, one single leader, namely the King. Truly, what power could oppress or trample upon any such body, so long as it remains one, without separation of any of its members, that is, the head which is the King, the shoulders and upper parts which correspond to the lords and princes, the arms which are the knights, the flanks which are the clergy, the kidneys and belly which are the burghers, the thighs which are the merchants, the feet and legs which are the common people. Incontestably, if this body, which God maintains, is prepared to hold together, it can face the whole world without fear.

The good prince must treat his people with gentleness.

Tully (Cicero) seemed to be prophesying the present time when he said that we can appreciate the strength and virtue of concord and friendship by contrast with the ills we have suffered through dissension and discord. Despite the faults and offences of the common people, and their being prone to foolish credulity and misplaced enthusiasms, the prince must respect them. Not that I advocate pardon for the principle miscreants who caused sedition, perverted their fellow men and incited them to evil.

A prince who is moderate has greater authority than one who is vindictive. Better a prince who is well liked for not being too rigorous in his exactions than one who is feared for his cruelty.

An address to the people instructing them, by examples from scripture, how displeasing to God is any rebellion or mutiny against the rulers by the commonalty.

What folly could ever have moved you to rebel against your superiors and believe that you could crush or destroy the nobility – a thing impossible to achieve, while the mischief of it would only rebound on you? You were blinded by great ignorance when you failed to recognise that nobility is so strong a tie that even kings hostile to one another would make peace in order to help their equals, and that you would be crushed if you rebelled, and rightly so, as is natural and pleasing to God. For, although all men are born and created equal, nevertheless you must realise that, by long habituation to different manners and usages, those who are of noble lineage have greatness of character and comportment that other men have not. And this is also to be seen among birds and beasts, some being of gentle manners and others not. If he please, each man can flourish in the estate that God has placed him in. You should be humble towards your lords and loyally do your duty, each according to his capacity.

It is not fitting that men of the lower orders should hold office.

On the pretext of being ill-governed and imagining that they will be better off if they cause commotion, the lower orders are inclined to act hastily – without due consideration and with no greater awareness than beasts of the evil consequences. On the other hand, please God they should not be enslaved by their rulers or be expected to bear outrageous burdens. How to proceed prudently so as to keep them in such a state that there is no cause for further anxiety about their unruliness? – but without ill treating them, for it is our Lord's will that they should be supported, and besides, their labours are necessary to the common weal. Do not elevate those who by nature's ruling are base. A stream that bursts its banks does more harm than a river. Do not elevate the common people and give them charges and positions of authority that do not properly belong to them. They should have no prerogatives in the government of town or city, since such things pertain to burghers of distinction and ancient lineage. The manual worker who all his life has never left his workshop – what good can come of his mixing with lawyers and suchlike? Such a simpleton, who barely knows his Pater Noster and can hardly control his own self in the tavern, who is he to govern others? God! with their little sense and proud ways, what greater mischief could there be than to be governed by such miserable fools? For what can you expect from a wretch who suddenly thinks he is master?

There is no end to the recital of woes attendant upon the exploits of the populace. Not that I would wish to exaggerate or put them in the King's bad grace, or yours, good prince, nor to denigrate them to those who, in time to come or when these events are forgotten or brought to a peaceful conclusion, may read or hear this book. My sole motive, and God knows it, is to bring peace and put an end to strife, and by the light of my limited understanding, I have tried to show how to control and govern the populace with such wisdom that those perils previously spoken of should never recur... So for the reasons already given civic office should not be granted to the lower orders. And if someone objects that the opposite holds true since this has been done in a number of Italian cities and elsewhere, I would reply that though this may be so, yet I have heard no one affirm that government by such people is good or that it remains peaceful for long... There is no greater folly, if I may say so, for a prince who wishes to maintain his sovereignty in honest and peaceful fashion than to allow the common people to arm themselves... It were better that a warring prince who had insufficient nobles and gentlemen at arms among his compatriots to employ in his campaigns, should enlist foreign mercenaries, as they do in Italy and elsewhere, rather than the populace.

Noblemen should at all times be well exercised in arms.

To this end the King should arrange for jousts and tourneys to be held regularly even in peacetime. For, as Seneca said, *"long preparation for war makes for swift victory."*

The parlous state of France as a consequence of the recent civil war, and how to prevent the recurrence of it.

For God's sake, most noble and excellent princes of France, knights and all other nobles present and to come, may this mortal peril never leave your memories – and this for your own sake – so that no more suffering may occur let it not be put out of mind as though it had never existed: the ruin, the destruction, the spilling of blood, the horrible cruelties, the pauperisation, the people's lack of reverence towards their sovereign lord: ladies and maids widowed and orphaned as a result of this great mischief.

How the prince must act not to keep the people from presumption and rebellion.

So that the people's vague desires cease, and previous ills do not recur, it seems to me desirable that the prince, as much to fulfil his duty towards God as to ensure that the people no longer air their grievances and be malcontent, that he govern justly, nor suffer them to be down-trodden or pillaged by the soldiery or anyone else; that he defend them diligently from all foes, as a good shepherd his ewes, and guarantee that nothing be taken from them without recompense. He should not entangle them in unnecessary wars but as far as possible guarantee them peace. He should prevent their being oppressed or ill used, so that they have no cause to rouse themselves or to be occupied with anything other than their own work. He should be gracious and benign when addressing them, lend a sympathetic ear to their petitions, be in no way disposed to show them cruelty but rather desire to treat them in all amity. And when he passes through the city or anywhere else he is likely to meet them, he should greet them with great kindness and with benign mien.

'Le Livre de la Paix' has been translated by Peter Khoroche.

Christine ardently believed in the efficacy of a virtuous ruler. Even as early as 1403 she had made a special prayer for the Dauphin, *'Oroyson de Notre Dame'* (Orison to Our Lady) and the last part of *'Le Livre des Trois Vertus'* was addressed to him.

'Le Livre de la Paix' is in blank verse and was written with a definite political objective in mind and directed at the Dauphin.

As the soul governs and maintains the body, so also an honest prince is the health of his kingdom, and as the body weakens when deprived of a soul, so too does a kingdom fall apart when governed by a weak or dishonest prince...

Christine praises the Dauphin for his attempts at civil peace. Once again, it was an effort to give him a picture of a model prince. In this book she judges events with a truly remarkable objectivity, detachment and vision. It is far too simple to say that Christine was "reactionary" because she stood against the movement of the Cabochiens, the **artisans who had never left their workshops and wanted to govern Paris.** She saw the picture as a whole: France, not Paris, was her concern. It could clearly be seen that the triumph of *les hommes de metier*, the artisans, far from bringing peace and unity to France, would accentuate the civil war, leaving the way open for England to conquer France completely. But they did not in effect avoid the blow, for Agincourt was only two years away and Henry V had already begun to assemble his bowmen and his navy for his assault on France.

In the independence of her spirit she sees, however, that a strong class of *moyens riches* is necessary for the stability of the country:

The rich and the poor cannot learn to live together as they are placed at the two extremities, but if between these two we find the "middle rich", order would be more conveniently retained... The discord between the rich and the poor could bring ruin to France...

Whatever contemporary ideas may be, the rising middle class during the close of the Middle Ages was one of hope and progress. They stood for citizens' rights against medieval privilege, and above all showed a far more enlightened attitude towards women. In the context of the early fifteenth century, Christine's perception about the role of the *moyens riches* was astonishing in its vision.

These sentiments, clearly, were ahead of their time in an age which was still feudal. In Italy where the Renaissance began earlier, the position of middle-class women was far ahead of those of France or England. Christine hoped that the rise of a middle class in France would see a more enlightened attitude to women. Neither of these hopes was to be truly realised until a very long time after her death.

'*Le Livre de la Paix*' was the last philosophic writing of Christine. In 1414 she must have felt her impotence in the face of the corruption in French political life. She tried to find refuge in poetry. In her book '*Autres Ballades*' (Other Ballads) are included some poems written at this time. With her whole heart in agony she had related the miseries of the people torn by civil war: but her warnings, her "lamentations", which during the whole of her life she addressed to the leaders of France, had brought no results.

Henry V invaded Normandy. The battle fought at Agincourt on 25th October 1415 was a resounding victory for the English. Amongst the prisoners taken by them were Charles d'Orléans and Jean de Bourbon, husband of Christine's friend Marie de Berry.

In December 1415, the Duke de Guyenne, who was central to all Christine's hopes for regenerating her *Dame Couronnée*, suddenly died. He was succeeded by his brother, Jean de Touraine, who in turn died two years later, and Charles, the last son of King Charles VI and Queen Isabeau, became Dauphin.

Among the most powerful figures in France from 1415 till her death in 1442 was Yolande d'Aragon, Duchess of Anjou and Queen of the Four Kingdoms of Sicily, Naples, Jerusalem and Cyprus, also Countess of Provence. She has been described as virtuous, wise and beautiful. While her grandson, Louis XI said she had, "*the heart of a man in a woman's body.*"

Yolande, the mother-in-law of Charles VII, practically ruled that part of France which was not occupied by the English armies. She negotiated peace treaties between the different belligerent factions in France, getting them to unite against the English. She sold her jewels, gold and silver vessels to pay for Charles' armies and for food for the besieged town of Orléans. In fact, she ruled as regent for a period and forced Charles (who at that time was influenced by the corrupt men around him) to face up to his responsibilities. Indeed, many towns like Tours refused to obey Charles unless his orders were countersigned by the Queen of Sicily.

If Jeanne d'Arc saved France by becoming the symbol of resistance, she was the inspired instrument of Yolande; for it was Yolande who gathered together the threads to build the unity and independence of France as she lay bleeding.

Yolande d'Aragon was not directly a patron of Christine, for she only came to Paris for specific purposes and for short periods, but Christine, as early as 1405, in '*La Cité des Dames*' says that **women like the Duchess of Anjou, Queen of Sicily, have a better understanding and a more lively consideration for government than many men, and if their husbands had counsel of men of equal quality it would greatly profit them...** She admired Yolande for the manner in which she governed her duchy in place of her husband when he was away and after his death. She followed a liberal policy, cut down the expenses of her court and forbade speculation in grain in famine-stricken France. She encouraged commerce, diminished taxes, and asked the bourgeois in the towns she governed to themselves determine the value of the tax they should pay (a remarkable decision by any standards). Out of the four faculties of the University of Angers, three of these, the faculties of theology, medicine and arts, were enlarged through the efforts of Yolande d'Aragon.

Paris was now ruled by the new Dauphin, who was still a child, and a regency comprising a moderate alliance led by the Dukes of Anjou, Brittany and Bourbon. It was not to last. On the night of 28th May 1418, the gates of St. Germain des Prés in the fractious city were secretly opened by treachery to eight hundred Burgundians who captured the mad King Charles VI. There was a massacre of all Armagnacs and sympathisers. Bernard d'Armagnac was killed. Many others fled, including the Dauphin, saved from certain death by the Provost of Paris, Tanguy du Chatel, who, at midnight, wrapping the sleeping prince in a blanket, rode with him through the night till they reached the safety of Melun. After two months of carnage, Jean Sans Peur entered Paris accompanied by Queen Isabeau. The cost of Burgundian victory was to be incalculable. In Paris everyone who could flee the massacre did so. Christine, however, had already left for the convent at Poissy, from where she was to write a poem on Jeanne d'Arc in the last year of her life in 1429.

While Paris was bleeding to death Henry V attacked and laid siege to Rouen and starved it into submission. Rouen had been in Burgundian hands and as such, Henry's task of conquest was a perilous one. The citizens of Rouen enclosed within the city walls, waited for their Burgundian saviours, at first with confidence but which by the end of a few months, turned to despair. Having endured a siege for six long months they surrendered to King Henry bitter in the knowledge that Jean Sans Peur, Duke of Burgundy, had abandoned and betrayed them.

Henry pressed on to Falaise and conquered it. At last the Burgundians realised the folly of having helped Henry in this conquest of France. They now knew the only way to arrest English progress was for all Frenchmen to combat the English menace together. Once more, in July 1419, a treaty was signed by the Dauphin and Burgundy, the two opposing factions. Henry's reply was to sack Pontoise, headquarters of the Duke of Burgundy, and to march to the gates of Paris.

Those moderates, like Christine, who regarded with abhorrence the loss of French independence, urged a meeting between the Dauphin and Burgundy in order to find a resolution to Henry's advance. At the meeting at Montereau the Armagnacs demonstrated that the murder of Louis d'Orléans by the Burgundians had been neither forgotten nor forgiven. On 10th September 1419, Jean Sans Peur was savagely murdered. Jean's son, Philippe le Bon, now found himself alone to deal with the murderers of his father, whose death he swore to avenge. His solution was to join forces with Henry of England and betray France.

The humiliating Treaty of Troyes between Henry V and Charles VI was signed in May 1420. Henry of England would gain the crown of France and the hand of the Princess Catherine. Charles VI would be allowed to continue to rule during his lifetime but Henry V would declare himself heir and regent of France. Queen Isabeau was persuaded publicly to disinherit her son, the Dauphin Charles. Henry V married Princess Catherine and in the Cathedral of Noyes he proclaimed himself heir and regent of France. The honeymoon was brief. Henry was soon subjugating the Armagnac strongholds to the south and west of Paris. This done, the two kings, of France and England, ceremoniously entered Paris, and the Parisians, thoroughly sickened by the ravages of civil war, proferred a warm welcome to their new sovereign. Henry had been away from England for three and a half years. His mission accomplished he now rode back to England with his French queen to a tumultuous welcome.

In 1421 Henry left England for his final campaign to subdue the Dauphin whose forces had defeated his brother Clarence at Baugé. He faced three hundred miles of hostile territory from Tours to Bourges, from where the Dauphin ruled. Henry fell ill and died at Vincennes on 31st August 1422, leaving behind a son just ten months old, and the regencies of France and England in the hands of his brothers, the Dukes of Bedford and Gloucester.

Chapter Twenty-Two

Last Years

> After your death there will come a prince with a courageous vision and boldness, who in reading your works will wish that you had lived in his age, and will long to have known you.
>
> Dame Philosophy in
> *'La Mutacion de Fortune'*

Moi Christine qui
ait pleuré
Onze ans en l'abbaye close

Où j'ai toujours depuis
demeurée
Quand Charles, c'est étrange
chose!
Le fils du Roy, si dire je l'ose

S'en fuit de Paris tout à coup
Par la trahison là enfermée

Maintenant d'abord, cela me
fait rire...

I Christine who have wept

Eleven years enclosed in the
Abbey
Where I have remained
since,
When Charles, how strange!

The King's son, if I dare say
so,
Fled suddenly from Paris
Where by treason held
captive.
Now, at first, I want to
laugh...

Et toi Charles, Roi de François

Septiéme de çe haut nom
Qui a fait si grande guerre
Qui te rapporte tant de bien

Que, grâce à Dieu, tu vois ton renom
Haut élevé par la pucelle,

Qui a soumis sous ton penon

Tes ennemis, la chose est nouvelle!...

Et toi, pucelle bien heureuse
Dois-tu être oubliée
Puisque Dieu t'a tant honorée

Que tu as la corde déliée
Qui tenait la France liée?

Te pourrait-on assez louer
Quand à cette terre humiliée
Par la guerre, tu as de paix dotée?

Hé! quel honneur au féminin

Sexe! Que Dieu l'aime il apparait!
Quand tout ce grand peuple parjure
Par qui tout notre peuple est ruiné
Par femme est battu et soumis

Ce que pas homme n'eut fait;

Et les traitres mis à l'écart,

And you Charles, King of France

Seventh of this noble name
Who made great war
Which brings you much good:
Thanks to God you see your fame
Carried high by the Maid who
Under your pennants has defeated
Your enemies, this is new!...

And you, blessed Maid
Must you be forgotten
When God has so greatly honoured you
Now that you have unwound
The rope that held France fettered?

Could one praise you enough
When you have given peace
To this humiliated war-ravaged land?

What honour is brought to the feminine sex!
Whom God seems to love
When this great perfidious race
By whom our people are ruined
Is beaten and overcome by a woman,
Which no man could accomplish;
And the traitors put aside,

Il est difficile de le croire!	It is difficult to believe!
Une fillette de seize ans N'est-ce pas une chose hors nature? A qui armes ne sont pesantes Il semble qu'elles y fut éduquée	A young girl of sixteen Is it not an extraordinary thing? Arms seem no weight to her As though she had been brought up to them
Tant elle est forte et dure!	So strong is she and with such force!
Et devant elle s'enfuient	And before her, her enemies fly...
Ses ennemis... beaucoup l'ont vu...	Many have seen it happen...
Ainsi rebaissez, Anglais, vos cornes; Car jamais vous n'aurez beau gibier. En France n'apporterez vos railleries Vous êtes fais mat en l'échiquier.	And so, you English lower your horns; For never will you win your quarry. France will never again endure your mocking words You have been check-mated.

Given this dictée by Christine in the year fourteen hundred and twenty nine.

When Christine fled Paris she was fifty-four. William Worcester, secretary to Sir John Falstaff, who lived in Paris during the English occupation tells us: *"One heard that Christine, who is a woman well-known for her birth and way of life, went into a religious house at Poissy near Paris..."*

At Poissy, she apparently did not take holy orders herself, but lived in the quarters reserved for those who, like her, wished to retreat a little from life. She was to stay there until her death in 1429. During this time she wrote *'Les Heures de Contemplation de la Passion de Notre Seigneur'* (The Hours of Contemplation of Our Lord's Passion) written in 1420 to console those women to whom this trying period had brought sorrow and who had lost children and relatives in the fighting. It appears to have been written at some particularly trying time in the life of France, perhaps after the shameful Treaty of Troyes in 1420.

This was also a painful time for Christine herself, not only because of the political situation but also because it must have been about then that her son, Jean du Castel, who had survived all the intrigues and dangers of the French court, died while on a diplomatic mission to Castille.

It appears that Christine was in touch with important people even in her retirement. Philippe le Bon, son of Jean Sans Peur, must evidently have asked her for copies of her work because she copied seven of her books all on vellum in folios of red leather and all dedicated to him. Among them were *'Le Chemin de Longue Etude'*, *'Epistres sur le Roman de La Rose'*, *'La Cité des Dames'*, *'Othéa'*, *'Cent Ballades'*, *'Le Debat des deux Amants'* – Philippe already had two copies of *'Lavision'* in his library.

The death of Charles VI followed that of Henry V in October 1422 and the infant King of England became Henry VI of England and Henry II of France. The King's uncles and Regents in France felt that their first duty was to establish the reign of their ward throughout France. At Bourges, the Dauphin, who had established a court had to be subdued, but on the route to Bourges lay the town of Orléans. In 1428, Orléans was besieged. The citizens of Orléans, led by Dunois, a bastard son of Louis d'Orléans, put up a heroic resistance. Meanwhile the Dauphin, as yet uncrowned, left Bourges and sheltered in the Chateau of Chinon. It was here that a seventeen year old maiden sought him out and convinced him that it was he and not Henry of England who was the true and legitimate heir to the throne of France, and that she was prepared to lay down her life to see him crowned King of France. Her name was Jeanne d'Arc. Now, dressed as a soldier and taking on a role not many Frenchmen dared to adopt at the time, Jeanne marched to Orléans at the head of an army and forced the English to lift the siege. Then, accompanied by the Dauphin, she entered Rheims on 17th July 1429 and watched the Archbishop of Chartres crown the Dauphin as King Charles VII of France.

It is often said that if France was brought to ruin by a woman, Isabeau of Bavaria, Queen of France, wife of Charles VI and mother of Charles VII, she was also saved by a woman., Jeanne d'Arc.

News certainly filtered into the sanctuary at Poissy; news of the civil war; the English occupation; the crowning of Henry VI as King of France; the raising of the siege of Orléans and the miracle of Jeanne d'Arc. In 1429, when Christine was sixty-four years old, the final page of her life coincided with the emergence of Jeanne d'Arc, who symbolised France rising from the abyss. Christine's last poem, all the more moving, was one glorifying Jeanne, and it reveals her undying love for France yet again. In it she refers in the first verse to Charles (now King Charles VII) and his escape.

It was ironic, perhaps, that Christine should die at the very time when France was to be freed from her bonds, and the English occupation was to be ended. She kept in touch with the outside world, even though she lived in seclusion at Poissy, and she saw Jeanne as a great figurehead round which the country could rally. To the last, Christine thought first of her adopted country, to which she was more fiercely loyal than many native Frenchmen might have been. Mercifully she was spared the horror of subsequent events. The Burgundians would deliver Jeanne to the English who would brand her a heretic. On May 30th 1431 in the old market square of Rouen, Jeanne d'Arc would pay the price for her loyalty to her country and devotion to the King. She was meted out the punishment reserved for heretics and burnt alive at the stake by the English, protesting her innocence to the last. Charles VII of France for whom she had given her life would stand by and do nothing to save her.

In 1435 the peace treaty of Arras was signed between the King and the Duke of Burgundy, Philippe le Bon, and the following year King Charles VII entered Paris in triumph. By 1453 the last of the English were driven out of France and Christine's beloved *Dame Couronnée* was once more free.

Christine, who was long admired for her poetry alone, had a profound influence on both French and English poets, but her views on life in general were far in advance of anything else written by her contemporaries, although she may have been frustrated by the lack of apparent effect her works had on those to whom they were addressed. She was a person deserving respect – not least because she was never afraid to speak her mind, nor did she cease to try to change contemporary attitudes and it is this force that continues to speak to us across the centuries.

She moved in a world which was brilliant, witty, artistic and voluptuous, and often imbued with the sentiments of chivalry. Chaucer participated in the same humane tradition as Christine and Froissart; the poetic world where the verse forms come from the troubadours... She entered this world, but she moved through it with a sense of doom.

In *'La Mutacion de Fortune'*, Dame Philosophy with insight and exactitude prophesied what the lasting impact of Christine's writing was to be.

I foretell that your works will have a varied reception; some will criticise their language in various ways, saying it lacks elegance; others will find your choice of subject matter strange; and others, more discerning, will praise them. In times to come they will excite more curiosity than they have in your own lifetime. Let me tell you that you were born into the wrong age, for in our times the acquisition of knowledge does not give one a reputation: it is as if the sciences had been born out of due time. For this reason few of them are in the ascendant. However, after your death there will come a prince with a courageous vision and boldness, who in reading your works will wish that you had lived in his age, and will long to have known you...

Important Dates

c.1363	Birth of Cristina da Pizzano
1364	Death of King Jean le Bon
	The Dauphin Charles becomes King Charles V of France
	Tommaso da Pizzano travels to Paris on the accession of Charles V
1368	Christine travels to Paris with her mother
1379	Marriage to Etienne du Castel
1380	Death of King Charles V
	The Dauphin Charles becomes King Charles VI of France
	Regency of Burgundy and Bourbon
1381	Birth of Christine's daughter
1385	Birth of Christine's son Jean
1388	Charles VI assumes control from the Regency of his Uncles
1389	Death of Christine's husband
1390-9	*Cent Ballades, Virelais, Rondeaux, Diverses Ballades*
1392	Madness of Charles VI
c.1393	Christine's daughter enters the convent of Poissy
1394	Return of Christine's brothers to Italy
1397	Salisbury invites Christine's son to England
c.1397	*Les enseignements moraux... à mon fils*
1399	Richard II is deposed and Henry Bolingbroke becomes King Henry IV of England. He invites Christine to his Court.
	Salisbury beheaded
	Epîstre au Dieu d'Amour
1400	*Le Dit de Poissy*
1401	*Le Debat de deux Amants*
	Le Livre du Duc des Vrais Amants
1401-2	*Le Debat sur 'Le Roman de la Rose'*
1402	*Le Dit de la Rose*

	Cent Ballades d'Amants et de Dame
1403	Birth of the future King Charles VII of France
	Le Dit de la Pastoure
	Le Livre de la Mutacion de Fortune
	Le Chemin de Longue Etude
1404	*Le Livre des Faits et Bonnes Moeurs du Sage, Roi Charles V.*
	Lettre à Eustace Mourel Deschamps
	Death of Philippe of Burgundy
1405	*Lavision Christine*
	Lettre à la Reine Isabeau
	La Cité des Dames
	Le Livre des Trois Vertus
	La description et définition de la prodomye de l'homme selon l'opinion de Mg Louis 1re duc d'Orléans par Christine de Pisan (unpublished)
1406	*Le Livre du Corps de Policie*
1407	Murder of Louis d'Orléans
1409	*Le Livre des Faits d'Armes et de Chevalerie*
	Sept Psaumes Allégoriques
	Civil War
1410	*Lamentations sur les Maux de la Guerre Civile*
1412	The Dauphin, Louis Duke de Guyenne assumes control. The Treaty of Auxerre is signed between the Burgundians and the Armagnacs. Failure of peace.
1412	Birth of Jeanne d'Arc
1413	Treaty of Poitoise. Temporary peace.
1412-3	*Le Livre de la Paix*
1413	Death of Henry IV
	Henry of Monmouth becomes King Henry V of England
	Revolt of the *Cabochiens* in Paris
1415	Invasion of France by Henry V, Agincourt
1417	Burgundian treachery betrays Paris
1418	*L'Epître de la Prison de Vie Humaine*
	Massacre of Orléanists in Paris
	Flight of Christine to Poissy
1419	Assasination of Jean sans Peur by the

	Armagnacs. His son, Philippe le Bon, becomes Duke of Burgundy
1420	Treaty of Troyes
	Les Heures de Contemplation de Notre Seigneur
1422	Death of Henry V at Vincennes, Paris. Death of King Charles VI. Henry VI is proclaimed King of England and France.
1425	Death of Christine's son, Jean.
1428	Siege of Orléans
1429	Jeanne d'Arc lifts the siege of Orléans Coronation of Charles VII of Fance at Reims
	Le Dittié sur Jeanne d'Arc
c.1430	Death of Christine
1431	Trial and death of Jeanne d'Arc.

Bibliography

Anslay, Bryan (tr.), *The Cyte of Ladyes*, London, 1521

Blades, W. (ed.), *Morale Proverbes, composed in French by Cristyne de Pisan*, translated by the Earl Rivers, reprinted from the original edition of William Caxton, A.D. 1478, with introductory remarks by William Blades, London, 1859

Boivin le Cadet, 'Vie de Christine de Pisan', in Keralio, Mlle de, *Collection des meilleurs ouvrages français composés par des femmes*, Vol II, Paris, 1787
'Bibliothèque du Louvre sous les rois Charles V, Charles VI, et Charles VII', dissertation historique prefacing Gilles Malet's *Inventaire du Catalogue des livres dè l'ancienne bibliothèque du Louvre*, reprinted Paris, 1836

Boucicault, Maréchal, in Michaud et Poujoulat, *Nouvelle Collection des mémoires pour servir á l'histoire de France*, Série 1, Vol. II, Paris, 1836

Bournon, F., L'Hôtel Royal de Saint Pol, *Mémoires de la Société de l'Histoire de Paris et de L'Ille-de-France*, Vol VI, Paris, 1879

Byles, A.T.P. (ed.), *The Book of fayttes of armes and of chyvalry, translated and printed by William Caxton* from the French of Christine de Pisan, ed. A.T.P. Byles for the Early English Text Society O.U.P., 1937

Campbell, F.-G.-C., *L'Epitre d'Othéa, Etude sur les sources de Christine de Pisan*, Paris, 1924

Castel, Mme Etienne du, *Ma grand-mére Christine de Pisan*, Paris, 1973

272

Champion, Pierre, *Histoire poétique du XVe siècle*, 2 vol., Paris, 1923
Splendeurs et misères de Paris, XIV-Xve siècles, Paris, 1934
La Librairie de Charles d'Orléans, Paris, 1910

Champollon, Figeac, *Louis and Charles d'Orléans*, Paris, 1844

Chottel, Jacques, *Charles d'Orléans Poet et Politique*, Paris, 1992

Cohen, G., *Vie Littéraire en France au Moyen Age*, Paris, 1949

Collas, Emile, *Valentine Visconti de Milan*,

Delanchenal, R., *Histoire de Charles V*, 5 volumes, Paris, 1901-31

Delpit, J., *Collection Générale des Documents Français qui se trouve en Angleterre*, Paris, 1847

Denifle, H., 'La Désolation des Eglises, Monastères et Hôpitaux en France pendant la Guerre de Cent Ans', in *Guerre de Cent Ans*, 2 volumes, Paris, 1897

Deschamps, Eustace, *Oeuvres complètes*, ed. by Le Marquis de Quex de Saint Hilaire et M.G. Raynaud, 10 vol., Paris, 1878-1903
Poésies Morales et Historiques, ed. G.A. Chaplet, Paris, 1832

de Silva Vigier, Anil, *This Moste High Prince, John of Gaunt*, Pentland Press (Durham) 1992

Douët d'Arcq, L., *Choix de Pièces Inédites Relatives au Règne de Charles VI*, Societe de l'Histoire de France, 1863-64

Dupont-Perrier, G., *Etudes sur les Institutions Financières de la France a la fin du Moyen Age*, 2 volumes, Paris, 1930

Froissart, J., *The Ancient Chronicles of Sir John Froissart, translated from the original French by Lord Berners*, 4 vol., reprinted London, 1814

Gérould, T., *La Musique au Moyen Age* Paris 1932

Guenée, Bernard, *Un Meurtre, une Societe, l'Assassinat du duc d'Orléans*, Paris, 1992

Hibbert, Christopher, *Agincourt* 1969

Hicks, Eric, and Moredu, Thérèse, *Le livre de Cité des Dames*, Paris, 1986.

Holinshed, R. *Chronicles of England, Scotland and Ireland* 1807

Juvenal des Ursins, Jean, *Histoire de Charles VI, Roy de France*, in Michaud et Poujoulat, *Nouvelle Collection des mémoires pour servir à l'histoire de France*, Série 1, Vol. II, Paris, 1836

Kemp-Welch, A., *Of Six Mediaeval Women*, London, 1913 *The Book of the Duke of True Lovers*, trans. with an introduction by A. Kemp-Welch, the ballads rendered into the original metres by Laurence Binyon and Eric Maclagan, London, 1908

Keralio, Mlle de, *Collection des meilleurs ouvrages français, composés par des femmes*, Vol. II and III, Paris, 1787

Laigle, M., *Le Livre des Trois Vertus de Christine de Pisan et son milieu historique et littéraire*, Paris, 1912

Lawson, Sarah, *The Treasure of the City of Ladies*, London, 1985

Le-Franc, Martin, *Le Champion des Dames*, 1530, reprinted Paris, 1874

Le Gentil, P., *Christine de Pisan, poète méconnu*, Paris, 1951

Lefèvre-Pontalis, G. (ed.) *Petite Chronique de Guyenne*, Bibliothèque de Chartres, Vol XLVII Paris 1886

274

Lorris, Guillaume de, *le Roman de la Rose et Jean de Meung*, ed. George Vertut Paris 1965

Lucas, H.S., *The Low Countries and the Hundred Years' War*, Ann Arbour, 1929

Lucas, R.H. (ed.), *Christine de Pisan, Le Livre du Corps de Policie*, Geneva and Paris, 1967

Luce, S., *La France pendant la guerre de Cent Ans*, 2 volumes, Paris, 1893

Machaut, Guillaume de, *La Louange des Dames*, ed. N Wilkins, Scottish Academic Press, 1972

Martin, H. M. R., *La Miniature française du XIIIe au XVe siècles*, Paris and Brussels, 1923

McLeod, Enid, *The Order of the Rose*, London, 1976

Meiss, Millard, *French painting in the time of Jean de Berry*, London, 1967

Metz, Guillaume de, *Description de la ville de Paris au XVe siècle*, ed. Leroux de Lincy, Paris, 1855

Meung, Jean de, *Le Roman de la Rose, mis en français moderne*, Paris, 1949

Michelet, J., *Histoire de France (moyen Age)*, 17 volumes, Paris, 1835-67

Monstrelet, Enguerrand de, *La Chronique*, ed. L. Douët d'Arcq, for the Société de l'histoire de France, 6 vol., Paris, 1857-62. *The Chronicles*, trans. by Thomas Johnes. 2 Vol. London 1840

Noël, O., *Histoire de la ville de Poissy depuis ses origines jusqu'à nos jours*, Poissy, 1869

Orléans, Charles d', *The English Poems of Charles of Orléans*, ed. Robert Steel, 1941

Palmer, J.J., *The Anglo-French Peace Negotiations 1390-99*, 1971

Paris, G., *La Littérature Française au Moyen Age*, Paris, 1913

Pernoud, Regine, *Christine de Pisan*, Paris, 1982

Perroy, E., *The Hundred Years' War*, English Trs., 1951 repr. 1965

Piaget, A., 'Chronologie des Epistres sur le Roman de la Rose', in *Etudes romanes dédiées à Gaston*, Paris, 1891

Pinet, M-J., *Christine de Pisan, 1364-1430, Etude biographique et littéraire*, Paris, 1927

Pisan, Christine de, *The Epistles of the Romance and the Rose and Other documents in the Débat 1401-02*, ed. C.F. Ward, Chicago, 1911

Pueschel, R., *Le Chemin de Longue Estude, par Christine de Pizan*, Berlin, 1881

Raine, R. R., *Les Sept Psaumes allégorisés de Christine de Pisan, a critical edition*, Washington, 1965

Rashdall, Hastindgs, *The Universities of Europe in the Middle Ages*, 3 volumes, 1936

Richards, Earl Jeffrey (trans.), *The Book of the City of Ladies*, London, 1982

Rigaud, R., *Les idées féministes de Christine de Pisan*, Neuchâtel, 1911

Robineau, E.M.-D., *Christine de Pisan, sa vie, ses oeuvres*, Saint-Omer, 1882

Roy, M., *Oeuvres poétiques de Christine de Pisan*, ed. for the Société des Anciens textes français, 3 vol., Paris, 1886

Solente, S. (ed.), *Le Livre de la Mutacion de Fortune, par Christine de Pisan*, publ. S. Solente for the Société des Anciens textes français, 4 vol., Paris, 1959-68
Le Livre des faits et bonnes moeurs du sage roy Charles V, par Christine de Pizan, publ. S. Solente for the Société de l'Histoire de France, 2 vol., Paris, 1936
'Christine de Pisan', in *l'Histoire littéraire de la France*, Vol XL, Paris, 1869

Thomassy, R., *Essai sur les écrits politiques de Christine de Pisan, suivi d'une notice littéraire et de pièces inédits*, (among which are the *Lettre à la reine Isabelle*, the *Lamentation sur les maux de la guerre civile*, and the Hymn to Joan of Arc)

Towner, M.L., *Lavision-Christine*, introduction and text, Washington, 1932

Ward, C.F. (ed.), *The Epistles on the Romance of the Rose and other documents in the debate, with a dissertation*, University of Chicago, 1911

Warner, G. F., *The Epistle of Othea to Hector, or the Boke of Knyghthode*, translated from the French of Christine de Pisan … by Stephen Scrope, edited from a manuscript in the library of the Marquis of Bath by George F. Warner, London, 1904

Willard, C.C., The Livre de la Paix of Christine de Pisan, a critical edition with introduction and notes, Gravenhage, 1958

Index

A

Agincourt, Battle of, 92, 170, 240, 259, 260, 269
Anastasia, 83
Anjou, Duke d', son-in-law of Charles V, 58, 169, 261
Aquitaine, Eleanor of, 82
Aragon, Yolande d', Duchess of Anjou and Queen of Sicily, 260
Armagnac, Bernard d', 241, 261
Arras, Treaty of, 96
Auxerre, Peace of, 248, 269

B

Berry, Duke de, brother of Charles V, 40, 51, 58, 83, 170, 193, 195, 224, 246, 247
Berry, Marie de, daughter of the Duke de Berry, 40, 107, 108, 169, 170, 260
Boethius, 62, 72, 226
Bourbon, Duke de, brother of Charles V, 51, 58, 104, 224, 261
Bourbon, Jean de, married Marie de Berry, 107, 108, 169, 170, 260
Burgundy, Jean "Sans Peur" (The Fearless) Duke of, son of Philippe "Le Hardi", 84, 195, 196, 200, 230, 241, 242, 248, 261, 266, 269
Burgundy, Philippe "Le Bon" (The Good) Duke of, son of Jean "Sans Peur", 190, 261, 266, 267
Burgundy, Philippe "Le Hardi" (The Bold) Duke of, brother of Charles V, xxv, 51, 53, 58, 68, 69, 83, 84, 92, 189, 190, 192, 193, 194, 195, 196, 200, 224, 242

C

Caboche, leader of the Tradesmen Rebellion, 248
Castel, Etienne du, married Christine de Pisan, 41, 42, 48, 53, 57, 58, 176, 180, 195, 268
Castel, Jean du, son of Christine de Pisan, 53, 91, 92, 195, 231, 266

—W—